W9-ANR-981

The Woman's Work-At-Home Handbook

THE
Woman's
Work-At-Home
Handbook

**Income and Independence
with a Computer**

•

Patricia McConnel

BANTAM BOOKS

TORONTO • NEW YORK • LONDON • SYDNEY • AUCKLAND

THE WOMAN'S WORK-AT-HOME HANDBOOK

A Bantam Book / November 1986

*Grateful acknowledgment is made for permission to
reprint an excerpt from* Cat's Cradle *by
Kurt Vonnegut, Jr. Copyright © 1963 by
Kurt Vonnegut, Jr. Reprinted by permission of
DELACORTE PRESS/SEYMOUR LAWRENCE.*

All rights reserved.
Copyright © 1986 by Patricia McConnel.
Book design by Ann Gold.
*This book may not be reproduced in whole or in part, by
mimeograph or any other means, without permission.
For information address: Bantam Books, Inc.*

Library of Congress Cataloging-in-Publication Data

McConnel, Patricia.
  The woman's work-at-home handbook.

  Includes index.
  1. Home-based businesses.   2. Microcomputers.
  3. Women—Employment.   I. Title.
HD62.7.M39   1986   004.16′068   86-47573
                ISBN 0-553-34324-6

Published simultaneously in the United States and Canada

---

*Bantam Books are published by Bantam Books, Inc. Its trade-
mark, consisting of the words "Bantam Books" and the por-
trayal of a rooster, is Registered in U.S. Patent and Trademark
Office and in other countries. Marca Registrada. Bantam
Books, Inc., 666 Fifth Avenue, New York, New York 10103.*

PRINTED IN THE UNITED STATES OF AMERICA

OPM   0 9 8 7 6 5 4 3 2 1

FOR BERNIE

We Bokononists believe that humanity is organized into teams, teams that do God's Will without ever discovering what they are doing. Such a team is called a *karass*. . . . If you find your life tangled up with somebody else's life for no very logical reasons, that person may be a member of your *karass*. . . . A *duprass* is a *karass* composed of only two persons. . . . A true *duprass* can't be invaded. . . .

> from the *Book of Bokonon*, as quoted by Kurt Vonnegut in *Cat's Cradle* (Dell Publishing, 1963)

A true *duprass* can't be dissolved, either, not even by the people who make it up.

> Patricia McConnel,
> a latter-day prophet of Bokononism

Contents

Acknowledgments

I don't like to work as hard as I had to work to write this book. That I did is due in large measure to the support and encouragement of two people: Bernard Conrad Cole and Ellen Levine.

Bernie has saved every piece of paper that ever crossed his path having to do with computers. Much of the research for this book began with his rummaging in the depths of a musty cardboard box in his back bedroom to find a reference he knew was there someplace. I might have written a good book without him, but it would have been a lot harder.

Bernie got excited and stayed excited about this book for the entire two years it took me to write it. He clipped and mailed to me every newspaper and magazine article he could find even remotely related to women and computers, and these clippings led me directly or indirectly to many of the women I interviewed, and to some of the experts whose advice and information were invaluable.

Ellen Levine is my agent, and definitely a person I am glad to have on my side. Some hard things happened to me in the course of writing this book. Ellen's professionalism, calm good sense, and warm support made those tough periods a lot easier to get through.

Many experts from several disciplines generously provided me with their research findings and/or their expert opinions. They educated me, and thus allowed me to write from an informed base. (Any errors and biases are my own, however.) These people may not be quoted directly, or may be quoted only briefly, but their contribution of background material is significant: Jan MacDonald of the Math/Science Network; Sue Block of the Community Memory Project; telecommuting consultant Gil Gordon; Dr. Margrethe Olson of the Center for Research on Information Systems at New York University; Ron Ahlstrom of the Utah Department of Employment Security, Labor Market Information Services; William Bielby, Professor of Sociology at U.C. Santa Barbara; John Schatzlein of HOMEWORK; Mary Brady of Trace Corporation; optometrist Michael Luby of Grand Junction, Colorado; Thomas Lecoq of the Optometric Extension Program Foundation; Kathy Kelley of the Association for Women in Computing; Kay Gilliland of EQUALS; and the folks at the National Science Foundation.

My most profound thanks and gratitude go to the women whose interviews you will find throughout the book. Without their stories this would be just another dry book of theory and fact. These women welcomed me into their homes and gave generously not only their time and energy, but sometimes very personal details of their lives, motivated by the desire to make the way easier for the women who follow. They have given of their hearts as well as of their minds; I wrote much of the book riding the crest of the inspiration I received from them. That inspiration and encouragement for the future of women are still with me, and so my life and my outlook have been permanently changed through contact with them.

This book was conceived and partially written during my year of freedom under a grant in literature from the National Endowment for the Arts. I was very productive and did some of my best work on this project and on my fiction during that year because I was free from any other demands on my energy. I am permanently and deeply grateful to the NEA.

Finally, thanks to the patient waitresses of Guido's and Pizza Hut in Moab, Utah, who brought me endless iced-tea refills while I sat working on this book on my Epson PX-8 lap computer, taking up a table that might otherwise have been occupied by someone who tipped better.

Preface

I bought my first computer for use as a word processor four years ago. It immediately changed my life by making my work at least five times easier and faster, thereby making *me* at least five times more efficient and productive. I wasn't prepared for such dramatic effects. I guess part of me thought that claims about computers must be exaggerated—nothing could be *that* good. But they are. Changing from a typewriter to a word processing computer is like trading in a horse and buggy for a car—you can go a lot farther a lot faster.

As dramatic as this change has been for me, it is nothing compared to what the computer has done for my future. It has changed me from a person with serious concerns about how I am to survive in my old age to a person with unlimited options from now till the day I die, even if I live to be ninety.

In this context it is important to mention that I am fifty-five years old, on my own, and, because of chronic health problems and a certain psychic battle fatigue, unemployable—at least in the conventional sense of working in a structured environment with an inflexible time schedule and a hierarchical chain of command. Fortunately, I love writing—it is my true vocation, and it gets me out of the structures I am unable to cope with, but I have no illusions about writing being something that can be depended upon for a steady income.

When I turned fifty I started to worry about my future: What if I can't always make a living as a writer? When times get rough, freelance writers are the first to be cut from the budget of almost any business that employs them. Even if I were capable of holding a job, the time is coming soon when I will be told I am too old. And what if my health declines as I grow older, and I can't leave my house? Old people who have to rely entirely on social security have a painful struggle just to survive. I am not willing to live like that.

I knew the time had come when it was imperative to train myself for a backup career—one that did not involve working at a traditional job. Until the year I bought my computer, my options seemed almost nonexistent. If I couldn't hold a job and couldn't support myself writing, what was I supposed to do—answer one of those ads for envelope stuffers?

Although these things have been on my mind since I turned fifty, they had nothing to do with my buying a computer. Rather, I had seen how a computer simplified life for my friend and technical writing partner, and when I received a small inheritance, I decided a computer would be an enjoyable luxury. Luxury—ha! I am now so dependent on it that I recently bought a second computer as a backup because I get so crazy and insecure when the first system breaks down. When I bought the first computer, I realized it had many possibilities for applications other than word processing, but I didn't think much about it at the time. I just had a vague idea that a computer would be nice since someday I might find another use for it. *That* turned out to be the underthinkment of the year!

My first computers were Osborne 1s. I chose the Osborne 1 because it is portable, because $1,795 bought me a system that included everything I needed except a printer, and because it came with a lot of free software (computer programs), including one of the best word processing programs available at the time, *WordStar*. I didn't pay much attention to the other software.

But that other free software is important to this story. I would never have bought an electronic spreadsheet (used for various kinds of accounting) or MBasic/CBasic (computer languages used for programming). But, because they were *there*, I experimented with them. I became fascinated with how many jobs the little machine (no bigger than a portable sewing machine) could do. My fascination led me to start reading books about computers and the popular computing magazines, which led to my interest in programming, which led to my taking a course in programming, which led to a better understanding of what computers can do.

The idea that in buying myself a computer I had bought myself a future was not something I didn't know one minute and did know the next. No big flash occurred—just a gradual expansion of ideas that came one at a time. At first I saw that traditional kinds of work were made much easier with a computer, work I would not have considered doing before because it seemed too tedious, boring, and/or underpaid—work such as word processing, bookkeeping, and income-tax preparation. A multitude of "user friendly" programs make these jobs easy and fast, eliminating boring, repetitive detail, leading the user by the hand through all the steps so that nothing is missed, providing checks against errors, and making corrections simple.

Later I realized I could learn to program and be a freelance programmer. I discovered I could buy a modem (equipment that allows transmission of digital data over telephone lines) and transmit my work anywhere in the country. Living in Moab, Utah, an economically depressed town of five thousand, was no longer as much of a handicap as it had been.

As my understanding of computers became more sophisticated, so did my ideas. With my intense interest in nutrition and health, I could create a nutrition data base and lease or sell it to an on-line service such as The Source. (A data base is a comprehensive collection of facts stored in a computer. On-line services allow anyone with a computer to get information out of the data base. For a fee, of course.) I could publish an electronic newsletter, a special-interest bulletin board, offer an editing service to writers or a nutritional consultation service—all through computer networks, and without leaving my home. I could even sell my soul to the devil and write those "personalized" sales letters that look like they are individually typed but in fact are churned out by computers by the hundreds of thousands. Those are not all the ideas I had, but they are enough to give you the picture.

Because of amazing technological devices that make computers accessible to the handicapped, I could do any of those things, even if I became bedridden in later years—all because of one small and relatively inexpensive machine! As long as my mind can work, *I* can work. There was a point, of course, where the significance of all this was at last quite clear to me, and I became a happier, more relaxed person.

One other thing besides the computer was vitally necessary before these options transformed the future for me: *My mind had to open to the possibilities*. This is an important theme in this book, and I'll return to it again.

So far I have mentioned only myself, but other things were going on at that time. Most of those things happened because I had purchased a computer and told people about it.

A woman in her seventies who works in my favorite second-hand store asked: "Do you think I should be learning about computers? It seems like it would be something I'd never get too old to do."

A friend who is a case worker for the welfare department asked: "How hard is it to learn to use a computer? What could I do to make money with it? I hate my job; I hate being a 'cop.' I'd like to do something where I could stay at home."

A writer friend with a very creative temperament said: "I want one! There's so much I just can't get on paper fast enough!"

Sounds good, except *not one of them has taken that first step to learn about or to acquire a computer*.

I registered for a computer science class, which was mostly about programming. About half the students were women, which both surprised and delighted me. But 30 percent of the class—all women—quit after the first couple of weeks. That is, *60 percent of the women dropped out*.

One of the women in that class had lost her husband the year before. She was one of the few who stuck it out. She told me that she and her husband had run a successful oil-drilling-equipment leasing service, and that she had a lot of ideas about using a computer to keep track of equipment in ways that would save a lot of time and aggravation. She was taking the class so that she could write these programs. I was very excited about this idea and asked her if she was going to buy a computer.

No, she said.

Well, how was she going to create her program and sell it?

Oh, she was not going to do that. She was going to try to find a job with another leasing company. She just felt that she had a better chance of getting a job at her age if she had something special to offer.

These things troubled me. Women are realizing that computers offer a potential for them, but somehow they are not really grabbing hold and making it happen. I started thinking in larger terms then—not just about myself, but about women in general.

In the late sixties I had to ask my ex-husband to take custody of our children. I had had a terrible breakdown of my health and mind because the strain of working and trying to raise our children and to be a whole person too was too much for me. Some women can do it; knowing that made it worse for me, because I felt that I must really be very inadequate if I could not do what so many women do so courageously and successfully (now we know that most of them pay a horrendous price in order to do so). I wondered: If a microcomputer had been available to me then, if I had been able to work at home at convenient hours and had been with my children, and had had the financial strain dramatically eased by not having to pay for child care, would I have been able to keep my family? Could I have been a better mother? It is painful when I think of how different it might have been, yet how out of reach any solution was at that time.

How many women are suffering in the same way today because they don't recognize the path that is open to them and the many problems that can be solved with one little machine?

I began to get very excited about the potential of computers to revolutionize the lives of women. I thought about all the problems working women face, especially working mothers, and began to see ways that computers could be used to solve these problems. I tried to find books and articles on women and computers, but I found that the subject had been hardly touched, except to explore the old idea that women are resistant to technology.

Then one day a friend came to my house so that I could show her how my computer worked. "I'm tired of my job," she said. "I'm also tired of driving an hour each way to work, and then coming home to cook dinner for my kids. Do you think I could make money with this thing? I'd love to work at home."

Although I had thought a great deal about the subject, I could offer only general ideas; I had not gathered information specific enough to help her in a concrete way. I had not yet met anyone who was making her living working at home with a computer.

That night I dreamed I was interviewing a large group of women—I seemed to be writing a book. The women were very excited; they had a lot to tell me.

In the morning I remembered the dream. Smiling, I said to myself: *Of course!*

PART I

What the Electronic Cottage Means to Women

ONE

The Funnel-Visioned Futurists

The pace at which technology changes has accelerated at a dizzying rate over the last thirty years. Since technology profoundly affects the way we live, almost everyone wants to know what is coming next, and books about the future are so popular that they sometimes make the best seller lists. *Megatrends*, by John Naisbitt, is the most recent example. Among the books on the future published since 1976 are *The Universal Machine: Confessions of a Technological Optimist*, by Pamela McCorduck; *Great Expectations: America and the Baby Boom Generation*, by Landon V. Jones; *Future Shock* and *The Third Wave*, by Alvin Toffler; *The Next 200 Years*, by Herman Kahn et al; *The Micro Millenium*, by Christopher Evans; and *The Telematic Society*, by James Martin—and that's only a partial list!

All these books have in common an assumption that technology affects men and women in similar ways. I went through the books named above while researching this book, and in some I found not a single listing under "women" in their indexes.

Yet women are affected by technology differently from men because their work is different. Women give birth—this fact alone forces an entirely different pattern on their work lives. Although men participate in the rearing of children much more than they did in the past, women are still the primary caretakers. In cases of divorce, it is usually the women who have custody of the children; much more often than men, they have the dual responsibility of supporting a household and raising the children. When women work outside the home, a variety of factors— including opportunity—leads them to work at jobs that are different from men's. When they do engage in the same work, they get paid less for it.

Thus, any book that undertakes to project what impact technological advances will have on work, the home, the family, and society in general must certainly consider in depth the special concerns and problems of women—especially those trying to combine work and raising a family—if it is to give a complete picture, since women constitute more than half the population. Yet, none of the books named above do this.

One would expect that books written by women would be more likely to serve women's interests. Yet, Pamela McCorduck, in her book *The Universal Machine*, which is specifically about computer technology, gives approximately two and a half pages to women as a group, and those pages have nothing to do with the impact of computer technology on their lives.

The author who mentions women most frequently in relation to cultural changes brought about by technology is Alvin Toffler. In his book *The Third Wave*, Toffler examines the shift of our culture from a manufacturing society to an information-processing one—that is, to a computer-dependent economy. The Third Wave is Toffler's name for this shift, and his book is perhaps the most important existing document about the future, not only because his projections are thoughtful, informed, and intelligent, but because he has reached a very wide audience and his ideas have been assimilated into the public's assumptions about the future.

But if Toffler is the most conscious of the futurist authors where women are concerned, we are in trouble. There are twenty-five references to "women" in the index of *The Third Wave*. Most of these references turn out to be phrases like *women's rights* or *feminists* ticked off in a list of political movements, or some other tangential reference.

Women are discussed at greater length in chapters where changes in sex roles and family structure are considered. Toffler describes how the "electronic cottage"—Toffler's now-popularized term for a home that is also the site of income-earning through electronic technology—might bring about a more equal sharing of power and responsibility between husband and wife. He briefly mentions the failure of existing institutions to take into consideration the special needs of women who work, but he explores the topic no further. He seems to recognize that women have special needs but never says what they are.

One of the most telling paragraphs in the book—in regard to Toffler's concern for the effects of the Third Wave on women—is this one, which appears in the chapter on the electronic cottage:

> Given the necessary tools, the [Institute for the Future] found, many of the present duties of the secretary "could be done from home as well as in the office. Such a system would increase the labor pool by allowing married secretaries caring for small children at home to continue to work. . . . There may be no overriding reason why a secretary could not just as well, in many instances, take dictation at home and type the text on a home terminal which produces a clean text at the author's home or office."

This is the only paragraph in the chapter about women working at home, and Toffler does not add any comment, thereby leaving us to conclude—taking the paragraph at face value—that the only significance of this situation is that the labor pool will not suffer. The profound significance of this new arrangement for the woman in question and for her children seems not to be worth thinking about, even though the effects on her and her children will in turn significantly affect:

- how well the new system works
- the psychological well-being of the children who grow up to be the new citizens of this society
- the general welfare of women and thus the evolution of feminism as a political force
- the economy, since women will have more money to spend from money saved by working at home
- mental health, as the multiple benefits of working at home free women from the great psychological and economic pressures of working away from home while raising a family (her increased well-being will make her a better mother, spouse, and worker)

The ripple effects are staggering to consider. But thoughts on this subject do not appear anywhere in Toffler's book, nor in the writings of any other futurist I could find.

I want to make excuses for Toffler, since he makes much more effort to be conscious of women than any other futurist. But a tough critique is called for: A futurist who does not consider that women comprise a special segment of the population, with many problems radically different from men's problems—and that the Third Wave therefore means very different things to them—is ignoring the concerns of more than half the population.

It is my contention that the Third Wave will affect women much more profoundly than it will men, and that women ought to be the guidon bearers of the new society, because they are the ones who may be most affected by it. I say *ought to be* and *may be* instead of *will be* because women won't lead the march if they are not aware of how much they have to gain by it; they won't be affected if they don't take advantage of the options open to them. Yet, *nearly all the jobs that can be most productively and economically transferred to the home computer terminal—secretarial, clerical, bookkeeping, data control—are performed by women in the vast majority of cases.* Nowhere in Toffler's book, nor in any other futurist's book I have read, is there a clue that anyone has thought for one minute in this direction.

To be fair, feminist writers, too, are missing the significance of Third Wave technology for women. Robin Morgan, one of feminism's most articulate, intelligent, and comprehensive thinkers, wrote the book *The Anatomy of Freedom*, which is about women and the future. But Morgan makes analogies between feminism and physics—computers and microprocessors get one paragraph. She writes nothing of the monumental changes this technology can make (and, in some cases, is already making) in the lives of women.

What about women journalists who write about technology? "Do Women Resist Computers?" was the cover story, written by a woman, for a 1983 issue of *Popular Computing*. The answer is "Absolutely not," as stated in the blurb above the article. The article itself has two main themes (both excellent ones): that computer anxiety is largely socially conditioned and can be overcome, and that women are entering the computer field in large numbers and doing very well there. What is not stated is that even larger numbers of women are *not* entering the computer field because they are *not* overcoming that socially conditioned computer anxiety. Again, the enormous potential of computers to make women free as they have never been before is overlooked.

Many articles are written about women who have made a fortune or risen to a position of power in some aspect of the computer industry. These articles are meant to be encouraging, but usually they focus on exceptional women, leaving the ordinary woman saying to herself, "That's swell, but I'm not an entrepreneur." Such articles also fail to note the significance of the fact that these women often started their entrepreneurship *working at home with a computer*.

An article in *Ms.* magazine some time ago describes many of the things computers can do for us; the author's main thesis is that women need to come to terms with computers because computers are going to change our consciousness and our daily lives. She sums up her theme: "It's not a machine, damn it. It's the future." Well, it most certainly is a machine, and for reasons I'll take up in chapter 21, which discusses technoterror, we'd better not forget that fact, even for the sake of an apt metaphor for the future. Nonetheless, her message is a valid one—as far as it goes. But elsewhere she says, ". . . computers are going to make it easy . . . for ever-larger segments of the population to work at home. If anyone has thought about how this is going to affect say, daycare, I haven't heard about it." And that's the end of that theme! Her next sentence, is, "Computers are already phasing out a number of traditionally female jobs. . . ." That's the last we hear of how computers are changing the lives of women. How could she come so close and still miss?

But the responsibility for recognizing what computers mean to women lies primarily with the futurists, because they help to bring about the future they predict. By planting ideas of the possible in our minds, they program us in that direction. They cannot send us along a path that does not potentially exist, of course—one that is not already in the process of evolving. But their ideas can speed us on our way and have a great influence on how our future develops.

I believe that unless futurists keep in mind that women have unique problems and special needs, they are not going to foresee, and thus design, a future in which the ramifications for women are of equal significance to those for men. They are going to funnel things, consciously or not, in the direction they have always been funneled—to male advantage. Women must participate in designing the future if they want to be included in it. It's as simple as that. The computer gives us more power to achieve this than we ever had before. The computer can't be controlled by existing power structures because anyone can own one. And anyone who owns one can be independent, and anyone who is independent has economic power, and economic power is political power.

So this book is about, in part, what the futurists have not said. It is also about how women can design the future for themselves, taking hold of Third Wave technology and allowing it to revolutionize their lives; how they can, if they will, make computers work for them in ways that may prove more effective in achieving their political and economic equality than activism and rhetoric could ever do. Economic power has always been, and is now, where true power lies.

Everything in this book, then, is meant to support two central, simple, and vital theses, interdependent and inseparable: (1) computers are tools with which women can transform their lives; and (2) computers will do nothing for us unless we grab hold and *make* them do something for us.

TWO

The Problems
of Working Women

The workplace is designed for the convenience and benefit of the employer, not the employee. It always has been and always will be. This fact, once stated, is so obvious that it hardly seems worth pointing out—but that's just the trouble. It's a situation we take so much for granted that no one questions it.

All of us, male and female, put up with many inconveniences for the sake of our jobs. We get up earlier than we want to, wear uncomfortable clothes, spend countless miserable hours on the freeway or on public transportation, eat unhealthful, overpriced lunches, and miss out on a lot of things we'd like to do because they happen during the hours we have to work. If we drive to work, we wear out our cars in three years. There are no figures on how fast we wear out our lungs breathing poisonous exhaust fumes. If we spend two hours a day commuting, that's fifty hours a week we spend for our jobs, not forty, and we don't get paid for those extra ten hours, which represent twenty percent of the time we spend away from home in order to work. Divide your salary by fifty hours instead of forty to see what you are *really* earning per hour. And two hours is just a mean figure. Many people in megalopolis areas spend even more time commuting; their hourly wage goes down accordingly.

It costs a lot of money just to have a job—wardrobe, transportation, parking, lunches—yet most of us can't claim any of these expenses as deductions on our income tax returns.

Women have added inconveniences and frustrations. On average, we are paid only 64 percent of what men earn for the same work. In spite of antidiscrimination laws and fifteen years of feminism, sexism remains pervasive. In the small city where I live, very few stores have women managers. Clerks are female, managers are men—those are the rules. When a managerial opening comes up, a man is hired from outside the company rather than promoting a woman. Overheard in a restaurant this spring: "Then he said, 'Why don't you stay home and raise your kids like you're supposed to?' " It's hard to believe this is still going on in the 1980s, but it is.

Sexual harassment on the job remains common, and some misogynous men still torment women even in high-level professional positions.

Funneled by high school and college counselors into already overcrowded traditional women's fields—teaching and the social services, for instance—women with college degrees can't find decent jobs. I know two women with master's degrees who work as waitresses; another is a bartender.

All these problems are compounded if a woman also happens to be disabled and/or a woman of color. Then God help her.

But a single mother has it the worst of all. Her day starts very early, since she must get her kids up, dressed, fed, and ready for daycare or school. She may have to transport them herself. Then she must get herself to work, where she puts in an eight-hour day. Her job actually takes anywhere from ten to twelve hours of her day, when you include commute time and a lunch hour. She then goes home to prepare meals, clean house, do the laundry, and try to find the time and energy to give her children the attention and love they need and deserve. She falls into bed exhausted, often without having done one single thing all day for her own benefit or enjoyment. There is little, if any, time for friendship, romance, entertainment, or any other of life's little compensations.

But that's just the beginning. Many single mothers pay out as much as 50 percent of their incomes on job-related expenses such as transportation or car maintenance, parking, clothing, and child care, so that it is impossible for them to have anything beyond the bare essentials of living, much less to save money, take an occasional vacation (badly needed), enjoy plays and concerts, or buy a beautiful dress.

If she is not fortunate enough to have a relative or friend to help out in times of crisis, the single mother may have to go to work leaving sick children in the care of someone who may or may not be competent. The emotional toll of this situation is enormous.

There are a few admirable women who have the strength and courage to cope with all this and somehow transcend it. They are paragons of strength and geniuses of adaptation. Those who are executives or professionals may earn enough to hire help to relieve some of the burden, but they, too, are pushed hard to adequately fill their multiple roles. Too many single mothers live their lives emotionally and physically exhausted, with few or none of the personal pleasures and gratifications that would make it all worthwhile. I often meet single working mothers who are depressed, bitter, and on the brink of mental and physical breakdown.

Yet I doubt if any of these women attribute their misery to the fact that they have to go out of the home to earn a living, even though most of their stress—financial, physical, and psychological—is directly related to that fact. They are much more likely to think of their problems as arising from their being single mothers.

Married women suffer some of the same problems as single mothers; the problems are just on a lesser scale. Often the net gain of working is hardly worth it after work-related expenses of working are deducted. The married woman has yet another role to fill—that of wife and partner. If her husband does not share the domestic burdens, she can be even more stressed emotionally and physically than the single mother, even though things may be easier financially; in addition to being responsible for the house and children, she has an extra person creating work for her. She may resent getting so little help from her husband, which will add to the already heavy emotional load.

It is the shared responsibility of all women (and enlightened men) to work to change these conditions—but in the meantime we must survive. And every one of the problems I have mentioned would be substantially alleviated if a woman could work at home as an independent contractor in her chosen field. But until recently, the only work that could be done in the home—typing, bookkeeping, ironing, sewing, or caring for other people's children—was so poorly paid as to be impractical. One type of penury was simply traded for another.

The microcomputer[1] has changed all that by creating new kinds of jobs that can be done at home, and by making it possible to do traditional kinds of work at home that could not conveniently be done there before.

There are two main reasons traditional jobs can be done at home more conveniently. One is that computers have changed the way information is sent from one place to another. A file of one hundred pages of text can be transmitted in minutes via telephone line from a computer in New York to a computer in Los Angeles, where the document can be read on the computer screen as soon as it is received, or, if desired, it can be printed on paper in less than an hour. Files of information can be kept in a main computer that can be accessed within minutes, via telephone, by any authorized person—if that person has a computer.

The other reason why the microcomputer makes it easier to work at home is that the computer can store records that would fill hundreds of sheets of paper on a single thin plastic disk, specially treated so that information can be stored on it in the form of electromagnetic charges. These disks vary in size and capacity, but the smallest capacity I know of is about fifty single-spaced pages. The contents of an entire four-drawer file cabinet can be stored on a handful of disks that would fit in a shoe box with room to spare.

Business records no longer take up very much space, nor are they heavy. A doctor or her secretary can carry home in a briefcase all the patient records for a small practice, and any of those same records can be transmitted in minutes from the secretary's home to the hospital or back to the doctor's office via telephone. Further, it is easy to duplicate records. Photocopying is slow and costly, but a computer disk can be copied in seconds—that's fifty to several hundred pages, depending on the capacity of the disk.

Because of the microcomputer, it no longer matters where certain kinds of work are done. In the past we had to go where the records were in order to do our work and to hand our work to other workers. Now, with a microcomputer and a telephone, most kinds of information-oriented work can be done just as well at home; this opens up innumerable new options for working at home, either as an independent contractor performing services for hire or by telecommuting[2] to a job. Banks and insurance companies are prominent among those now experimenting with telecommuting programs because it is so easy to do routine data entry, such as processing insurance claims, from a site remote from the main office.

The computer also changes the *way* work is done. It does many things for us that we used to have to do ourselves, and does them faster. It does not make mistakes unless a person has programmed a mistake into the computer to begin with. Once a program[3] is set up, it guides us through complex operations in such a way that we can't leave out or forget something, and in some cases it will even tell us if what we enter on the keyboard is not correct. The computer also enables us to do what we don't know how to do. For instance, a horse race handicapping program will ask us (by printing questions on the computer screen) for certain facts about the horses in a race. When we enter them, the computer will use criteria included in the program to pick a likely winner. We don't have to know how to handicap; we just need a program written by someone who *does* know how, and we need certain facts to be available to us. The computer does the rest. Consequently, we don't need as much expertise to do certain jobs as we did in the past, and this in turn widens our options for work we can do at home.

A more relevant example (unless you intend to take up bookmaking) is the way we write letters. Say you have written an angry letter to your landlord, but after thinking it over you decide you really ought to take out that line that refers to his "flea-infested bundle of crates you are arrogant enough to call an apartment house" and simply say "your apartments." If you have written your letter on a typewriter, the whole letter must be retyped. But on a computer with a word processing program (so called because *typing* is too limited a term to describe all the ways in which words can be manipulated on a computer), you move a little pointer on your screen called a cursor to the beginning of the word *flea*, then you push a certain key 13 times—once for each word to be deleted—and then you type in *your apartments*. That's all. The text stored in your computer's memory is changed, and all you have to do is press another few buttons to print out a new copy. You can do this any number of times you want. The value of this streamlined revision to writers is beyond calculation.

Because computers change the way we do work, they also change the amount that can be charged for traditional at-home work. Word processing can be billed at a much higher rate than conventional typing because of the speed and efficiency with which the work can be done and because of the expanded services the computer makes possible, such as sending copy to be typeset directly to a printer over the phone, which saves typesetting charges. More detail on why word processing is so fast and efficient will be given in a later chapter. The important thing to note at this point is that a person who makes $5 to $6 an hour as a typist can earn $12 to $18 an hour doing word processing.

The computer streamlines bookkeeping and accounting in similar ways, making these jobs easier and faster and allowing users to perform sophisticated acccounting functions with relative ease. The result is that bookkeeping has become a more lucrative freelance pursuit.

A number of new occupations have evolved simply to support microcomputers. Writing programs, advising people which computers and software to buy (*software* is a collective word for *programs*), designing ways for people to use microcomputers to do their work, training people to use computers, and writing instructions for computers and software are some of the more common support services. All of these services are usually very well paid, and all can be done by an independent contractor working from a home base.

So, the microcomputer not only allows work to be done at home that was not practical before, it also opens up new kinds of jobs and makes old jobs more profitable. However, from a woman's point of view, the most important single advantage of the computer revolution is that it opens up possibilities for self-employment (independence!) for women who otherwise might not have that option for lack of capital, lack of education, or because of family obligations. None of these is an insurmountable handicap if you can scrape together enough money for a microcomputer. Further, a computer allows a woman to make two to four times more per hour as an independent contractor than she did as an employee, doing the same work. No one skims a profit off the top: what she earns is what she gets. Add to this the elimination of all the problems arising from working outside the home, and without looking deeper it almost seems silly to have a "normal" job.

However, there are special problems with working at home, too, so I don't want to sell you the idea of the microcomputer as an economic panacea. There are tradeoffs to be made, and being independent makes greater demands on our characters than do most jobs. People who work at home end up working harder. And working at home is not for everyone—some people just don't like working alone; others lack the qualities of self-discipline and organization that are essential to working independently. We'll look at these things in depth later on, but obviously I think the gains are worth far more than the tradeoffs or I wouldn't have written this book. In the next chapter we'll examine in detail how running a business at home can solve problems particular to women, and some additional benefits.

---

[1] Microcomputer is the term used to distinguish the small *personal, home,* and *desktop* computers from larger, more powerful *mainframe* and *mini*-computers used in big business. These small computers have been made possible by the miniaturization of internal circuitry, and all their control and processing functions are usually contained on a single chip called a *microprocessor.* If the computer doesn't have a microprocessor it isn't a microcomputer.

[2] Telecommuting is the substitution of telecommunications for travel to and from a job. Telecommunication is the transmission of information by any device using electric or electromagnetic signals, such as radio and telephone.

[3] A program is a set of instructions that tells a computer how to receive, process, and deliver information.

THREE

The Benefits
of Working at Home

The reduction—and sometimes the elimination—of work-related expenses is the most apparent benefit of working at home, but there are many others. A few were briefly mentioned in chapter 2; a more detailed examination will make their full import apparent.

Additional Financial Benefits

TAX ADVANTAGES

Working for yourself at home allows substantial tax benefits, particularly important to women because (1) women earn substantially less than men do, and (2) even if a single-mother receives child support, the cost of supporting a single parent household is crippling. As an independent contractor you can claim as business deductions your telephone, supplies and equipment, business entertainment, travel, and part of your rent as business deductions.

During all the years I worked as a secretary I deeply resented the fact that my bosses, whose income was four times more than mine, could deduct their "business" lunches, including two whiskey sours, while I had to *pay* tax on mine. This resentment came to a critical point when I found out that a man I knew deducted all expenses for his luxury motor launch as a "research" vessel (it was never used for anything but pleasure), while I was not allowed to deduct the $5,000 a year I spent helping my daughter through college. I want to see this unfair system changed completely, but that won't happen soon; until it does, I'll see to it that I'm in the category that does the deducting!

Since I became self-employed I pay far less income tax on the same amount of gross income, simply because expenses I could not deduct as a salaried employee are now deductible. Tax inequities are a major reason I decided never to work for a salary again, and I believe that this is one of the most compelling reasons why anyone who can work for herself should do so.

EARN MORE PER HOUR FOR THE SAME WORK

Employers make a profit on your work. You get only a part of what your efforts bring in. When you work for yourself there is no one skimming profits off the top. You get it all, less only your overhead, which is a very small amount when you work at home. As a self-employed person you could be earning 50 to 100 percent more for the same work. Employed word processors make $5 to $6 an hour in one city; independent word processors in the same city make up to $18 an hour.

SECURITY

It's ironic that many people don't want to start their own business because they want the "security" of a job. Yet, losing a job is a total catastrophe, while as a free-lance or independent contractor you may lose one client, but rarely all of them. The loss of one client is seldom devastating if you have several customers, since one account represents only a percentage of your income, not all of it.

The Freedom of Flexibility

FLEXIBLE HOURS

Working at an employer's site usually means working the hours set by the employer, a certain number of hours per week, indefinitely. Even flex-time jobs usually are flexible only within certain limits. But mothers working at home can schedule their work while their kids are at school or sleeping. Work time can be adapted to each family's unique priorities. If you want to schedule a game of tennis at 10:00 A.M., or a college class at 2:00, you can.

Students on limited incomes and with scheduling problems can work between classes, late at night, on weekends, or whenever their other activities slow down. Artists, actresses, writers, and other creative people who have a hard time making a living at their art can schedule income-producing time in and around the demands of their artistic pursuits.

As part of my research for this book I interviewed more than thirty women who work at home with computers. Almost everyone I spoke with said one of the principal advantages of working at home was flexibility. Working by someone else's clock and in someone else's office locks your life in a rigid format, with your schedules tailored to your employer's needs, not your own. The potential for customizing your life to suit your own unique circumstances is one of the most powerful incentives for finding a way to work at home on your own schedule.

FREEDOM TO WORK ANYWHERE

Many businesses can be run from almost any location. This is of tremendous importance to your personal morale, and it allows you the freedom to choose the environment in which your children grow up. People with urban burnout can move to small towns and go into the city only when necessary to call on clients.

Public relations agency owner Kathryn Hubbell lives in Eugene, Oregon, but uses her computer and telecommunications networks to market her services nationally.

I have an ancient (1968) step-van that I have fixed up as an RV, complete with a desk and four-drawer file. I installed a DC-to-AC current converter, which allows me to run my portable Osborne 1 from an auxiliary auto battery. I can work anywhere—even on a remote mountaintop miles from the nearest electrical outlet. Because a few diskettes (the magnetic storage media resembling little phonograph records on which all working data is stored) take the place of reams of paper, it is a simple matter to take my work with me wherever I go. Hundreds of pages fit into a little box or a briefcase.

Stephen Roberts is a writer who is traveling the United States on a bicycle, financing the trip by selling stories about his adventure. He carries a Tandy Model 100 lap computer weighing only 8 pounds. He writes his stories on the computer, then hooks up with a public telephone wherever he happens to be, calls CompuServe—a computer network service—and uploads the story to his own special workspace he gets as a CompuServe subscriber. His assistant back home then uploads the story to her computer and prints it out for mailing to his publisher.

I carry my 8-pound notebook-size Epson PX-8 in my rucksack and hike into the Utah Canyonlands wilderness. I can work sitting in the sun with a rock as a backrest, occasionally resting my eyes by lifting them to gaze at the red rock canyons. While I think, I can watch a raven drifting on the air currents. I also take my PX-8 to my favorite restaurant in Moab, which has an outdoor patio where I can work in fresh air and enjoy the excellent iced tea. Working in restaurants eases the loneliness of writing, yet I am uninterrupted.

Lap computers can be used to turn long trips by plane or car into productive time. The possibilities are limited only by the user's imagination.

WORK AS LITTLE OR AS MUCH AS DESIRED

Many single individuals with a low-key lifestyle do not need a full-time income, yet part-time jobs are not easy to find. Others are workaholics and like to commit the major part of their lives to their work. Both types can customize their work lives to suit their needs by working for themselves.

Computer programmer and consultant Heather Ellin, of Truckee, California, is one of the first type. She works hard (and gets an excellent fee) for a few months a year, then spends the rest of the year traveling.

TIME FREED FOR OTHER PURSUITS

An immense amount of time is saved by the elimination of commuting (usually two hours or more daily), shuttling children to and from daycare, frittered-away lunch hours, and by working only as much as needed to produce the income you want. That time can be used for exercise, rest, and recreation; for quality time with your children; for self-education leading to career advancement; or for any other productive activity you now have no time for. Saving two hours a day is equivalent to an entire workday weekly. What could you do with an extra day each week?

KEEPING LOVED ONES OUT OF INSTITUTIONS

Many elderly persons, handicapped or retarded children, and chronically or terminally ill people must be kept in hospitals or institutions because no one in the family can afford to quit his or her job and stay home to care for them. The morale in such institutions is very low, so people feel guilty about placing a loved family member in such a place. In addition, the care is expensive beyond all reason, and if there is not insurance coverage the cost may keep the family in financial slavery. The care is often scandalously bad. My eighty-three-year-old mother lay in her nursing home bed with a broken hip for three days before I discovered it on a visit. She had fallen and someone had just dumped her back into bed without an examination. I was nearly homicidal with rage and pain, but at the time there was no way out of the nightmare because I could not stay home to take care of her.

Ironically, many institutionalized persons don't require much care; they just need someone to be there in case of need.

Caring for such a person is easy to combine with working at home with a computer. It's an alternative that might allow many to come home.

WORK CAN BE ADAPTED TO MARRIED LIFE

In some marriages both partners have careers. When a career is a top priority for each partner, it can be a severe strain on the marriage, especially if one spouse is transferred to a different city. Many couples solve this problem by maintaining separate households and visiting on weekends—an extreme measure, but better than dissolving a marriage that otherwise may be working well.

For those whose jobs require a lot of personal contact and visibility, working at home all the time is not feasible. But people with jobs in information-related fields may be able to do a certain percentage of their work at home with a computer, then transmit their work to the home office by phone, even from another city. Such an arrangement would allow partners separated by their careers to spend more time together, perhaps extending the two-day weekend to three or even four days.

Another common situation is that one partner has a career and the other is committed first and foremost to the marriage and the family, with earning money or pursuing a career coming second. In such cases, working at home can be ideal, since that work can be custom-fitted to the career of the other partner and to the demands of family life.

Carla Govreau lives in Moab, Utah. Her husband works for Union Oil in oil exploration and expects to be transferred every few years. Carla has a degree in computer science, but it isn't practical for her to hold a career job because (1) she has chosen to give her husband's career first priority and (2) she wants to be at home with her two daughters while they are small. So, Carla does programming at home and teaches computer classes at the local university extension, which satisfies her need to do something in addition to mothering and housekeeping.

WORK IN COMFORT

It is ninety-six degrees outside right now. I am working stark naked, with a glass of iced tea—endlessly refillable—at my side, classical music playing softly in the background. A fan hums soothingly in the corner, aimed just the way I want it. I have an air conditioner, too, which I keep at a temperature I consider healthful and comfortable. I don't have to accept someone else's idea of what is good for me. I don't have to put up with cigarette or cigar smoke, or people I don't like, or noise or distractions. I have an upholstered chaise-type chair, so I can sit with my feet extended and lean back comfortably with my computer keyboard in my lap. My kitty Millicent is snoozing on the back of the chair. If I need a purr, I reach up and stroke her back. My office is a mess. I think I don't like it that way but I must since I never clean it up. No one says anything to me about it. It's my space, absolutely.

If I get stuck or bored or lonely, I can quit for a while and call a friend. No one cares. When it's lunch time I'll fix myself a glorious salad with my favorite homemade dressing. It will be twice as big as a restaurant salad and cost one-third as much. It will have in it exactly what I want.

Writing requires quite a lot of cerebration, as do many other kinds of work, and while that is going on the body is idle. I get up and do some mindless chores around the house. Pulling up weeds is an amazing stimulator of creative thought, as is taking a shower or washing the dishes. Sometimes I just sit and stare out the window at the desert behind my house. There is no one to say I am not working just because my hands aren't typing.

When I take a break it is a real one. I drive down to the store or take a walk in the spectacular red rocks that are the reason I live in the Canyonlands. I get up in the middle of the night to write things down, and I take a nap in the middle of the day.

These pleasures can be yours.

Psychological Benefits

CHILDREN GET THEIR MOTHER BACK

A mother who works at home is there when her kids come home from school. She does not have to leave sick children, and she is available when accidents or other emergencies arise at school. The several million latchkey kids—children who come home from school to an empty house—are a major problem in our society. They are more likely to get into trouble and are more vulnerable to molestation.

The psychological well-being of both mothers and children should be considerably improved with the stress of being separated at critical times removed.

REDUCED STRESS

The cumulative psychological stress of spending two hours a day or more on the freeway, of having to leave sick or unattended children, of financial worries, and of coping with corporate madness can have profound effects on morale. Working at home has its own set of stresses, but most of the women I interviewed for this book felt that they had been relieved of tremendous psychological pressures—especially sexism—by becoming home-based workers.

PERSONAL GROWTH AND DEVELOPMENT

There are incalculable rewards to be reaped from putting to use all the potentials that are often actively discouraged in women's job environments (unless they are in management, and sometimes even then): initiative, creativity, responsibility, and self-discipline.

For many, the necessity of overcoming socially conditioned dependency in order to work independently leads to an overall improvement in all levels of their lives.

In the next chapter you will meet some women who discuss how working for themselves has changed them, and a few who have undergone complete transformations.

INCREASED SELF-ESTEEM

Many of the women I talked to while researching this book mentioned higher opinions of themselves as an unexpected result of their entrepreneurial efforts. Management attitudes toward women in secretarial and clerical positions are too often condescending; when we live with these attitudes day in and day out, our self-regard erodes away, even though we may know better. But women who work for themselves are seen differently and treated differently by other people in business.

Kaye Ireland, of Gallitan, Tennessee, left her job in a hospital to start a business providing computer services to medical offices. She says, "When you're a secretary or an office worker, they [the doctors] take you for granted; you're about as important as a typewriter. As long as the work's produced, they don't really care about you; they even take their rage out on their employees sometimes. Now their attitude toward me is completely different. They relate to me as a person on their level, another professional, and it makes me feel good about myself."

RELIEF FROM BOREDOM

As a home-based businessperson you must wear many hats. You must be your own PR person, advertising manager, bookkeeper, supply manager, and receptionist, in addition to performing the main services for which you are being paid. Even those services will have considerable variety, because you will be doing them for many clients, not just for one company as you do in a job. Although any business has chores that are routine and monotonous, changing hats often and having a variety of clients is much less boring than most jobs.

Nina Feldman, who owns a word processing service in Oakland, California, says that although word processing itself is not that exciting, she never knows what she will be doing next, and that anticipation keeps her interested. One of her most interesting jobs was typing the manuscript for the autobiography of a woman scientist—something she would not have had the opportunity to do in a conventional typing job.

Expanded Horizons

OPPORTUNITIES THAT WOULD NOT BE OPEN OTHERWISE

To open any kind of business in a commercial location costs a great deal of money. Not only are commercial rents high, but furnishings must be bought, services contracted for, signs erected, and permits obtained. Because monthly overhead is high, most businesses do not make a profit for at least the first year. That's why business experts recommend that you have a year's living expenses in reserve in addition to the substantial amount of capital required just to open your business.

Many women do not have that much money, nor do they have the credit base to borrow it. But a business run from home can be started with a minimal amount of cash, and because the overhead is extremely low (you are using facilities you already have), you can start making money immediately. Many women who never could have even dreamed of owning a business can now do so if they can come up with enough cash for a microcomputer and a printer—roughly $2,000 to $4,000—and a few months' living expenses. Prices for small business computers are dropping fast, and by the time you read this book you may be able to get started for even less. If you have a mate or have someone who is willing to pay your living expenses for a few months, then all you need is the equipment.

MORE POTENTIAL FOR CAREER ADVANCEMENT

When you work for yourself, advancement is automatic. As long as a market exists for your services, your own initiative, talent, and dedication will bring you automatic rewards in the form of more and more business. Many women are stuck in jobs that offer no openings for career advancement, no matter how talented they are. We are all familiar with the plight of the secretary who has all the responsibilities of an administrator without the title or the pay and is never promoted. With your own business you get the credit *and* the money.

Even if your business should fail or you decide that working at home just doesn't work for you, you have a whole new set of the most marketable skills you could possibly have—computer skills. Joan Gough, of Moab, Utah, provides a wide range of computer services, from computer tutoring to mailing list maintenance, through her business, Access. But Moab is a very small town and its economy has been devastated by the closing of its main industry, a mineral processing plant. It is not certain that Joan's business will ever flourish, although she is holding on. Joan says, "I'm having fun, but I'm still not sure I'll survive."

Joan has also discovered that she doesn't like having to knock on doors to hustle up business: "I'm not a businessperson. I'm not really good at aggressively marketing my services. I'm not suited to it temperamentally."

Joan may eventually give up her business and take a job again. However, she insists that the time she is investing now will not be lost. Joan is a teacher and librarian, and she'd like to work in a school or a library again. She says, "I really love library work, and my experience with computers would fit in beautifully. Libraries are going to computers, and that's what I would do. I know how to tutor students on the computer now, and I know I would use that in any job I took. I know that everything I've learned how to do on the computer and the skills I've developed can be used in some way. This time and experience wouldn't be lost at all."

SELF-SUFFICIENCY FOR THE PHYSICALLY AND EMOTIONALLY HANDICAPPED

Handicaps that prevent people from earning their own livings can range from moderately impaired eyesight to the almost total disability of quadraplegics. Many of these people can't do ordinary work of any kind because they either can't speak on the telephone, can't write or type, or can't read, depending on their particular disability.

There is an exquisite paradox in the fact that a person who cannot even hold a pencil may be able to operate a computer. That computers are the greatest thing that ever happened for the handicapped is already widely recognized. Several very good programs exist to train the disabled to use computers as well as to make computer use easy for those who can't use their hands or eyes.

For the visually impaired, there are computer screens that display oversize letters, and programs that, in conjunction with voice synthesizers, vocalize everything entered on the keyboard. Other hardware/software combinations produce Braille print-outs from ordinary English keyboard input.

For those who do not have full use or control of their hands, there are a variety of devices. One program, called *KEYLOC*, is for people who can't hold down more than one key at a time—it converts all momentary-action keys to alternate-action keys. Another product uses Morse code to allow all keyboard functions to be controlled by two switches.

Quadraplegics and cerebral palsy victims, who have very limited control of their movements, can use a variety of devices such as a stick held in the teeth or attached to the forehead to tap on special keyboards, or ingenious blow-and-sip devices held in the mouth and controlled with the breath.

Computers quite literally enable handicapped people to work who could not work before. To move from complete dependency—and often a state of hopelessness—to self-sufficiency results in a degree of improved morale and self-esteem that can't even be imagined by those who have not been in that position. In chapter five you will meet a handicapped woman whose life and personality were completely transformed by learning to support herself with computers.

Not only can handicapped people now enter the job market with computer skills, but telecommuting makes working possible even for those who are too disabled to leave their homes or beds—something that until now has been unimaginable.

EXTENDED WORK LIFE FOR THE RETIRED

Many people are forced to retire before they want to, and age discrimination in the job market makes it very difficult to find even a part-time job to supplement a retirement income. I am not the first to comment that our retired elders are a vast national resource of experience and wisdom going to waste.

Computer work is not stressful physically, does not have to be done full-time, and, as we have already seen, can be done even by people who have lost significant physical capacities. Once again, the fact that computers allow a wide variety of work to be done in the home means you can't get too old to earn money.

Helen Sobell was fifty years old when her son, age sixteen, got her interested in computers. Because Helen had a teaching background, she saw very quickly that computers could make it possible for people to learn in a much more individualized way. After taking a course in programming, she found a job as a programming apprentice at Teachers College of Columbia University. She also started working for her master's degree in science education and taught a course called "Computers in Education—Problems and Issues." Later she worked as a systems analyst (an expert who figures out how to solve large "system" problems with computers). Finally, in 1980, at the age of sixty-two, she received her doctorate in science education.

Helen was sixty-six and still teaching when I interviewed her. Her doctoral dissertation was "A General Systems Approach to a Language for Problem Analysis." Her central idea was that the kind of thinking one must do in order to write computer programs can be usefully applied to other kinds of problems we encounter in all sectors of our lives. This philosophy gives Helen a special slant as a teacher of computer skills.

Helen feels that people can undertake a computer career at any age, but warns that it takes "a willingness to stand naked in the bright light of knowledge. I have seen older people, both men and women, who could not tackle a computer problem because they felt they had a certain status to maintain and they felt vulnerable when they moved out of their own area of expertise and found themselves inferior in computer knowledge to younger, less experienced, and less educated people. But if one can do that, it is a very worthwhile accomplishment."

Mary Furlong and Greg Kearsley, authors of *Computers for Kids Over 60: Keeping Up with the Computer Generation* (Addison-Wesley), gave a series of computer literacy workshops in senior citizen centers and nursing homes in Washington, D.C. Mary told me she was surprised to find that her students enjoyed writing their own programs more than playing computer games or using off-the-shelf applications such as word processing and budget management programs. She has taught people in their eighties and nineties to program and says that older people make excellent programmers because they are more patient and persistent, more relaxed, and follow directions better than middle-aged adults. She comments, "The employed person coming in from a job to a class doesn't have much time and wants to learn very quickly." One thing retired people have is plenty of time!

I know of a number of courses that were created for older people. Check your town's senior citizen center or retired people's organizations for computer courses especially designed for older people; perhaps you won't have to stand naked in front of anyone but your peers.

A WAY TO DROP OUT—PRODUCTIVELY—
FOR THE ALIENATED AND THE BATTLE-FATIGUED

Many Vietnam veterans suffer from a condition known as *post-trauma stress syndrome* (PTSS). They were so emotionally brutalized by the war that they can no longer cope with the ordinary stresses of interfacing with society, much less hold a job, and often they are not able to handle personal relationships. Some are so damaged that they retreat to the wilderness, living in huts or abandoned mines and getting by any way they can.

Although little recognized, this same syndrome, in a milder form, shows up in all kinds of people who have been brutalized by life in one way or another. Not exactly crazy, they are just worn out. The "hobo jungles" are full of them. However, the inability to cope is not always that extreme. Some people escape to drugs or booze, or become dependent on welfare or family, or take jobs far below their capabilities because they are easy and low on stress.

I often see signs of PTSS in women. To the world at large they may appear apathetic, to have just given up. The battered woman who goes back to the man who beats her may simply not have the strength left to make it on her own. The world is full of secretaries who have all the skill and good judgment needed to make good managers, but who will not seek promotion because they know they can't handle the responsibility. Such women may have difficult marriages, or may be single parents who are exhausted by their double roles, and they may have any of a thousand additional problems—a bad childhood or financial difficulties, to name two common ones.

People can deal with occasional huge traumas, such as the loss of a job or the death of a loved one, better than they can with an endless succession of lesser tribulations. There has to be a letup between traumas; we must have rest. If there is no rest, some essential core of the spirit wears out. Women and minorities are prime candidates because of the constant, never-ending stress of discrimination and the resulting problems with poor self-esteem and resentment that undermine morale.

I often meet PTSS victims in the small towns where I have spent the last ten years of my life. These people have to get away from the freneticism of big cities and are drawn to the laid-back lifestyle of small towns. But often they are hard pressed to support themselves in limited small town economies, and it is sad that they often must leave the country, which they find healing, and go back to the city to earn a living—back to the same environment that may have had a lot to do with the condition they are in.

Obviously, the opportunity to work at home—away from the constant stresses of interaction with people, commuting, competition, office politics, and overt prejudice—offers an excellent solution for such people, whether they are in the country or in the city.

COMPUTER TRAINING PROGRAMS
GIVE PRISONERS A NEW CHANCE

In 1981, Best Western Hotel headquarters in Phoenix had problems meeting its need for reservations clerks in its 1,900 hotels during peak seasons. Somebody had a brainstorm: the Arizona Center for Women (a euphemism for *prison*) was only seven miles away; why not teach the prisoners to operate computer terminals and let them make reservations from the prison, entering the information into the hotel's mainframe computer from the terminals at the prison site? At first the idea was laughed at, but after a while it was taken seriously. At least the prisoners were certain to be available on call!

Best Western contacted the prison administration, which went for the idea. After all, the women would learn new skills, earn some money, and help support themselves at the prison.

Today, twenty to fifty women (depending on need) work at terminals supplied by Best Western, earning $3.75 to $3.98 per hour. They receive two weeks' training before starting work, and they have the option of becoming Best Western employees upon their release from the institution. Several graduates of the program are now working on the regular staff at Best Western headquarters. Whether or not the women from the program choose to work for Best Western when they leave prison, they have learned marketable skills that can help them get a new start.

It is only because of computer technology and the ability to communicate from terminals at the prison to the mainframe at Best Western headquarters that this program is possible. The Best Western program is unique, but is an exciting model of how the business world can help itself and help prisoners too if it wants to, and of how computers and telecommuting can open up life-transforming options not possible otherwise.

FOUR

How Women Have Used Computers to Change Their Lives

Scientists use the word *elegant* to describe a solution that is both sophisticated and simple. They say all "real" solutions to scientific and technological problems have this characteristic of elegance. Consider the helixical structure of DNA. Consider the wheel, or the simple wood screw.

The microcomputer is an elegant machine. It is sophisticated because it can do more work in ten seconds than a team of mathematicians can do on paper in a year. It is simple because a microcomputer is nothing more than a series of electrical circuits with thousands (soon to be millions) of little electronic off/on switches.

But, as impressed as I am by computers, it would be ridiculous for me to claim that if you buy a computer all your work problems will be solved. The computer is only a tool, and problem-solving begins with human ingenuity and will. Initiative and the will to triumph are not enough if the *means* for solutions do not exist, however. In many cases, the computer provides that means. I do claim that in the hands of a person with imagination, initiative, creativity, and the will to triumph over her problems, the computer becomes a powerful enabler. It becomes a tool for transformation.

Chris England owns Writers Inc., an agency that contracts

technical writers for the computer industry. Chris started out as a technical writer twelve years ago, writing user documentation.[1] She was eventually promoted into management, which she didn't like. "Fortunately," she says, "the company went bankrupt."

At her "retirement" party, she received a year's subscription to *TV Guide*, a box of bon-bons, and bedroom slippers. "In six weeks' time I was going crazy," she says. "I thought I was going to wallpaper the garage. I had a lot of energy and I was used to being very productive. So I decided to go back to my first love—technical writing. But in the meantime I had fallen in love with my free time, so I decided to go back on a consulting basis."

Chris did not plan to start an agency; it evolved because she knew a lot of people in the computer industry, and she received more calls for her services than she could accept. She saw that there was a real need for an agency just for technical writers and that she was well qualified to evaluate portfolios and match writers to the special needs of computer companies. That was four years before I interviewed her; she now rates her business as "very successful."

Chris has an IBM Displaywriter, which is a dedicated word processor.[2] Chris says it is a vital tool. "Because my people change contracts so much, their résumés are constantly being updated, so I put their résumés on the IBM and I can easily add each new job without retyping the whole résumé. If I had to do that on the typewriter, it would be a full-time job. I also store common business letters and my invoices. What I need now is a data base for my people so I can search easily for the special skills to match a client's job. Now it is a tedious, time-consuming job of going through all the paper files."

Working at home made it possible for Chris to work while pregnant right up to her due date. She says, "Being pregnant slowed me down a little bit, but it did wonders for my business." All the world loves an expectant mother, and Chris found it got her instant empathy, which in turn helped get business.

When the baby was born Chris found she needed full-time help. "For the first six weeks after the baby came, I'd put the phone on the answering machine for the better part of the day and return phone calls during nap time. But I found I couldn't really be productive that way. This is a very competitive business and you really can't do it by halves. So I started bringing someone in to take care of the baby. It was great, because she could take care of him—his nap cycle really didn't matter—but I could stop, put the phone on the answering machine, and nurse him. I nursed him until he was a year old. Since I stopped nursing him I've been sending him to a daycare center two days a week for his own good—for his socialization.

"The flexibility of my work is absolutely great in terms of the baby. I can schedule my work around doctor's appointments. The daycare center called me the other day to tell me I forgot to take my baby's favorite blanket with him. I just put the answering machine on and in five minutes I was down there with his blanket—they're right down the street. There are times when I miss him and so I take a whole day off just to be with him. I see much more of him routinely, too, than if I had a job. I don't have an hour commute at either end of my day.

"It's very important for work-at-home mothers to find out what services are available to them. Through the American Association of University Women I found a cooperative daycare center. I look at leaflets in the obstetrician's office to find out what services are available and how I can use them."

Note that although Chris England ultimately chose to have full-time help with her baby, working at home still offers many benefits for her as a mother—including being able to nurse her baby for a year.

When Chris first decided to work from home as a freelance technical writer, and later when she formed her agency, she wasn't a mother. She was looking for a way to enjoy her freedom and, at the same time, work at something she liked. The benefits that came to her as a new mother were extra.

But serendipity didn't end there. Chris's husband, Art, was an executive manager of systems and programming at a major food chain. When he resigned from his job in 1983, he knew that the next job he took would probably be the one he would retire from in ten or fifteen years. Chris's business made it financially possible for him to take several months off to enjoy his new baby and to relax. He was still on his "sabbatical" when I interviewed Chris. During the interview, Art came in to ask what tablecloth Chris would like to use for the dinner he was preparing for company that evening. Art enjoys cooking, and Chris says she hasn't had to cook for three months. "This has been a wonderful hiatus for him," she says, smiling happily. Obviously it has been wonderful for Chris and the baby too.

By taking advantage of opportunities in the computer world, and by using a word processing computer to make it possible to handle a great deal of clerical work in jig time, she has exploited all the computer's potentials so that her life is exactly the way she wants it.

Miriam ("Mim") Hawley runs an editing service from her home, using her EXO computer. She also does occasional transportation consulting. She went into business for herself because she couldn't find a job. Since she is an extremely qualified person, she knows she hasn't been hired because of her age: fifty-five when I interviewed her. She would have preferred a job but had been frustrated so many times that she got fed up and started her own business.

Miriam had a B.A. in economics when she married and dropped out of the job market for fifteen years to raise her children. When her children were old enough she went back to school and earned a master's degree in history because she likes the subject and because she knew that it would take too much time to catch up with economics after fifteen years out of the field. But when she received her master's degree and applied for a teaching job, she was asked, "Why should we hire you? You haven't worked for fifteen years. What makes you think you can come out of school now at the age of forty-four and go to work?" All she was able to find were part-time teaching jobs.

It took Miriam a year and a half to find a full-time job. She was finally hired to work on the federally funded impact study of the BART transportation system in San Francisco, stayed with it five years, and wrote their final report. When that project was finished, she had considerable expertise in the field of transportation and land use, and went to work for a transportation-consulting firm, where she stayed until they went out of business.

This time job hunting was even harder. Miriam says, "No one was saying out loud, 'My, aren't you kind of old?' People think I should be retired, or the people who interview me are twenty-five and they think I'm their mother or grandmother. I didn't get jobs I know I would have gotten twenty years ago—jobs I know I could do. I found all this very difficult and distasteful. I looked very hard for about six months. I may have given up too soon, but I was just very irked about the situation. Sometimes I think that maybe I really need to fight that fight [against ageism] to show myself I can do it; but on the other hand, if I can do it this way, if I can actually work my children's way through college and be relatively interested and happy in what I'm doing, then I prefer not to fight."

So Miriam began freelance consulting. She has done performance evaluations of local public transportation systems and a national study of business location decisions in relation to the transportation available.

Miriam bought a computer because she thought it would be useful for word processing and statistical analysis in her consulting business. She says, "I spent about three months getting acquainted with the equipment and the programs, and waiting for customers to come to me—I wasn't very aggressive at that point." When she found that consulting jobs sometimes came months apart, she decided to exploit the computer's potential by starting a word processing business to fill in the gaps in her consulting income and to help pay for the equipment. Eventually she stopped actively looking for consulting jobs and concentrated on the editing services that now comprise the major part of her business.

Of working for herself, Miriam says, "It's nice to work at home. I like the flexibility of being able to go out and work in the garden a bit or work in the evenings if I need to. I like the ability to accept or reject jobs; there are some people I really don't want to work for and I simply turn them down. When you work in an office you don't have that choice."

Like most of the other women I interviewed, Miriam takes advantage of women's networks and organizations and cooperates with other women who do word processing. "I've met a number of people who have become my friends through the networks. Several of us can connect with modems, and if we get overloads of work or want to go on vacation we can get someone to take care of our business. That's a nice feeling, to work in that kind of cooperative arrangement. Also, I like knowing how to deal with computers. I feel like I'm keeping up with the world.

"It's important to feel competent, to be able to feel you can go out and learn a new skill and make it work. Just making a business go to the extent that I can pay my expenses, buy the equipment over time, and make some money feels like more of an accomplishment than when I worked at a full-time job where I earned much more money. I have more of a feeling of being in charge when I'm doing it on my own."

Miriam doesn't wait for customers to come to her anymore. She advertises in local newspapers. She also receives referrals from previous customers.

We live in a culture that has a myth, perpetuated in hundreds of movies and TV shows, that those who do not fight injustice directly are failures, perhaps cowards. Other cultures, notably Far Eastern ones, esteem very highly the ability to "let go" and find another path to an objective. Miriam chose to avoid a battle against ageism in the job market that might have left her exhausted and bitter, and chose instead to put her positive and creative energy into an alternative solution. That solution has turned out to be more rewarding to her than the employment she sought.

Mary Dum had been working at home for many years, doing the office work for her real-estate-appraiser husband, when she became excited about computers and bought one. She taught herself to use the computer for all aspects of the real estate business, which involves a great deal of manipulation of data. Mary exploited all the knowledge and skills she already had, adapting them to the computer.

Mary says, "The computer enabled us to handle a lot more work in the same amount of time, so we were able to generate more income without hiring more people. Because I was in it ahead of a lot of people in the real estate field [Mary got her first microcomputer in 1978], I got a lot of calls from people who needed help setting up their computers. I threw myself into it and spent a lot of time with computers, so I learned a lot in my first year, and I was helping people to set up computers in my first year. I began to realize that I was giving away my time and putting a lot of energy into helping other people. I realized there was a niche to be filled." So, Mary became a consultant for real estate computer applications, a specialized service that brings a very respectable fee.

Mary feels that becoming a computer expert has had a significant impact on her marriage. "Computers have changed my life: although I am married to the same man, I am treated as an equal now. We were Midwestern people and he was a farmer before we were married. Without meaning to be, he was very much the traditional male. He used to say, 'My wife, who is my secretary,' but I was never his secretary. Now if he were to say such a thing other people besides myself would make fun of him. I'm definitely carrying my half. I do all the public relations, much of it by public speaking. I spoke at the NAR [National Association of Realtors] convention, and they still play the game of asking Tom to speak too, on the same topic, at the same time. But now he refuses, and says 'I don't talk on that.' I speak on implementing computers in the business province. One of my main topics is how to choose software. I also edit a newsletter for a real estate group.

"So my computer expertise has changed my relationship with my husband. We get along a lot better; he may not think so, but I think so. It took time. The first week that I began to get as many calls as he did, he decided we had to have another phone immediately. He couldn't possibly share that. But he got over it.

"I have a great deal more self-confidence. I always knew that I could do things. I was raised with that belief, but I hadn't found the thing that I was going to do until I was past forty. I was a pre-med student before I got married, but I gave it up when I married Tom because in the fifties a career in medicine and motherhood didn't mix. It's hard now, but it was harder then."

Part of Mary's consulting service involves teaching people to use computers and software. Age fifty-two at the time I interviewed her, she says, "In the type of consulting I do it's a definite advantage to have gray hair. It makes you seem like everybody's mother, and that's all they want, somebody to hold their hand and say, 'I'll take care of you, don't worry about it,' and they go away happily believing that. Hell, maybe I can't do it either, but I'm not worried about it, and I take it easy and we eventually solve all the problems one way or another. And they pay me to do that."

Mary Dum now owns five computers.

Miriam Liskin wanted to be a scientist from the time she was eight years old, but by the time she was in college as a biochemistry major she was developing values that alienated her from what she calls "mainstream middle America." It wasn't that she had chosen the wrong career, exactly, but by the time she got her master's in biochemistry and discovered what she would have to put up with in order to do the work she wanted to do, she felt the price was too high.

"I realized that being a scientist in reality means you have to work sixty hours a week for the rest of your life. You have to compete for grant money, which is very scarce within this little cutthroat academic world. I hate the fact that it's like that, but it is. My ideal from the start was to find a little niche which would not be on this high-power track and try to exist on that level and just do some interesting research, but there wasn't very much money for the kind of research I was doing: enzyme mechanisms. Not a hot field. I didn't want to get into genetic engineering because I was politically opposed to it, but that's where all the money was, and is. I would have had to move anywhere in the U.S. they offered me a job, because jobs were so hard to come by, and it was going to be a sixty-hour-a-week struggle forever and I would have had to be constantly competitive. I didn't lose interest in any of the things I was studying or working on, and I worked really hard when I wanted to, but I didn't want the end result, I didn't want to live like that."

While Miriam was working on her master's degree the biochemistry department acquired a desktop IBM computer. The secretaries in the department wouldn't touch the computer (!), so it ended up down in the lab. Miriam had taken some programming courses in high school and had used mainframe computers, which she didn't like because, since they were used by everyone, there was usually a long wait to get things done. But when the IBM desktop came to the lab, Miriam wrote some programs for it. "When I was a teaching assistant in biochemistry I got interested in educational programming and I wrote a whole series of programs to simulate experiments for the under-graduate lab classes.

"Nobody ever read the handouts in advance the way they're supposed to. I got the idea that a student could go to the computer and step through the whole thing before doing the experiment. You would tell the computer how to set up the experiment, it would give the results, you could interpret the results, and then the program would ask you some review questions. You would go through the whole process without having to manipulate the physical equipment. If the students could do that in advance they would really understand what was going on, so when they actually got in the lab they could concentrate on learning how to do it physically. I wrote all these programs and people in the department were really enthusiastic but nobody wanted to actually do anything with it because to use it effectively required buying ten terminals.[3] At that time, it wasn't even clear that the big computer would accommodate ten more terminals. But that got me interested in programming."

Miriam's disenchantment with the competitive academic world of science led her to quit school when she earned her master's degree, without knowing what she was going to do next. To pass the time while she decided what to do, she started fixing cars.

It was during this period that the Apple II, the first widely popular and commercially successful personal computer, appeared on the market. Some friends of Miriam's loaned her one for a month, and this was the turning point. "I thought, this is it. This is how it's all going to come together. I love programming, I love computers, and here is a small computer that I can have total control over. I don't have to wait for hours to get on a system. I also saw the opportunity to get a job other than with one of the huge companies. During the time I was working on cars there were only two of us in the shop, and for a time I worked alone, and I liked that a lot and realized that I wanted to be self-employed or work in a very small business. I didn't want to work my way up through the power structure of a large corporation, playing politics, working for years for a boss who is not as smart as you are and who doesn't give you credit for your ideas, as my father did for so many years. I knew I could never make it in that kind of environment.

"Computers were something I had always liked, and I liked

the small ones even more. The small computer could make it possible for me to work in an environment I could nearly completely control. I saw that I could live separately, the way I wanted to live, outside the mainstream of American culture, and not be bothered by the system but still get what I want out of it because this [small-computer skills] is something that they need."

So Miriam worked for ComputerLand for a year and a half while she learned about small computers. ComputerLand gave her the opportunity to use many different systems. "The people who worked there were really into computers, and we'd close the store and stay until midnight just playing around. The important thing was to have four or five hours to sit there and try things. That job was definitely important and gave me a chance to learn a lot of specific things."

Miriam is now teaching, consulting, and writing a computer trouble-shooting column for *Computer Currents*, a biweekly Bay Area magazine in newspaper format. She works out of her pleasant woodframe house in Berkeley, California. She does, indeed, work the way she wants to. "I am a night person—for some reason programmers are almost always night people—and I have the freedom to stay up until three or four in the morning. I have to dress up for certain clients, but when I don't have to, I don't, and when I get home I can forget about it. I don't have to be somewhere every day at nine o'clock, and I hope soon to have the freedom to say I'm not making any appointments in the morning at all. I like working any hour of the day or night, or being able to start and stop at random. I like to stop working at five or six in the afternoon, see friends in the evening, and start again at ten at night."

Miriam wants to expand her business, and she says that, ideologically, she likes the idea of taking on partners who would have equal interest, equal responsibility, and equal profits. But, smiling, she adds, "For the same reason that I wouldn't want to work for a boss, I now want to have an employee. I'd like to have control over what's going on in the business but not do everything myself. I feel attracted to the idea of having an employee who will do what I want even if it turns out to be stupid."

Miriam does not regret the years she invested in an education in science. "When I was an undergraduate, I was trying to learn as much as possible about every kind of science, and I'm glad I did that. I hope to put it all together in an integrated world view, and I couldn't possibly consider it a waste to have studied everything I did. Because of my science education I learned to break down a problem into pieces and how to think about solving each piece, and applying the same method to programming was just a matter of hacking away at it until it began to work. What I liked about science was figuring out at a microscopic level just how things work. Programming is just reversing that process, making a microscopic little machine solve a problem to make something work. If the truth were known, the reason I'm in it now is that someone's paying me to sit around and solve puzzles."

Miriam is a prime example of how the computer can be used by society's nonconformists (often our most creative people) to get out of a system that stifles them, to find a way to be independent and productive, and still to contribute something to the whole.

Nina Feldman likes to sing and play with local music groups, listen to music, and hang out with her friends. "I do a variety of things, from jazz to sixties rock. It's a hobby. I never had the idea that it would be a paid career; I wouldn't even want it that way." Since Nina didn't want to go professional with her music, she had to do something else to earn a living, but music is a stay-up-late-get-up-late lifestyle that doesn't mesh well with conventional jobs.

A few years ago she worked as a cook, but found it too exhausting to be on her feet all day. She signed up as an office clerk with a temporary agency, since that would get her off her feet and give her some flexibility to accommodate her lifestyle, but temporary work didn't pay very well for people without typing skills, and so Nina went back to school to brush up on her typing.

Nina hadn't been working long as a typist when she learned that word processing, which was very new at the time, paid much better than typing. At that time, however, about the only way to learn word processing was to take a full-time job and be trained by the employer. So that's what she did. She was hired and trained by Bank of America, and she was the single word processor for twenty-five people. But having to be at work at eight o'clock didn't fit Nina's life. "I never got enough sleep. I can't say how much that affected me. Some people seem to be able to stay up late and get up early, but I was constantly a wreck."

Nina's job was phased out when Bank of America decided to buy word processors for all the secretaries. Nina was told she would have to become a secretary, which she didn't want to do, so she quit. "I went back to working temporary. Word processing for temporary agencies is pretty lucrative. It's eleven dollars an hour now.

"In the meantime, my father, who is a math professor, was working on a math textbook, and he said, 'What if we find a place where you can rent time on a word processor and put my book on the machine? Then I can revise it as I go along.' So we looked around for someplace where I could do fifteen hours a week on someone else's equipment, but we couldn't find a place cheap enough. It was more practical to invest in the equipment, so he said, 'If you want to go into business for yourself, how about this?' The idea of going into business for myself had always sounded good to me, but the scary thing was, 'Where am I going to get my first job, and how am I going to manage to go even two weeks without an income while I'm trying to get my first job?' This way I had someone to foot the bills to start with, and a consistent amount of work I could depend on for the first year. My parents talked me into it. They really helped me. They lent me the money and said, 'Take your time paying it back.' "

As you might guess, Nina likes being able to set her own hours. "It's made my life more flexible. Not having to be at work at 8 o'clock has made a world of difference in my life. I don't have to start work until 9 or 10 o'clock if I don't want to, and I can work at 10 or 11 at night if I want to. I feel that now I have the freedom to do all the little things I enjoy. I just like to have my life free-flowing and flexible."

Although Nina sees flexible hours as one of the major benefits of working for herself, owning her own business has changed her life in other important ways. "The work tends to be a lot more interesting than when you are working for an employer.

Almost everything I get has something of interest in it, whereas in an office the same things came through all the time and it was boring." As an independent, Nina has done work for a best-selling author and for a woman scientist who was writing her autobiography.

Nina feels that working for herself has developed her character. "I find myself working harder, being more careful. I won't goof off on the client's time. When I worked at the bank, I'd get distracted a lot, and they were paying me for that. But now, the minute I get distracted, I stop charging. I spend a lot of time hanging out with my neighbors and I love being able to do that. But when I used to do that at work I felt guilty or I'd get in trouble. Now I know that when I'm charging I'm doing my work, and that makes me feel better about work in general.

"Another thing I like is that once in a while I get a chance to edit, and I feel I have helped to mold something, to make it sound different and better. Also, I get to work for my friends. Occasionally, when I can afford it, I give them a good deal on something like a résumé, and I feel good about doing something for someone I like.

"There's a difference in the way I feel about myself, and a difference in the way the public seems to feel about a person who is in business versus a person who is working in an office, even though they may be doing the same work. When you're in business they see you as a person who has her stuff together. In an office, I was given the benefit of the doubt much less often. Especially as a temporary, a lot of people treated me like a scullery maid.

"I'm getting a different self-image working for myself than I had as an employee, but it's slow in coming. I find that I can still fall into a subservient role, as if each customer that comes in is a new boss. That's why I feel guilty when they say, 'Why did this take so long?' But I'm gradually getting more assertive and saying, 'This is how much it costs,' and I'm working on my sales pitch, my self-confidence, and how I come off to my customers. I sometimes feel as if I am stammering and stuttering, but my boyfriend overheard me talking to a customer once and he said, 'I was listening to you sounding so professional with that guy, and I was really impressed.' "

Judith Oppenheimer is another word processor turned entrepreneur, but she started on a grander scale. She convinced
family and friends to finance her in the amount of $30,000 for
equipment and operating capital. Judith had been working for a
law firm and was frustrated because she never saw the final
product of her work—she was an intermediate in a process that
was finished by someone else. But she had not thought of going
into business for herself until, reluctantly, she attended a moti-
vational seminar (FACA) because her boyfriend insisted that she
go. But, in spite of her resistance, the seminar helped her see
that she needed to be independent, to strike out on her own.
Once the insight came that she could do the same work and
make money for herself instead of making it for someone else,
she was confident and excited. Her confidence communicated
itself to her backers and they came across with the money.

In 1979 she formed O.A.S.I.S., Inc., which provided word
processing services to attorneys, engineers, and major corporations such as Sony and ABC. O.A.S.I.S. kept twenty to thirty
people busy (depending on workload), some as full-time staff
members and others as contractors. When I last talked with
Judith she was in the process of changing over to direct mail
project management and consulting, which has a higher earning potential for her. Project management, consulting, and contracting mean that Judith takes over a whole project for a
company; she contracts for and deals with all vendors, hires the
technical people, plans how the project is to be done, and
oversees it through to completion.

Judith says the main difference that working for herself has
made is that she is no longer unhappy. "When I was working
for other people I was sick all the time and my energy level
wasn't good. There was no satisfaction in my work, no sense of
purpose. I was just given a task that was a piece of something
that had no beginning and no end. I had no idea why these jobs
were being performed, because when you're doing secretarial
work nobody bothers to tell you. But when you're doing things
for yourself, or even if you are just in a position of authority and
responsibility, you see the whole and not just the pieces, and
you get a sense of purpose and some satisfaction. That's the
major difference.

"Running O.A.S.I.S., I tried to keep in mind that when people worked for me, they would work better if I could somehow give them that view. When somebody worked for me as a gal friday or a gofer and they had an inclination for marketing or sales or research, and they showed me that they wanted to do something, all they had to do was bring it to me and lay it out and let me help them define it in terms of what we were doing, and they got the go-ahead. 'By all means, go ahead, let's see what you can do.'

"Being in business for myself has made me stronger and more responsible."

Judith's policy, as an employer, of letting people have room to grow is an example of how women who know both ends of the professional ladder can change the climate of business when they get power of their own. Judith's concern doesn't stop there. She is a founding member and director of the New York chapter of the National Association of Women Business Owners, and she edits their newsletter. She says, "I think I have a lot of excitement to share. I'm excited about the potential for women to create, to be independent, to be wealthy, to do whatever the hell they want."

Judith sums up her philosophy this way: "Everybody starts with the same thing—twenty-four hours in a day. What you make of it is up to you. You can play victim or you can take control and be happy. Taking control doesn't necessarily mean you have to be an independent businessperson. I have been a business owner and am now a consultant, but there are as many different ways of being happy in the world as there are people. The main thing is to do what makes *you* feel good and not what someone else thinks you ought to do. One thing my parents taught me was that if the majority of people are doing it, it's probably wrong. That rule has proven itself out to me. So when people say, 'Naw, it will never work,' then I go ahead full force. Maybe five percent of the people in the world are really doing well, so obviously the majority is not the group to follow."

Maxine Wyman is a technical-writing consultant. She writes instruction manuals, user manuals for computer systems, and systems manuals for programmers and other technical personnel. At the time I interviewed her she was working under contract to an accounting department of a major bank, writing a report analyzing computer systems throughout the bank.

Maxine has always been a writer. She's worked as a reporter, has done writing in connection with her job with a U.S. senator, and has done political and economic analysis as an employee of Wells Fargo Bank. It was while working for the bank that Maxine learned technical writing. "When they moved the department that was doing political and economic analysis to London, I applied for a job as a technical writer in the same bank and got the job on the strength of my skills as a writer. I didn't have any background in computers at all. They trained me. I found I did well and enjoyed it.

"Then I thought I wanted to do programming, so I went to work for a subsidiary of Firemen's Fund, which has a training program for programmers. But I found I didn't like it. I realized that I liked writing and working with people. When the subsidiary I was working for moved to Texas, I was left with the choice of taking another position with the company, or finding an alternative.

"I began to examine my goals and what kind of life I really wanted. There are frustrations in working in a large corporate structure. You have to play games to move forward in the bureaucracy. I needed to make some real changes in my life and that pushed me to break with a standard job.

"I opened my mind to the possibilities of freelancing and saw that it was viable. I explored ways to get involved in it and then I did it.

"I was thirty when I went through my transition. I looked at my life and said, 'I am no longer a child, I am not going to be thirty forever, and my life is moving on. If I am going to accomplish the things that I really want in my dreams, if I haven't gotten there by now, I'd better get down to it.' My ambitions as a writer extend beyond technical writing to poetry and fiction. It's very difficult to have the time you want to spend on writing if you work at a regular job. What you must do is find a balance point in your life where you can earn enough to support yourself and still give yourself some portion of your time to create. Up to this point, the only time I had like that was unemployment.

"The knowledge I gained while learning programming made

me a better writer, so it wasn't time lost. I became more knowledgeable about computers and I am better able to communicate with technical people.

"I'm doing well. I've been working steadily and I've had no shortage of employment. My income as an independent is twice what it was when I was working for companies. In a capitalist society what you are worth is viewed in terms of how much you can command in dollars, so what you charge a premium for, they will value.

"I don't have an agent. That's my personality, I guess, or a product of my background as a black woman. I've always had it stuck in my mind that I've got to do things on my own. Working as an independent you must have more than your skills in the profession, which is why a lot of people use an agent. An agent who has been out there for years has more contacts, but most of my work comes through references from people I've worked with in the past."

I commented to Maxine that some people want an agent because they don't like to deal with soliciting business, they just want to do the writing and not worry about the rest of it. She replied, "It's difficult for women to have to be aggressive; we aren't trained that way. But my life has taught me that you have to press yourself forward and say 'I have the skills.' As an employee I have had to sell myself to people, to say 'I am competent, I do have skills, I can accomplish things,' because when a black woman competes for jobs she has to prove that she is competent.

"People deal with me differently as an independent. I can't say that sexism and racism have gone away. But people approach me in a completely different manner, which is like water to a dying flower for me. When you're an independent contractor you have automatically the cachet of expertise; people assume you're competent and skilled. There is no question about it. When you're an employee and a part of an organization that's not automatically assumed.

"Working for corporations I did not experience racial barriers per se, although they exist in any corporation. Blacks are underrepresented in the computer field. At the time I was the only one in my group at Wells Fargo, and there were only two other black writers in the systems division. You encounter racism with individuals but you deal with that. I don't let someone else's racism block me.

"I think a person's sex is a greater barrier than their race in the computer industry. It's changing now, but I've certainly encountered problems with managers, who were of course men. Most of the technical writers are women, and there is a tendency to look on the position as a secretarial one, and you are treated accordingly. In corporations you have to push hard to get past that." [Chris England told me that technical writers are sometimes looked on as skilled clericals.]

"I find a difference between the way I am treated by a software vendor and a major corporation. The software vendors know what they're doing. They're not looking for a secretary; they're putting together a software package they must market. They don't assume secretarial skills go along with what you've been hired for."

By striking out on her own, Maxine got out of the corporate politics that frustrated her and impeded the progress of her career. She has doubled her earnings. She is given more respect and taken more seriously as a professional. Although no one can entirely escape racism and sexism, as an independent contractor these problems become more manageable. The flexibility of independent contracting would have allowed Maxine to give her creative writing more time, had she not involved herself with another creative activity: she had a baby girl, Patrice Zora, in September 1984. But independent contracting means that Maxine can stay home with her baby and still work. She says, "I am becoming adept at doing two things at once. I write poetry or read aloud while I nurse her. I practice walking meditation with Patrice in my arms, lulling her to sleep for her nap. And watching my child change each day is worth all the cabin fever of working at home."

Going into business for herself has affected Maxine's life in more ways than anyone else I interviewed.

Sue Rugge was not allowed to graduate from high school because she was pregnant—not an unusual thing in the 1950s, when abortion was dangerous and illegal and unmarried pregnancy was considered a disgrace. At seventeen, she married the boy—also not unusual in those times—and by the time she was eighteen she was struggling to survive, picking prunes for twenty-five cents a box. Sue was not the only young woman who was prevented from continuing her education, trapped into marriage too young, forced to work too young, and robbed of the fun and adventure of her young adulthood. It's a familiar story to many women. Only the details change, and any woman who has been through that experience knows it would be handicap enough if the story stopped there. In Sue's case, as in many others, things got worse. Her husband was killed in an automobile accident in the early sixties, leaving her with two small children to support.

Sue had found a job as a clerk typist for General Motors when she was twenty, before her husband was killed, and was assigned to type acquisition slips for their technical library. Based on the three years' experience she gained in that library, when Sue decided to leave Santa Barbara she looked for a position as a corporate librarian. Because she could type, she was hired as a typist/librarian and continued at this work for a decade, helping engineers and scientists with their research. She became a skilled technical librarian, but in 1970 her job was phased out as a result of a corporate takeover.

Sue decided that the only way she could have security and make the kind of money she felt she deserved was by working for herself. "I set out not to make a company but to make a living," she recalls. "I was trying to keep myself together. I had two kids to support."

Sue and her friend Georgia Finnigan, a professional librarian, put together the organization that would eventually become Information On Demand. Running the business out of her bedroom, Sue Rugge physically visited libraries to search out technical information in directories, indexes, and abstracts for corporate clients, engineers, and scientists.

I wish I could tell you that Sue started her business with a computer, but she did not. She did the same dreary job that reference librarians have always done: she painstakingly searched directories, abstracts, and indexes, compiling lists of references for her clients and providing them with copies of articles in which they were interested.

Changing over to computers in the mid-1970s allowed her—by means of computer networks and databanks—to process in minutes information that previously would have taken her days or weeks to chase down by searching laboriously through printed indexes. Computer networks also offer more complete and wider-ranging indexes and lessen the chance of missing something important through human oversight. Computer searches are highly accurate, provided that the user knows how to use key words effectively.

Doing her research more efficiently enabled Sue to earn much more money for the time she invested. Doing her work more quickly also enabled her to take on more clients, which again meant more money.

Today, the clients of Information On Demand (IOD) include such companies as Amoco, Chevron, Exxon, General Electric, Westinghouse, and Xerox. IOD uses Texas Instruments terminals to access more than three hundred data bases, providing information from all over the world. But small clients are served as well; for instance, IOD furnishes cancer research information for families of cancer victims.

About 50 percent of the company's work involves delivery of documents to clients. IOD maintains personnel in major research libraries throughout the United States and has established working relationships worldwide, including one with the Lenin State Library in Moscow. Delivery of copies of documents located by the computers is still the slowest part of the business, but with the perfection of telecopying systems this, too, will be accomplished in minutes, from any part of the world.

Rugge and Finnigan went into business by putting up $125 each for letterheads, business cards, and a listing in the Yellow Pages. In 1978 the partners split due to a disagreement over whether the company should grow by seeking outside investors. Rugge took over, and with no investment capital increased business 100 percent over the next few years. IOD is now one of the largest as well as one of the oldest information brokerages in the country. In September 1982 Rugge sold her interest to the Pergamon Group of publishing companies. At their request, Rugge stayed on as president. The company did a volume of $1.5 million in 1982.

Not bad for a high school dropout, unwed mother, and twenty-five-cents-a-box prune picker.

Sandra Kurtzig left a successful career in marketing with General Electric to work part-time at home and start a family. She installed a secondhand desk in her bedroom and began writing computer programs for small firms.

In June 1984 her 28-percent interest in the company she founded, ASK Computer Systems, was worth $46 million, according to *Fortune*.

Sandra's background is very different from Sue Rugge's. Sandra has bachelor's degrees in mathematics and chemistry and a master's in aeronautical engineering. Her move to work at home was motivated by different factors: She wanted to start a family, and working independently at programming from her own home was her solution to combining a career and motherhood, both important to her.

When she began in 1972, Sandra's first part-time project was writing programs that allowed newspapers to keep track of their newspaper carriers. Within months, she was working full-time and had hired several people to develop software for business applications. She had her family anyway (two boys), but had to abandon working at home in order to continue along her path to becoming a millionaire. Now incorporated, ASK Computer Systems, Inc., topped $65 million in sales in 1984 and employs about 350 people.

The services offered by ASK have also grown more complex. The company buys computers from Hewlett-Packard and Digital Equipment Corporation at a discount, installs their software system called MANMAN (for "manufacturing management"), and sells the entire package to manufacturers. The concept that has made ASK successful is what is known as a "turnkey" system: the purchaser buys a fully installed, working system and simply "turns the key" to be up and running. The systems range in cost from $125,000 to $300,000. So far ASK has installed more than seven hundred of its systems. The MANMAN system is also available on a time-sharing basis to firms that can't afford their own system, for a fee of $4,000 to $8,000 a month.

Not everyone who starts a business at home using her bedroom as an office will become rich, of course. Women like Sandra Kurtzig are exceptional, but they're not rare, either. Some of the following women started businesses at home; I have included some who did not, because they all started from unlikely—and in some cases extremely disadvantaged—positions, and their stories help make my point that any kind of restrictive circumstances can be overcome with enough determination.

- To qualify her for computer industry entrepreneurship, Lore Harp had a degree in anthropology, a year of law school, a husband, two children, and six months' work experience—in a bank. She knew nothing about computers. She and her friend Carole Ely each put in $6,000 to start Vector Graphic, Inc. to market a memory board (a circuit board for computers that stores information) designed by her husband. Harp turned a bedroom and bathroom into an office/ warehouse, with the shipping department in the shower. In 1981 the company had sales of $30 million.
- Ann Piestrup is a former nun who started an educational games software company in 1979 with a grant of $1,000 and an Apple computer. The Learning Company has attracted $3.5 million in venture capital.
- Ann Winblad was bored with her job as a systems analyst with Federal Reserve Bank in Minneapolis, so she quit. After teaching computer science for a while, she founded Open Systems, Inc., with three friends and $500. The company develops accounting software and in 1983 was sold for $15.5 million, with Winblad staying on as executive vice-president. Winblad's photo has appeared in *Fortune*; she is shown barefoot, in jeans, sitting on top of a conference table.
- Portia Isaacson was raised on a dairy farm in Oklahoma. She left home at eighteen with $25, intending to work her way through college. When she figured out how long it would take her to get a degree working full-time and going to school at night, she got discouraged and joined the army instead. After the army, Portia married and had three children. Her husband later deserted her. Portia resumed her education while working full-time to support her children (she also received assistance from several welfare programs), and with awesome energy and determination she eventually earned master's degrees in computer science and computer engineering and a Ph.D. in computer science.

Along the way she went through three more husbands. By the time she was thirty-five she was famous in the computer industry, writing and lecturing widely and gaining considerable experience in the business. In 1980 she founded Future Computing, a company that gathers information on the dynamic and fast-paced computer industry and sells it back to the industry for big bucks. (She was soon joined by her fifth husband, Egil Juliussen.) In 1984 the company was sold to McGraw-Hill for a reported $8 million; Portia's personal net worth is $5 million.

• Roberta Williams wouldn't even touch a computer until her husband, Ken, insisted that she try the adventure game *Colossal Cave*, which he had called up on his home terminal from an IBM mainframe. Once she tried it, she was hooked. She became obsessive about the game. But once she solved it, she couldn't find any other games difficult enough to challenge her. She decided to write her own. Ken did the programming and designed primitive graphics from Roberta's sketches, and they sold the result, *Mystery House*, by mail order. Sales were $167,000 the first year. Next Roberta wrote *Wizard* and *The Princess*—which Ken also programmed—the first adventure games in color. Their company, Sierra On-Line, was formed in 1980; in 1983, games and software sales totaled $10 million.

With computers, rags-to-riches stories are so common that they are considered characteristic of the industry. Luck has something to do with it—being at the right place at the right time with the right service. Character is another prime requisite: willingness to take a chance, astute judgment, the ability to be a self-starter and be self-disciplined. It helps to be intelligent, but not necessarily educated, as the case of Sue Rugge amply illustrates. (I am talking about formal education. Sue, of course, has educated herself.)

Although not all of us can be a Sue Rugge or a Sandra Kurtzig, almost anyone can accomplish the same goals on a more modest scale. Most of the women profiled above sought to solve a personal predicament by leaving a traditional job to work at home. Another thing these women have in common is that most of those who are impressively successful did not foresee success on the scale they finally achieved it. Each hoped only to make enough money to get along.

The message is not that women can succeed in business; they have always done so, when circumstances allowed them to go into business at all. The message is that the computer has changed the circumstances.

----

[1] **Documentation** is the instructions to the user on how to use the computer and/or software.

[2] **Dedicated** means designated for a special purpose. A dedicated word processor is a computer that is designed primarily for word processing.

[3] **Terminals** are keyboards and monitors that allow you to operate a computer from a remote location. *Remote* can mean across the room or across the country.

FIVE

How Handicapped Women Have Used Computers to Become Independent

Perhaps no other group has as much to gain from learning to work at home with computers as disabled women. Handicapped persons of either sex must surmount overwhelming problems in order to become independent, but these problems often are worse for women. The majority of women are still encouraged to be dependent—the influence is sometimes subtle, and it is everywhere. Overcoming this conditioning is tough for any woman, but add to this the barriers to independence inherent in being disabled, and you have a set of deterrents that can be overcome only with heroic spirit and gargantuan effort.

Here are three women who have used computers to transcend their limitations to become totally independent:

Joan Orke had arthritis for many years before it totally disabled her. She had been working in Minneapolis as a genetics-research field worker for the University of Minnesota. But by the time Joan was twenty-eight she was not only too sick to work but could not even care for herself. She moved to Rochester to stay with her mother and spent the next two years in bed. When it seemed clear that she wasn't going to get well, Joan applied for social security disability benefits, which gave her barely enough to get by.

The Department of Vocational Rehabilitation (DVR) sent Joan to a program called HOMEWORK, administrated by Control Data Corporation, which trains disabled people to work at home with computers; the training is done in the home as well. The DVR paid Joan's tuition.

Joan was one of eight people who graduated from HOME-WORK's first class. "It was the first class and so it was still experimental. It took eight months to complete the training and another eight months to find work. I sent out hundreds of letters but had only two interviews in that time. CDC [Control Data Corporation] had a placement program and they tried to get interviews for us, too. The entire class had a hard time. CDC tried to convince other companies to hire us, but there was a lot of resistance. I don't think the situation has changed much yet, but I believe it will change as telecommuting becomes more common and as people see that similar programs do work.

"When I started the HOMEWORK program my arthritis also started getting better. When I finally got my job as a telecommuting programmer for Honeywell Corporation, I was able to move back to Minneapolis. The job gave me the opportunity to live independently and to have my own apartment again, which is important to me.

"I am the only official telecommuter at Honeywell at this time, although other people have informal telecommuting arrangements. Women who have had babies, for instance, have been able to telecommute part-time. I work a full forty-hour week, and I go into the office about once a week. Honeywell gives me a desk and two terminals that hook into their mainframes. They pay for my phone line for the computers.

"I'm treated exactly like everyone else. I think Control Data has had a lot to do with that. They were very responsible about helping us to find jobs, and there was no way they were going to let us get involved with any business that would exploit us. They insisted that we be treated as normal employees. Not only do I not feel exploited, I feel very lucky.

"I know that I'm paid exactly the same as the people doing the same work in the office. I'm making more now than I was making at the university before I got sick. When I was on disability, I got about $360 a month in the beginning, and the most I ever got was $600. Now I *clear* about $1,200 a month. I get company benefits, and I'm paying back social security, since

I am now a taxpayer and I contribute to the social security fund instead of taking money out of it.

"I do feel isolated sometimes. I try to maintain contact with everyone at work. I talk to people on the phone several times a day and I try to talk to different people each time. My co-workers have been extremely helpful. They make sure I get calls when important things happen, and they have me come in for lunch. It's important to have a network of people who are willing to help you. It isn't easy working at home, because I don't have a computer background and I've never programmed in an office. A lot of informal learning goes on when you're looking over someone's shoulder—you need a network of people sharing information. But if I go in to work, I have a hard time concentrating because there are a lot of distractions. At home it's easier to get things done without people talking, telephones ringing, and activity going on all around you.

"I have full range of motion in my hands and don't require any special equipment to work. I'm on a special diet that makes it very difficult to eat in cafeterias. I have a little trouble getting around, and some days I have to use crutches. But my main limitation is fatigue.

"One of the things I like about working at home is that I am not so tired all the time. I get up in the morning and make coffee and feed the cats, and I'm at work. I don't have to get dressed (I can work in my pajamas), I don't have to take a shower, and I don't have to fuss with breakfast. If I have to get straight out of bed and do all that stuff right away, it takes me at least an hour, and by then I'm already tired. Now it takes me ten minutes from when I get out of bed until I'm 'at work.' Not only is it less time-consuming for me, since it takes me so long to do things, but it doesn't tire me out. I have a beautiful apartment across the street from the park. I have natural sunlight. Everyone I work with in the office is in a dark place with no windows.

"My health has improved dramatically since I started this job. Telecommuting has played an important role because the flexibility allows me to get the maximum amount of rest.

"Working with computers allows women to have financial equality with men. This is the best-paying job I ever had. I was never paid at the same level that men were, and now I am.

"I really do enjoy what I'm doing. It allows me flexibility about when I work. There's no supervisor breathing down my neck. I am much more in charge of my life. I make it or break it myself."

Polly Taylor had been a psychotherapist for twenty years when, in her late forties, she underwent a number of changes, physical and political, that for a time caused her life to disintegrate.

As Polly's egalitarian feminist consciousness grew, she found that she could not incorporate her ideals into her work. "I decided that psychotherapy is not feminist. I couldn't see any way to avoid the one-up position of the therapist." She also became depressed and discouraged because in Buffalo, where she then lived, there was little feminist activism. "The same few women were doing everything."

At the same time, Polly was developing severe environmental allergies. She became progressively less able to cope with ordinary things in the environment—cigarette smoke, natural gas, perfumes, pollution, soap, even photocopy paper. When she tried to find other jobs, she found she could not tolerate office environments. Discouraged, she and her woman companion sold "everything but thirty-three cartons of books," bought a motor home, and migrated across the country to San Francisco, taking a year to make the trip and eating away at twenty years' savings.

In San Francisco Polly continued to search for a way to make a living, and took a CETA job editing for *Broomstick*, a magazine for women over forty, where she is now a co-editor. By the time the CETA funding for her job ran out, Polly knew she was not able to hold a conventional job, and she applied to the Social Security Administration for disability benefits. "I was clearly disabled, but the application was denied. With environmental disability, people simply don't believe you. You spend all your time arguing how sick you are. But what happens is that you convince yourself that you are totally incapable of doing anything. I'm capable of doing most things as long as I am not where the environmental garbage is. But during the time I was trying to get disability benefits—and it took over a year before they finally turned me down—I was making a career of being disabled. I was hit by a car during that time, so that was a factor, too. I finally decided I could either make a career of being disabled, or I could try to handle that as best I could and find something else to make a career of. I said, 'I can't do this. I can't think in terms of convincing people I am disabled anymore.' "

While all this was going on, Polly had come in contact with the National Women's Mailing List (NWML), which made their computer facilities available to women's organizations. They taught her to use the system, and she computerized the *Broomstick* mailing list. Then the NWML hired Polly to enter data for them. Since she was not allergic to computers, she began to see the potential for earning a living at home with her own computer. She decided to take what was left of her savings and buy a system. She took a course with the Women's Computer Literacy Project, where her awareness of what can be done with computers was expanded, and when she told them her idea, they counseled her and helped her choose her system.

Polly now has her office set up in her kitchen, where she works in a controlled environment doing mailing lists and word processing. Most of her work comes from contacts she has made through women's organizations in the city. She lives in the least-polluted part of the Bay Area, and can ask people who bring work to her apartment not to wear perfume and not to smoke and to try not to bring animal hairs in on their clothing. She says, "My energy level and the number of hours per day I can be up and about have vastly increased. When I first came to San Francisco I used to spend at least two or three days a week in bed, just barely getting up and around to get something to eat. Now I keep going pretty well and work four to five hours a day." Her morale is dramatically better. "My state of mind depends very much on being able to control what I'm breathing. The psychological effect of knowing that I'm going to be all right because I'm in a safe place is terrific." She is still co-editor of *Broomstick*, which provides a meaningful, creative outlet for her feminist sentiments. Most important of all, she is not dependent on anyone other than herself.

Polly has a dream of setting up a communal living arrangement with other allergic women. "I can't work more than four hours a day, so the system sits there unused twenty hours a day. If I lived somewhere in this fantasy motel where my quarters and the computer's quarters were separate, someone else could use the computer. I know people who could do very well with a computer but don't have the money to buy one. There could be a reasonable way to share the expenses. You can live much less expensively with other women. Environmentally ill people need to be in their own [controlled] environment."

Polly, like all the other women interviewed in this chapter, has used the computer to customize her life to her own special needs. In her case, it was a matter of survival; and it's difficult to imagine what her options might have been without the computer.

In 1980 Dian Lehmann, who has muscular distrophy, had withered away to a mere seventy-five pounds. She was completely dependent, without hope or spirit, and had no will to be otherwise because she expected to die.

When I interviewed her four years later she was working at MEDLAB (a medical software firm) in Salt Lake City as a technical writer and programmer, and despite being confined to a motorized wheelchair she was fully self-supporting and living independently in a house with her eight-year-old daughter, Michele. She was enthusiastic about her job and completely responsible for her own life and for raising her daughter. It was hard for me to believe that this vibrant, lovely woman had been willing herself to die four years before. Now she talked excitedly to me of her plans to go into marketing because, she explained, "marketing is exciting, and that's where the bucks are."

What happened? The most important thing that happened was the tapping of Dian's own latent strength and courage; but the catalyst for the transformation was a training program that taught Dian to use computers, which in turn revealed to her that not only did she not have to live a life of dependency, she could have a career and be competitive, and that she had qualities and resources that were valuable to others. It taught her, in other words, that she could lead a rich and full life despite her physical disability.

It is not surprising Dian was in the spot she was in in 1980 if you consider her history: She contracted muscular distrophy when she was ten years old. Her family assumed she was not going to live very long, so instead of encourging her to learn skills of self-sufficiency they tried to make life as pleasant as possible and demanded little of her. But Dian survived adolescence, and in 1968, still ambulatory, she married.

Dian's physical condition had been relatively stable for some time, but after bearing a daughter the disease became active again and she began to deteriorate. In 1975 she enrolled in college, but she was losing strength in her legs and at times found it necessary to use a wheelchair, although she was still on her feet much of the time. Her marriage was also deteriorating, and in 1980, when Dian fell and broke her leg, she hit the nadir of her life. She thought she was dying, believed she would not live to see her daughter grow up, and could see no point in living, because even if she survived she would be confined to a bed or a wheelchair, doomed to total dependency for the rest of her life.

Although Dian had been taught to be dependent, she had an independent personality, and the prospect of lifelong dependency simply killed her spirit. Compounding the problem was her marriage—she had married a man who needed a dependent woman. She explained, "In order to maintain that marriage I had to turn off everything independent in myself and just not feel in any way. The only way I survived was by turning off all the switches." She was faced with a lifetime of total physical dependency and no visible way out of the marriage which suffocated her. She had no work experience and no skills. A lot of the things that you normally can do without training, such as waitressing and odd jobs, were closed to her because of her disability. She had no transportation from her isolated country home and she couldn't drive. Dian gave up.

If Dian had not exactly willed herself to die, she had stopped fighting to live. At one point she was extremely weak and was admitted to a hospital for psychological and physiological testing. When her hospital counselor discovered that Dian's marriage was probably on the rocks, he encouraged her to find a way to learn some job skills. But Dian resisted. Since she was convinced that she would die soon, all she wanted was to stay home and be a mother to her daughter. But under pressure she finally agreed to undertake training if the counselor could find something she could do in her home.

The hospital brought in Department of Rehabilitation counselor Jess Kappel, who recognized a potential in Dian that she did not see in herself. He proposed her as a candidate for the HOMEWORK program, a project of Control Data Corporation that trains disabled persons to work at home with computers— the same program that trained Joan Orke. It was well suited for Dian because training also takes place in the home.

A representative of HOMEWORK gave Dian tests to determine if she possessed the basic mental skills to learn programming, and she passed. Dian laughs when she explains that even though she didn't believe she could do the work, her self-regard was so low that the only way she could feel good was by pleasing other people, and she would do anything to win approval. To please her counselor, she agreed to apply for the program; to please the HOMEWORK representative, she did her best on the tests. HOMEWORK accepted her; she then worked hard on her studies to—what else!—please her teacher. Yet, at no time did she believe that she could do the work, despite high scores in the most important areas of her testing: math ability, logic, and verbal skills.

A number of serious problems were still to be overcome. Control Data Corporation's PLATO system, the principal tool of the training program, requires a private phone line and a reliable power source, both of which were not available on the farm where Dian lived. But Dian's counselor and the HOMEWORK representative kept at it. The phone company eventually cooperated and the system survived the fluctuating rural power supply.

Dian says that the support from HOMEWORK went far beyond what she considered reasonable. They not only had to solve extremely difficult logistical problems to install the system, but they had to cope with Dian's negative attitude toward her ability. Fortunately, Dian's need for approval led her on. "My husband was encouraging me, and I wanted his approval, too. I went into it for all the wrong reasons."

Dian's belief that she could not learn, compounded by the strain of a disintegrating marriage, affected her studies. She progressed very slowly. Another crisis was inevitable.

"I left my husband and moved to Portland. When I left my husband I weighed seventy-five pounds. There was not much left of me, physically or psychologically."

Moving to Portland meant that the terminal had to be moved

and the lines reconnected. "CDC [Control Data Corporation] was wonderful. They came and moved everything and gave me total support. They would have been justified in giving up on me at that time. I was progressing very slowly. They could have said, 'You're taking too long and it's too much trouble.' But they didn't. They continued to support me. If they hadn't, there's absolutely no way I would have made it. The only thing left for me would have been welfare."

But, about midway through the course, Dian realized that she was indeed learning and that she had a future in programming. The prospect of becoming self-supporting and independent revived her will to live and excited her. She forgot about pleasing others and began to work for herself and for a future with her daughter.

That was a scant three years before I interviewed her. Today Dian supports herself and her daughter and maintains a home in Salt Lake City, Utah. But here's the surprise: when Dian completed her training she decided she did not want to work at home. Her muscular distrophy had stabilized again and she was able to get around in a motorized wheelchair. Her courage was so renewed and strengthened by the self-confidence she felt as a skilled specialist that she wanted to return to the world and try the new wings of her spirit, and she accepted a job as a programmer with MEDLAB in Salt Lake City. After six months she applied for a higher-paying technical writing position and received it. MEDLAB has provided her with a terminal so that she can work two days a week at home, which eases her transportation problems and lessens the babysitting expenses.

Dian has been active with various advocacy groups for the disabled. She is spokesperson for AWARE (Association for Winning Accessibility, Rehabilitation and Education), an advocacy group for disabled people. She was first runner-up in the Miss Wheelchair Utah pageant in 1984. She sits on several governmental committees, including the Governor's Advisory Council, the Utah Transit Authority Specialized Transportation Advisory Board, and the Salt Lake City Handicapped Issues Committee.

When I met Dian in 1983 I saw only a vibrant, enthusiastic woman who had learned to thrive on the competition in the corporate environment—a woman with plans. "I want to go into marketing because that's where the bucks are. Marketing's harder for people in wheelchairs because you have to be able to get around. To that end, I have recently bought a van, which is being fitted out with hand controls, since I can't use my legs to drive. Another disadvantage for disabled people in marketing is that in a wheelchair, you have to watch out for people's toes in a crowded conference room!"

Since my interview with Dian she has accepted a consulting position with Control Data's Disability Services Division, helping them to develop software for the disabled and for the marketing of HOMEWORK. She says, "My dreams are coming true!"

Summing up, Dian says, "I had no idea when I came to Salt Lake City that I would be so in the thick of it. I am pleased with the way the choices I made have turned out. I want to keep my professional life and my advocacy for the disabled separate, but it is exciting how the respect I have received from such professional organizations as the STC [Society for Technical Communications] has given me opportunities to have an impact on the disabled person's environment. Now, with this new consulting position with Control Data's Disability Services Division, the two can truly complement each other—I can serve the interests of the disabled as I achieve my goal of breaking into the marketing world."

I asked Dian to talk about the problems of independence for disabled women:

"It is very difficult for me to allow myself to be seen outside of my wheelchair. I know that people see me and a few see my chair along with me, but I put my chair between myself and other people; no one else does. How I deal with that determines how they see me. When disabled people are angry, I understand their frustration and I empathize with it. But they are choosing to be angry. If you're going to cry about it, you won't get anywhere. You have to be able to say, 'I am a worthwhile individual,' and accept that some people are going to hate you [for being disabled] because that's how the game is played.

"But, given all that, a woman in a wheelchair can get away with saying more because everyone knows she has to be assertive in order to make her world work. And everyone says, 'Hey, she's out there doing it. And look at all the strikes against her, but she's out there doing it.' They respect and admire you for that. I have many people backing me, so if I fall on my face, it will be my own fault. So many people respect what I'm trying to do, and they don't see me as aggressive, they see me as making my world work.

"A woman has a hassle getting high up in any business, whether she is disabled or not. I am disabled, I am a woman, and I am taking some fairly strong political stands in my organization. A lot of the other people are being earmarked as troublemakers. I am not. Why? I firmly believe that a woman in a wheelchair has an advantage if she knows how to use it. When issues come up in the corporation that are controversial, I can take a stand, and because of all the things I've been through I have perspective—I can sit back and be objective and not see things as a win/lose situation. It's a loss that I'm in a wheelchair, but it's a win that I'm alive, so it's not either/or. It's both.

"A disabled woman may be hired as a token, but if she can get a foot in the door and sell herself as someone who can be an asset to the corporation, and can learn the communications skills that are involved in that, it's wide open. There are some pros to going into the computer industry, because your physical limitations don't prevent you from sitting at a keyboard.

"No matter what the odds look like, no matter how difficult the situation is, there's always a way to change it, but you have to have the ability and the determination to do that. It's just like a program that's not running. You can just keep looking at it and looking at it and playing with it and it just doesn't compile, but if you go home and get away from it and think about it a little bit, in the morning you come in and try something new, and it's that constant trying something new that works. Maybe whatever you're doing is a lot of drudgery. Once you get into that drudgery mode, you're in danger of slipping back and not making life work, because you lose the desire, and desire is what it takes to make life work.

"A woman has to make the decision to make it on her own, totally and absolutely on her own. She can be married and have kids but they are separate people, they are not with her in her adventure, and she has to make that decision and take full responsibility for it. You can't slough it off and say, 'Oh, I had to do it this way because of something.' It's a choice.

"I've been independent less than four years, on the job market less than two years. And sometimes I find that I'm out in the middle of the ball park and I've got this ball, and I don't know what to do with it, I don't know the rules. I have to be very careful that I don't overstep my bounds, but at the same time I have to hold my ground. So far I haven't had too much trouble, because most people understand the challenges I'm up against and they admire and respect me for what I've overcome. But I also realize that this is coming to an end. The people at work see me as a productive individual; they no longer see my chair. So now I have to compete on an equal basis. Equality—that's what we're all in this for, right?"

Resources

THE HOMEWORK PROGRAM

A number of programs teach disabled people to work with computers, but HOMEWORK is unusual because the training can be done in the student's own home or in a hospital on a schedule adapted to the individual's needs, using a terminal connected by phone lines to a central computer.

Potential students are recommended by insurance companies, government-funded rehabilitation centers, or employers. The candidates are tested for motivation and mental ability, and the home environment is evaluated for suitability. There must be a private telephone line available and a quiet place to work. This screening is quite thorough, since it costs $25,000 to train each student and there must be some reasonable expectation of success. (This cost is borne by the referring agency or employer.)

A PLATO terminal is installed in the student's home, where she receives personal instruction in its operation. PLATO is Control Data Corporation's computer-based educational system. Through this terminal, the student communicates with her instructor, with the mainframe computer that contains the training programs, and with other students in the program. She also receives a considerable amount of text material to study.

Once the student is comfortable using the terminal, her coursework begins. She learns data processing concepts; number system theory and computer applications; BASIC programming; networking; batch processing; COBOL programming; structured analysis and design; validating, sorting, and updating sequential files; business systems analysis and design; IBM 360/370 computer orientation; and IBM job language control. The coursework takes about five hundred hours to complete—about six months if the student works twenty hours per week. The student receives personal and telephone visits from her instructor, as well as direction, assistance, and support from several on-line consultants. When the course is completed, the student is qualified for an entry level job as a structured COBOL programmer.

At this point HOMEWORK assists the student in finding a job as a home-based programmer. Now, as at all times during the program, counselors are available to help students with job search strategies and psychosocial problems arising from disabilities, and to give support and assistance in achieving personal goals.

The HOMEWORK program was originally developed so that Control Data Corporation would not lose the experience and skills of employees who had become disabled. Later the program was offered to other businesses and organizations.

The cost of maintaining a disabled person who cannot work can run into hundreds of thousands of dollars. Since the cost of retraining through HOMEWORK is only $25,000, the program has a very practical economic value as well as the obvious humanitarian one.

Joan Orke and Dian Lehmann are both graduates of this program, and their praise for it is extravagant.

If you cannot leave your home or hospital and would like more detailed information about HOMEWORK, write or call:

Control Data Corporation
HOMEWORK
P.O. Box O
Minneapolis MN 55440
(612) 853-4946

Another program that trains disabled people in their homes is LIFT, Inc. LIFT also trains programmers using terminals connected by phone lines to a mainframe computer (mainframes are the giant computers used mostly by big business, universities, and government). Graduates are initially hired for work that LIFT has negotiated on contract, but the ultimate goal is for the companies to hire the graduates directly.

LIFT
350 Pfingsten
Northbrook IL 60062
(312) 564-9005

Other such programs may soon be in operation, since these two programs have been successful. Check with your state vocational rehabilitation counselor to find out what options are available in your area.

Persons who have lost almost all motor ability can be trained to use computers with special adaptive devices. Dr. David Rabin, profiled in Peter McWilliams's book (listed below), operates a computer using *one eyebrow*! As long as you have one muscle group under control, you can operate a computer. If you are such a person, or know someone in that predicament, contact:

Trace Research & Development Center on Communication, Control and Computer Access for Handicapped Individuals
University of Wisconsin—Madison
314 Waisman Center
1500 Highland Ave.
Madison WI 53706
(608) 262-6966

Ask for their list of publications—it's a treasure chest.

For those able to get to schools and vocational training centers, there are *many* options. Check with your state vocational rehabilitation counselor for computer training centers for the handicapped.

IBM has supported many computer training centers for the disabled since 1972. To find out if there is one in your area, write:

IBM Project to Train the Disabled
Rehabilitation Training Program
Federal Systems Division
18100 Frederick Pike
Gaithersburg MD 20879
(301) 840-4980

Personal Computers & Special Needs, by Frank G. Bowe (Sybex),
is a thoughtful, knowledgeable effort to make the disabled
aware of the many ways in which computers can revolutionize
their lives. The book explains special devices available to make
computers usable by even the most severely handicapped; training programs that teach the disabled to use computers; and the
possibilities for employment, education, and independent living
for the disabled through computers. The author himself is
disabled, and he includes many profiles of disabled people who
are utilizing computers to work, learn, and live independently.
The author is an authority on his topic, and although I found
some puzzling major omissions of information, the book is
highly recommended.

Personal Computers and the Disabled, by Peter McWilliams
(Quantum Press/Doubleday), is a carelessly assembled, skim-
the-surface book. Nevertheless, his list of resources covers some
that Bowe misses, and the captioned woodcuts and steel engrav-
ings are entertaining.

HOW (Handicapped Organized Women) is a self-help and
support group founded by Deborah McKeithan in 1979 because
she was dissatisfied with existing groups for the handicapped.
HOW encourages mutual support, growth, and strength. There
are chapters in several major cities; if there is none near your
home, contact Deborah McKeithan and start your own!

HOW
1100 Blythe Blvd.
Charlotte NC
(704) 376-4735

HEX (Handicapped Educational Exchange) is an on-line databank
that lists many resources for the disabled and serves also as a

general information bank. There are also on-line conferences. For information about how to access HEX with your computer, write:

HEX
11523 Charlton Drive
Silver Spring MD 20902

The Handicapped User's Database on CompuServe contains news of events and issues of interest to the handicapped; profiles of handicapped people who are doing interesting things; employment opportunities; descriptions of resources, organizations, and products useful to the handicapped; and much more. This is a huge compendium of information that is being continuously updated. Access to this database alone is worth signing up with CompuServe. Once on the system, type GO HUD at any ! prompt.

Exploring Computer Careers for the Handicapped, by Marilyn Jones, available from The Rosen Publishing Group, Inc., 29 East 21st Street, New York NY 10010; phone: (212) 777-3017.

PART II

A Multitude of Possibilities: Ways to Work at Home

SIX

Your Own Computer Business: General Services

Most computer-based businesses that can be run from the home fall under a few general categories, such as word processing, bookkeeping and accounting, mailing lists, information retrieval, and consulting. However, the variations and specializations that can be adapted under any of these general headings are almost limitless. There are also some unique specialized services, such as horoscopes, biorhythm charting, and nutritional counseling; some of these will be discussed in chapter 7. *Virtually any business that is based primarily on the processing of information rather than merchandising can be done at home with a computer.* Therefore, almost anyone can find a special way to capitalize on her unique combination of interests, skills, and experience.

Summarized below are the most common types of general computer-service businesses suitable for home operation, with an explanation of the services offered by each and the role the computer plays. Where appropriate, the background required to operate such a business is given.

Word Processing

If you can type words into a keyboard, you have a highly marketable skill. The difference between typing words on a typewriter and typing them into a computer keyboard is a few hundred dollars a month, since you can charge about three times more per hour for word processing than you can for "just typing."

Of all computer skills, word processing is the easiest to learn. The transition from typist to word processor involves little more than learning how to manipulate text on the computer screen by using a variety of command keys. As with any skill, it takes time and experience to get fast at it, but most people can learn enough in a week to turn out professional work—partly because the computer allows an infinite number of fast and easy corrections before you commit your text to paper.

Word processors make much more money than typists because the computer allows a great variety of auxiliary services to be offered that can't be done with a typewriter. For example:

- Copy that needs to be typeset can be sent over the phone directly from your computer to the printer's computerized typesetting equipment, saving your customer substantial typesetting charges since no one at the printer's has to reenter the copy.
- A résumé customer may require ten originals. A typist must retype the résumé ten times, but a word processor types it only once and instructs the computer to type out ten copies, each one "original." The résumés will be printed six to eight times faster than they can be typed, so you can be doing something else with your time.
- Computer programs are available that will automatically index a book, create a bibliography, and number footnotes and put them in the right place.
- A typist can edit and check for spelling errors, but a computer can do it faster and won't miss anything. Text can be saved on disk for the customer, and can be revised, updated, and reprinted without doing the whole job over— only the changes need to be entered.
- If a customer instructs you to print out text with two-inch margins, and then decides she doesn't like it and wants inch-and-a-half margins, the change can be made with a couple of keyboard strokes, and a new copy is printed in the new format without retyping a single word.

The market for word processing services is virtually limitless because the need to record words on paper is universal. As futurist Alvin Toffler and others have pointed out, we have changed from a manufacturing society to an information-management society, and words are our stock in trade. Sixty-five percent of the work force in this country is employed in information management.

College students, teachers, writers, lawyers, and doctors are excellent sources of word processing work. Many offices with full-time secretaries occasionally need extra help because the secretaries are too busy with office management duties or large projects, or because someone is on vacation or out sick. As a word processor you might get subcontract work from large secretarial services.

You can offer general word processing to a broad public, or you can zero in on a particular market, such as doctors or public-relations firms. The good spelling-checker programs allow you to add your own selection of words to the basic dictionary the computer uses, and these words can be the special technical language of medicine or engineering or whatever you choose. You can offer error-free copy to businesses and professions with the most arcane jargon, a strong selling point since such businesses have a hard time with general secretarial services because of the spelling problems associated with specialized vocabularies. Even in large cities where secretarial services abound, you can compete by finding something special to offer.

All you need to start a word processing business is a computer, a good word-processing program, and a letter-quality printer. Later you can add a modem so you can transmit copy over the phone, and buy more sophisticated programs to do a variety of specialized word processing tasks.

Bookkeeping and Accounting

The computer has revolutionized bookkeeping and accounting as much as it has word processing. Until the computer came along, figures had to be entered into ledger books by hand, and calculations were done on a hand-operated calculator and therefore were subject to human error, either in reading the figures or in punching them into the calculator. Bookkeeping was a slow and laborious process, especially since the same figures sometimes had to be recorded in several places. The computer performs calculations automatically with lightning speed, and they are error free. With one of the more sophisticated programs, a figure need be entered only once to be recorded on as many records as necessary.

For example, when an order is entered from Acme Ambershoots for three wibble wodgets, the computer can automatically (1) look for the price of wibble wodgets, calculate the total price for three, subtract Acme's discount, if any, and add the sales tax; (2) add the charge to Acme's account; (3) deduct three wibble wodgets from inventory; (4) determine if the supply of wibble wodgets is getting low and, if so, flag them to be reordered. It will do all these things in a few seconds, a task that would take a person several minutes. At the end of the month Acme's statement is already compiled and the computer needs only a command from the operator to print it out.

Payroll is a matter of entering the employee's name or ID number and the number of hours worked, or the basic salary. The computer calculates the total pay, all the deductions, the net pay, and prints out the check. It may also compute accrued vacation and sick leave and send them to the employee's permanent record. Some programs even send the deductions to their respective files so that each quarter the figures are already compiled for quarterly reports—all the F.I.C.A., income tax, health insurance, etc.

Speed and accuracy are obvious benefits, but there are others as well. One of the most important reasons why computers are so liberating is that they allow us to overreach our own skills. The computer itself does not make errors in math or logic unless it is malfunctioning. Software has correct structure, procedures, and information built into it. A well-designed program will guide the user through a process step by step so that even a novice can perform some jobs that she would be unable to do on her own.

But, although computers can allow us to perform skilled tasks that we may not know how to do, they can't make up for human experience. There is an important difference between bookkeeping and accounting. Bookkeeping is a matter of recording figures in the proper places. Good software makes it practically impossible to do it incorrectly. Any reasonably intelligent person, even one with no prior experience whatsoever, can keep a set of books. I know because I've done it.

Accounting is another matter altogether. An accountant not only records figures, she analyzes them. She prepares tax returns and statements of net worth, and is prepared to advise clients on how to manage their businesses for maximum profit as well as tax benefits. Although accounting programs can do most of the routine work for her, there is no program that provides the wisdom, intuition, and experience that are so important in honing decisions for an individual business that is not exactly like any other. These qualities are found only in a trained and experienced person. Bear this distinction in mind when planning a bookkeeping and/or accounting business.

Many general accounting packages are available, as are programs specifically designed for doctors, lawyers, retail stores, and specific industries. Large professional offices often have their own computers, but small practices and small businesses often require bookkeeping services.

Accounting software packages tend to be very expensive, and some are not very flexible. A less expensive and more flexible alternative is to acquire a good spreadsheet program and buy templates for it, or create your own forms customized to the business you are serving. (A spreadsheet is a worksheet that you can set up yourself any way you want. Spreadsheets and templates are explained in more detail later.)

Mailing Lists

Mailing lists are created from lists of names provided to you by your customer. Once the names are entered in the computer they never have to be retyped. Maintenance of the list involves merely deleting and/or adding names from time to time. Whenever your customer wants to do a mailing, you load his list into the computer, update it if necessary, and print it out on peel-off mailing labels that come on fanfold continuous paper. The only equipment you need, besides your computer, is a printer with a tractor feed. Even a very cheap printer will do, since the printing does not need to be of high quality.

In order to create mailing lists on your computer you need a program for that purpose. Programs are available designed specifically for mailing lists, but many data-base programs will also run lists for you. (A data base is information stored in an organized manner.) Lists can be set up to be sorted alphabetically, by zip code, or by any other criteria that you may want to incorporate. If you have a list of all the people who live in Coocoo County, Tennessee, and want to run off only the names of one-legged blue-eyed astronauts who live there, you can do so, provided you set up those criteria in your original list. The National Women's Mailing List is programmed to indicate each woman's special interests and who she wants to have access to her name. Since you don't get on this list unless you sign up for it, the special interests are defined by the women themselves. So, if a political candidate wants a list of all the women who are interested in women's health issues, she can get it, but the list will exclude those who have said they don't want to receive mailings from political candidates.

Mailing lists can also be used to do form letters. Those obnoxious mailings from people who want you to buy magazines, and who have your name reprinted twenty times per page, are an example of this capability carried to psychotic extremes. Used reasonably, you can send identical letters to all the customers of a particular firm, but each letter will be an "original" typed letter with the individual's name and address at the top. An enterprising man in my computer-users group talked some automobile dealerships into sending their customers followup letters three months from the date they purchased their cars. The letters say, essentially, "How's everything going? Any problems? We hope you're satisfied with your car, and be sure to let us know if we can be of service." Each letter is "original," using a form letter with a mailing list program. My friend keeps track of the dates (on his computer, of course), and sends the letters automatically. The dealerships don't do anything but provide him with the names of their customers and dates of sale. Customer response has been excellent and the dealers are delighted. So, with a little initiative you can create your own market.

Any business that does direct mail advertising or regularly sends out form letters is a candidate for a mailing list service. Public relations firms, printers, and advertising agencies are the

best sources of business, but individual small businesses sometimes design their own advertising matter and have it printed,
and these too are good candidates for a small mailing list
business. It is hard to compete against the giant direct mail
firms. The niche for the home business to fill is doing the small
and highly specialized mailing lists that are too small for the
big firms to bother with.

In large cities a living can be made by doing nothing but
mailing lists, but in smaller cities it may have to be an adjunct
to other services. Mailing lists nicely complement word processing services. You may find yourself typing the advertising copy,
sending it to the printer over a modem, printing out the mailing
list, attaching the labels to the envelopes, stuffing them, and
taking them to the post office. If you design and write the copy
too, you have become a direct mail advertising firm. You can
define your services as narrowly or as broadly as you wish.

Agency Services

An agent is simply a person who helps a person with a need
to get together with a person who can fill it. Without the agent
the two people might never meet, or at least it might be a lot
more difficult. You can get a person who has lost a dog together
with the person who found it, a person with a ranch to sell with
someone who wants to buy it, a starlet with a producer, a
lonely boy with a lonely girl (or another boy!). The possibilities
are almost infinite.

The computer is ideal for such services. If you want to buy a
car and know that you have only $1,000 to spend and that you
prefer Fords, you must read all the ads in the classified "Cars
for Sale" section because you have no other way to find a single
ad for a Ford priced at $1,000 or less. But if you tell a computer-
ized data base what you want, the computer does the scanning
for you at thousands of words per second and comes up with
only those ads that meet your criteria: all Fords for sale for
$1,000 or less.

One of the most promising applications for the search-and-
find capability of computers is for rental housing in metropolitan areas. The searcher pays a fee to get a list of all rentals
available in a certain area, and can specify that it must have

two bedrooms, a garage, allow pets, and rent for less than $500 per month. The landlord may or may not have to pay a fee to have a house or apartment listed, depending on the demand in the area. The agent may also charge a percentage of the first month's rent from the landlord—depending, again, on the supply/demand ratio. Landlords may specify that the agent do initial screening for desirable applicants before the house is shown, in which case the percentage charge is more justified.

As an adjunct to being a rental agent, you might offer a roommate finding service. Again, desirable characteristics and compatibilities can be listed, and only those people meeting the customer's criteria will be selected.

Computerized dating services are big business, but there are some variations on that idea that haven't been tried yet. Many people aren't necessarily looking for romance but would like to meet others who share their interests in photography, horticulture, semantics, or any other subject. Such a service would be wonderful for people newly arrived in a city.

Providing house sitters, babysitters, freelance writers and artists, people who want to barter goods and services, janitorial services, plant rentals, shopping services, dog walkers, or just about any other kind of service that is normally done by an independent contractor is a logical basis for an agency, and the computer makes it fast, easy, and efficient. People who specialize in finding rare and out-of-print books are now using computers. You will remember that Chris England exploited her expertise and experience as a technical writer, combined with her contacts in the industry, to found a temporary-employment agency for freelance technical writers.

To start such an agency you need a database management program, and you need to understand how to use it fairly well. You must also advertise effectively to attract your clients. Only a fair-sized city can support any kind of agency on a full-time basis.

Information Search and Retrieval

Nearly all human knowledge is recorded somewhere, but getting at it can be tough, as you know if you have ever tried to find any bit of information that is the least bit obscure. As this century progresses, the amount of information being recorded is increasing exponentially, but it has been only in the last ten years or so that a serious effort has been made to computerize a major part of it. It will take a long time to enter the enormous backlog of records into computers, and some sources may be too huge even to attempt—the entire contents of the Congressional Record or the Library of Congress, for instance. But most records of widespread importance have at least been *indexed* on computer, so, although you might not be able to use your computer to retrieve the entire text of a research paper published at Harvard in 1903, you can use a computer at least to find out where it is and how to get it.

The past masters at information retrieval were research librarians, whose specialty was knowing which index to look in. It took years for them to become familiar with all the reference works they needed to do their jobs well. But considerations of space made it necessary to limit the number of ways in which a work was listed. Author, title, and topic indexes have been the norm, and still are in printed indexes. Yet the computer makes it possible to index an article by all the authorities quoted in it, the locale where experiments took place, or the names of all the chemicals used in the experiment. Consequently, searching for information has become not only incredibly faster and more efficient, it has become more thorough and precise. Additionally, it is now possible to quickly locate an article, book, or research paper in a library that may be on the other side of the continent or even the world. What took weeks or even months can now be done in hours. Once you have located your document, the major troubles are over. You need only have someone on site to make a copy for you, and that's usually possible.

If you were to call up each and every data base that might have the information you need, however, the time and expense would almost negate the advantage of using the computer. So now there are indexes of indexes, and information-retrieval services that will search all available indexes for you and come up with a list of references.

You recall that Sue Rugge was a technical librarian who started an information service in her bedroom. Later she started using computer terminals, and her business, Information On Demand, now grosses $1.5 million a year. IOD is accessible through CompuServe, The Source, and ten other electronic mail (E-mail) systems. Sue's company is the oldest and largest such service in the country, and you would have a hard time competing with it on a national level. However, people like to deal with hometown businesses, and a Houston businessperson is more likely to call on a Houston–based information retrieval service than one in San Francisco. (She might not be a CompuServe subscriber and therefore would not know about IOD.) Another way to compete is to specialize. If you live in the same city as one of the megacorporations, find out what their research needs are, and specialize in that area as a way of attracting their business.

Specialized information retrieval integrates well with specialized word processing and/or bookkeeping services. The more service you can offer to a select market segment, the more competitive you can be. A nurse, for example, might start a service for doctors combining medical record keeping, word processing, and medical research services. Her own medical background and expanded specialized offerings to health-care professionals will give her a distinct edge over the general word processing services.

To operate an information service, you need only supplement your computer system with a modem, the software to run it, and subscriptions to the appropriate database services. There are several guides to on-line data bases, and new ones are being published all the time. New data bases are being launched continually, too. This is an industry that is growing fast, so there's stiff competition. The secret to success is finding a special market segment you can serve better than anyone else can.

Consulting

Consulting is advising people how to do things, and computer consulting can range from projects as simple as helping someone select a word processing program to complex systems analysis. Systems analysis is setting up an entire system by analyzing the client's information-management needs, choosing the computer best suited for them, selecting the programs for it (and in some cases customizing them), and teaching the client's staff how to use the system.

Your past experience in any business combined with moderate computer experience can qualify you for computer consulting, a growing and very lucrative service profession. Fees range from $15 to $100 an hour, with most of them falling in the $25 to $50 range. It's an easy service to run out of your home but generally requires that you spend a good bit of time visiting clients in order to study their methods of operation.

You will remember that Mary Dum was doing the office work for her real estate appraiser husband when she got excited by computers and bought one. She taught herself to use the computer for all aspects of the real estate business. She is now earning handsome fees as an independent computer consultant for real estate applications.

Carol Frazer has been a programmer since the early 1960s. She now owns a software store in Salt Lake City, but she is also a software consultant. All her programming expertise gives her an immense advantage over stores whose owners and employees don't know how software is written. In addition, Carol can customize software for the customers who need it.

There are many levels of computer expertise, and you don't necessarily have to be an expert programmer or systems analyst to be a consultant. You simply need to know how to do one thing well. For instance, if you learn word processing (which is easy and doesn't take very long), you can hire yourself out to a company and teach their staff to use their word processing programs. Even though these programs are easy to learn, the majority of people will not teach themselves, and this creates lucrative work for consultants.

If you have experience in a particular field such as inventory control, grocery store management, or payroll, you should exploit that experience when you choose a consulting specialty. Because of your experience you will have a thorough knowledge of how information must be handled in that business, and you will be able to set up an efficient and trustworthy system.

Off-the-shelf programs are available for almost every business you can think of, and it is seldom necessary or desirable to write an original program for a business, principally because the cost is prohibitive to all but the large companies. The key is to select the right program, because if the program isn't adaptable to a company's unique needs it is a waste of their money. The better business programs allow the user to define forms and functions within the limits of the program. So, consulting does require a thorough knowledge of the programs available for your specialty, and the ability to adapt a program if necessary. When a company's needs cannot be met with an off-the-shelf program, it is often possible to customize one of the standard database management or spreadsheet programs. (These programs will be explained in detail in chapter 19.) Customizing requires some expertise with these programs, but is not as technical and difficult as programming. Depending on how fast you learn and how intensely you are willing to apply yourself, what you need to learn about customizing data-base managers and spreadsheets can be mastered in a few weeks to a few months.

But in most instances an off-the-shelf program will do, even for extremely specific applications. Just to give you an idea of how specialized some programs are, there is one called *pc-CUT*, which computes cutting, pricing, and inventory information for wood truss design and construction. It takes some digging around in software catalogs to find such programs—catalogs that your client probably doesn't know exist. If you are serving the construction industry and have a client who wants to do computer-aided wood truss design, she is going to be very impressed when you come up with this program. However, you must be sure that the software will run on her computer, figure out how to use the program yourself, and teach your client to use it.

Services are advertised in computer magazines that catalog thousands of programs. Such services are invaluable aids to consultants.

Creating and Marketing Your Own Data Base, Newsletter, or Special-Interest Group for Public Networks

Commercial subscription on-line computer services such as The Source and CompuServe provide access by telephone to their huge mainframe computers. They charge by the hour, usually with a monthly minimum, and sometimes they charge an initial sign-up fee. The range of services they offer is vast and growing all the time. These services will be discussed in chapter 11, but what concerns us here are the on-line newsletters, data bases, and special-interest groups they offer.

An electronic newsletter is like any other newsletter except that you receive it by accessing a remote computer by telephone and then read the newsletter on your computer screen. You can also download it to your own computer for storage on disk and/or print it out.

A data base is nothing more than a reference book in a computer, and it can be as specialized as the batting averages of major league players for the last fifty years, or as general as the *World Book Encyclopedia.*

A special-interest group is a computerized bulletin board where people who share a common interest exchange information. Sometimes valuable connections are made. Any subscriber can access the bulletin board to leave messages for the entire group or for individuals and can read any messages that are not marked *private.* Usually each group will have its own data base for storage of information useful to its members. These groups are coordinated by system operators, or sysops.

With a modem to connect you with the commercial on-line services, you can sell a newsletter or data base to services such as The Source and CompuServe, or offer your services (for pay) as the sysop of a special-interest group. For the newsletter or data base, you get a percentage of the fees the service receives for the actual time their subscribers spend accessing your data. Therefore, the more successful your project is, the more money you get. The fees are similar in principle to the royalties authors receive for books.

To publish an electronic newsletter you need only have an interest in a particular topic and the ability to gather information about it. You can write it all yourself or invite contributors. Norm Goode, a member of the Work-at-Home special-interest group on CompuServe, publishes a newsletter about working at home called the *Micro Moonlighter.* He publishes it both in the traditional fashion (printing and mailing to subscribers) and on CompuServe. He prints articles on any topic of interest to people who work at home with computers. Some of his contributors come from the Work-at-Home special-interest group.

For a newsletter to succeed, of course, it must have a broad-based appeal. Once you subscribe to a service like CompuServe, you can check the index for special-interest groups and existing newsletters. When you see an active special-interest group, the topic around which the group is formed is a likely basis for a newsletter. Then you can write a sample issue and submit it to the service to see if they are interested in publishing it.

To write a data base you need to be either an expert in a particular field or an intrepid researcher. If you don't have credentials—that is, if you don't have an advanced degree or several years' experience in the field—you should carefully reference the sources of your data. Of course, you should have a working knowledge of how data bases are structured. Before undertaking to write a data base for sale to an on-line service, you should query them to find out if they are interested and to obtain guidelines for setting up your data base so that it will work on their system. Check existing data bases on the system to see how they are formatted.

The subject of your data base should not be too esoteric. A general reference data base on nutrition will attract a wider readership than one on the molecular structure of vitamins.

To set up a special-interest group (SIG) on one of the on-line services, you must find an area of interest not already covered by existing groups, one that has a broad base of appeal—such as fitness and health or investments—and one about which you are fairly knowledgeable. Once you sell your idea to the service, you must become familiar with the system and be prepared to answer many, many questions from users about how to use the system and what the group is about. The sysop is expected to intervene if any abuses of the system occur, such as offensive language or hostile messages. You will arrange to have guests for special on-line conferences and will post notices of news that is relevant to the SIG's topic. Another job of the sysop is to make people feel welcome and draw them into "conversation." You will need to spend time on line every day.

Any special interest can become the basis for a data base, newsletter, or SIG: stamp collecting, history, politics, nutrition, astrology, horse racing, car repair, East African gourmet cooking. Your own unique experience and interests combined with a computer and modem result in a home business especially tailored to you. Subscribe to The Source or CompuServe and find out what people are doing. You'll get lots of ideas. You can also set up your own electronic bulletin board and charge people to access it, but the potential is much better through an established base that has hundreds of thousands of subscribers.

Financial Management

Perhaps because of our long recession, many people are deciding they need professional help to plan for future security, and financial management consulting is a fast-growing specialty. People want to know what insurance they need, what kind of investments to make, how to provide for the education of their children, how to plan for retirement, and how to manage their money so that they can do all these things.

To be a financial management (FM) consultant some training is needed, of course, unless you already have a background that gives you ready-made expertise. Courses and books on the subject are available.

The bulk of FM software is very sophisticated and is meant for professional financiers or for business managers. Many of these programs are designed to be used with on-line investment information data bases like Dow Jones News/Retrieval and Warner Computer Systems. But less sophisticated (and less expensive!) programs are available for individual investment analysis and forecast, loan amortization, and related functions. The main value of these programs is the "what if" function, which makes it possible to try out different strategies to compare long-term results.

For example, one program, *Financial Planning Diagnostic Program*, is available for TRS computers and produces a fourteen-page financial evaluation for individuals who have an income of $20,000 or more. Evaluation is based on a four-page questionnaire. Other financial analysis programs are listed and described in the various software catalogs available from computer dealers and bookstores.

Income Tax Preparation

This is not something to undertake if you have no prior tax training, but it's not all that hard, either, for the simple reason that people who have very complicated forms have them prepared by their CPAs. Many people pay to have simple returns prepared, with the deluded notion that returns prepared by commercial services are not audited, or that if they are audited the preparers, not the taxpayers, will be responsible. Also, although the average family tax return is extremely simple to fill out, the IRS seems to run their instructions through a scrambler before printing them, so the impression one gets from reading the instructions is that no one but a CPA should attempt to fill out a long form.

There are many tax programs, and most offer yearly updates for a moderate fee (since there are changes in the tax structure every year). However, like accounting packages, these programs tend to be very expensive if they are very detailed. You may be better off buying a good spreadsheet program and setting up your own forms. Many books are written on the most popular spreadsheet programs, with detailed instructions and illlustrations on creating templates. You will find these books in any computer bookstore; you will need one for the particular spreadsheet you plan to buy. (See chapter 19 for a detailed explanation of spreadsheets.)

Since tax work is seasonal, you can't rely on it for a full-time income, but it's an ideal service for someone who wants to earn extra money working hard for two or three months a year, or to supplement other services such as financial planning, bookkeeping, or accounting.

If you don't have a tax background there are several ways to get training. Large commercial tax-preparation chains, such as H&R Block, offer training programs for their employees. You could work for them for a season to receive the training and some experience. You could also apprentice yourself to a local CPA to help with the overload at tax season.

Tutoring

A natural moonlighting project for school teachers, especially during the summer, is tutoring. Not only are there hundreds of educational programs available for tutoring in school subjects, but kids will get valuable experience on the computer. Most schools don't have enough computers to allow students adequate access time, and many computer-conscious parents are willing to pay to have their children get an early edge on the competition.

I know one person who bought an Apple IIe and Logo, the programming language that is designed to teach children how to think math, and started tutoring the same month she got the computer. By staying two chapters ahead of the kids in her Logo manual, she never got caught. Of course, she now knows Logo very well, once again confirming the old law that says the best way to learn a subject is to teach it.

You can tutor adults, too. I was contacted not long ago by a woman who had a part-time job in an office where there was a computer, but, she told me, "No one there has the time or the interest to teach me to use it." She was looking for tutoring so that she could take advantage of the computer to do her work. Many people find themselves in this situation and may prefer tutoring to a class because they can learn at their own pace.

Tutoring is one of the few businesses you can do at home that involves constant contact with people, so it's ideal for those who like to teach and to be around people. However, the financial return for your time is not nearly as high as other businesses.

Renting Computer Time

Even if you have a full-time computer-based business, your computer will sit idle some of the time. Some extra income can be earned by renting time on it. If you live in an area near a university, you have a ready market, since most schools do not have enough computers to provide adequate access for their students. Students are likely to want to use the computer at just the times you won't be working on it—evenings and weekends.

However, you would have strangers working in your home, and this can interfere with your privacy and relaxation.

If you start renting time and find a considerable demand, you might dedicate a room in your house to the purpose and buy more computers. You can't charge more than about $8 per hour for computer time, but if you have three computers you will bring in $24 an hour with very little effort. Of course, you won't make money until the computers are paid for.

Renting computer time is a practical adjunct to tutoring, since it allows your students to practice what they have learned, and you are on hand to give advice and answer questions.

Any home-based business may be subject to local zoning laws, but many cities do not strictly enforce these laws if there is no traffic to and from the home. When considering a business where people come and go regularly, however, you should be careful to find out what zoning laws apply and how your neighbors feel about the traffic.

Computer Programming

It takes a long time to develop enough expertise to work as an independent programmer, but if you truly like computers and are serious enough to invest some time in learning to program, your future for a number of years can be absolutely secure, and the groundwork is laid for security indefinitely. The reason I don't want to assure you that programming is a guaranteed career for more than a certain number of years is that currently it is not clear how programming will be done ten years from now. Some people in the industry claim that there will always be a need for people to do special applications programming, while others say that the computer itself will do all the programming in the future. Programs to write programs, called program generators, already exist.

Professor Magreth Olson of the Center for Research on Information Systems at New York University did a study on telecommuting ("Overview of Work-at-Home Trends in the United States," New York University, NY, 1983). She reports a severe shortage of experienced programmers in the United States and believes this situation is likely to persist. Magreth is involved in the study of the impact of computers; hers is certainly a knowledgeable opinion.

But programmer Dian Lehmann, who works for a big software developer (MEDLAB), has this advice for would-be programmers: "It's important for anyone coming into the computer industry to realize that they are going to need the capacity to continuously change. You can't just learn one programming language and leave it at that, because if you do you're going to be out of a job. Computers are eventually going to do all the programming. You're going to have to learn systems analysis or something else that the computer can't do. Anyone who comes into the industry and expects to maintain their job at the level they're at for even two years may as well quit. They're going to have to be ready for change."

No matter who turns out to be right, though, programming is an excellent base for branching into other specialties, particularly systems analysis, which the computer can't do and probably never will be able to do. Systems analysts will continue to be very highly paid for a long time to come. If you follow Dian's advice about staying flexible and ready for change, programming is a valuable skill that lays the groundwork for an openended career in computing.

Heather Ellin started programming in 1958 at the age of seventeen. She is now an independent systems analyst and consultant who works hard a few months of the year and spends the rest of the year traveling. Heather thinks one of the best ways to prepare for a career as a programmer is to work for a large company that has a training program. "Unfortunately, some of the best learning environments are places like Firemen's Fund Insurance where you have dress codes and all that. But they send you to training programs, hold seminars and classes, and have good programming standards, which is extremely important. They may not take absolute beginners anymore since now there are more people available who have had some classes, but it's easy to take a few classes."

Heather believes there is not much of a job market for independent programmers for microcomputers because people are not willing to pay a programmer a couple of thousand dollars to develop a program for a $2000 computer. She suggests, instead, learning to program for minicomputers. (Minicomputers are larger and more expensive than microcomputers and are used primarily by large businesses and institutions.) "A software package for a minicomputer usually costs ten thousand dollars or more. There are lots of jobs for freelance people and there's money in it. You can hook a terminal up at home over a phone line or a lease line and work there, if you want to."

When Heather advises against programming for micros she has in mind the kind of programming that consultants do—special applications software for businesses. One program, one client. However, developing programs to sell to the general public is another ball game.

For example, some women have done very well by developing and marketing their own games software for microcomputers. Joyce Hakansson became involved with a computer education project at the Lawrence Hall of Science in Berkeley, and later joined the Children's Television Workshop to create a gallery of educational games for Sesame Place (Sesame Street's games annex). She saw a need for nonsexist, nonviolent games that would be interactive, entertaining, and educational, and eventually formed her own software development company. Texas Instruments and Spinnaker Software are now distributing her products. I know of at least four other women who have become successful games-software entrepreneurs—most of them motivated by the desire to improve on the violent, aggression-based, noneducational games that glut the market.

Competition is tough for independents who try to market their own products because large software houses hire teams of programmers who work months and even years to develop a top-of-the-market program, and the companies then invest as much or more money in marketing as they do in developing the programs. There just isn't any way an independent can compete on that level.

However, individuals can do very well on other levels. One of these is developing a special program for a special market where the need is not currently met. I am presently looking for a data-management program for a friend who is a river-raft-trip operator; so far I haven't found one. If none exists, I'll write one for him, which I can then market to quite a few other pack-trip operators. It's not a large market, so it won't make me rich, but since the same program could easily be adapted for excursion operators of all kinds, it might feed me for a while. Quite a few people have done very well with programs they have written because they couldn't find a commercial one to meet their needs.

You can try to market your programs yourself, but you may be better off selling them to a software distributor, as did several of the games programmers mentioned above. Book publishers are now distributing software, and programmers may now work under much the same terms as book writers, earning advances and royalties from the sale of their programs.

Another area to explore is becoming an expert with one of the major popular database or spreadsheet programs like *dBase II* or *SuperCalc*. These programs can be customized with what are called *templates*. In computer jargon a template is a "program" that works with another program to save the user work.

An example of a template is a program for doing income tax with *dBase II*. *dBase II* is an extremely popular system that is an odd hybrid of a data-base manager and a programming language. It has all the ability you need to do income taxes, but you must design the forms and the math formulas yourself. Once they are set up, they can be saved and used over and over. The forms and formulas you create are called templates because they "fit over" *dBase II*.

Creating templates is not programming in the purest sense of the word, since templates won't work unless they are used with the mother program. But we do speak of "programming" *dBase II* to do certain specific jobs.

Creating and marketing templates for people who don't have the time to develop their own forms and procedures is a lucrative form of programming. Of course, you must buy a database manager or spreadsheet and become an expert at developing applications for it. There are seminars and courses on this specialty in most major cities, and many excellent books are available on the subject.

Programming of any kind requires an ability to break a problem down into its component parts, a logical mind, extreme patience, and a tolerance for frustration. If you like solving puzzles, you might like programming. The best way to find out is to take a class or two and fool around on your own computer. Advice from professionals on how to learn programming varies. Some, like Heather, insist that to learn good programming techniques, you must take classes. But many successful programmers are self-taught. While in high school Miriam Liskin had a class on programming large computers, but she taught herself microcomputer programming. She believes that the best way to learn about micros is to buy one and use it.

Real-estate-applications consultant Mary Dum was forced to teach herself. "When my son was a senior in high school he needed a calculator. I went to a computer store and they had a Commodore Pet. It was the first small computer I had ever seen, and it was doing all sorts of fancy things on the screen. I looked at it and said, 'I have to have it. I don't care what it costs, I don't care whether I can do anything with it, I don't care what happens, I have to have one.' So I came home and told my husband, and he thought, 'She's off again.' Then I decided that the Pet wasn't enough, that I wanted a full-size business computer, so I started looking.

"I had been going in and out of Computer Center in Berkeley because they had some computer magazines, and I got to know the owner, Pete Hollenbeck. When I wanted to buy a business computer Pete wouldn't sell it to me because he thought I didn't know anything. It was true, I didn't. I thought I could develop an application that would justify deducting it from my income tax, but my main motivation was simply that I wanted it. I was just fascinated with what it could do, and I wanted to learn about it. I love tools, and this was another tool.

"I asked Pete if I could use the computer and he said, 'Probably not.' At that time [1977] using a computer was a matter of learning to program. There were no spreadsheets, and only one word processing program that was worth anything. If you wanted to use a computer you had to do the programming yourself. Pete was insistent that I learn to program before buying the computer, so I did. I didn't take a course, never have. I taught myself from books, and Pete helped me. I'd go down to the store in the late afternoon and he'd help me. He couldn't do that now, of course—he's too busy. I spent a lot of time and read a lot of books. It took me until March 1978 to teach myself to program to the point where Pete would sell me a computer." Mary was forty-six years old when she started programming, by the way.

Anyone who is going to teach herself to program would do well to have a knowledgeable person to answer questions and troubleshoot programs, as Mary did. My efforts to learn programming on my own ran into a considerable number of snags when I encountered problems that just aren't covered in the books.

Several of the women profiled elsewhere in this book are programmers. In addition to those named above are Carla Govreau, Carol Frazer, Joan Orke, Mary Ellen Siudut, and Lisa Walker.

Programmers find jobs in a number of ways. You can list yourself in the Yellow Pages, call on local businesses to leave a card and résumé, contract with a software-development house, or sign up with an agency.

Technical Writing

In the computer industry, technical writing most often refers to the writing of manuals, also called *documentation*. Documentation is of two general types: one tells the "end user" how to operate the computer and/or how to use the software; the other tells the technical person how the computer is designed and how to fix it or modify it. The two types often overlap.

Unless you are very fortunate, the manuals you will receive with your computer equipment and your software are going to be very badly written. That's because there is a dearth of competent technical writers. Part of the reason for this scarcity is that the computer industry has created a demand for technical writers on a scale that has never existed before, and there just aren't enough trained technical writers to go around. This is good news for anyone who wants to get into the field.

The other reason is not so readily apparent. An odd schism in our society separates art and science, and for some reason competency in the English language falls on the art side. Because of this schism, engineers don't learn to write decent English, and most writers are intimidated by technical language. (When I studied power and transportation at a university, the industrial arts building was the only place where no one ever posted notices of concerts and plays; industrial-arts events were never posted in the humanities building.)

Anyone who can keep her balance with a foot in each world can make a very nice living. I earn $25 to $50 an hour for my technical-writing services.

Unless you are already an engineer, technical writing requires a willingness to struggle to make sense of technical processes that you may be totally unfamiliar with, explained to you by people who leave out crucial steps or who present them in an incomprehensible jumble of technical jargon. Technical writing requires a particular temperament, and I suspect it is the same temperament required of a programmer—a high tolerance for frustration and a great deal of patience.

If you like both language and technology and you earned A's in English, you might do very well as a technical writer. Most technical colleges now offer courses on the subject, and I would not be surprised to see technical writing offered as a major in most colleges in the future.

Although some training is desirable, it is possible to enter the technical-writing field by the side door. **Sandy Emerson** knew nothing about computers when she went to work for The Community Memory Project, a nonprofit organization that is designing a public computer-access system that will operate much like a public telephone. While working there she wrote pamphlets and publicity for the project and published their magazine. She also learned a great deal about computers. Sandy left the project to become a full-time writer. She is the co-author, with Jean L. Yates, of *The Business Guide to the Unix System* (Addison-Wesley).

Sandy says, "Technical writing is an excellent conjunction of women's language skills and the computer. Because technical writing is an expanding and lucrative field that lends itself easily to working at home, I think women should jump on it if they have any interest in writing at all. Manuals for computers continue to need a lot of work, there are over two hundred computer magazines that need articles, and there is the computer-book market."

You will remember that Maxine Wyman was working as a political and economic analysis writer at Wells Fargo Bank when the department moved to London. So Maxine applied for a technical-writing job in Wells Fargo and got it on the strength of her writing skills. She knew nothing about computers at the time, and it took some time for her to consider writing as an independent; and when she left her job it was as a result of a reappraisal of her life and where she was going. Maxine now earns twice as much as an independent as she did working for corporations.

She says, "I think you have to have special training to do technical writing, but special training is not necessarily a prerequisite for getting into the field. I've seen people come into this field two ways. One is from a strong writing background, and the other is from a technical background where they have no writing experience but a lot of technical knowledge. I think the latter is more difficult than for a writer to pick up the additional technical knowledge needed to write well and fluently on a subject. But technical people get caught up in the jargon without realizing that the jargon doesn't mean anything to anyone not in the inner circle.

"As a reporter I learned to go in and research and investigate and then write what I needed to write. Those skills stand you in good stead no matter what kind of writing you do. If you've got broad experience as a writer, especially if you have experience in the mass media, you understand that there's a difference between writing a memo to your peers and writing something that is going out to the general public. You have a better grasp of how to direct things to the audience you've targeted. People who come from a technical rather than a writing background often don't understand that.

"For a novice technical writer, I'd recommend a job with a company where you can get some experience and a technical background. My background as a technical writer with Wells Fargo and a programmer with Firemen's Fund Insurance has been invaluable to me. The companies sometimes will support your attending classes. Another way to enter the field is to sign up with an agency; it's hard to get independent contracts if you have no track record."

Another way to break in is to find documentation that is badly written, partially rewrite it, and submit it to the company with a proposal that they hire you to rewrite it completely. Badly written instructions come with everything from bench tools to kitchen appliances. If you can produce something much better than what the company already has and put the proof of it in their hands, you don't need to worry about an impressive résumé. This plan requires that you invest some time and energy with no guarantee of a return, but it's worth the investment in the long run.

The technical knowledge can be picked up as you go along. I took two years of electronics courses before I started technical writing, and once I was in the field I found the level of technology was so advanced from what I studied in school that my classes were of no help whatsoever. I just had to struggle until I comprehended the material. I was fortunate to have a mentor who helped me out when I got stuck. If you can find such a person, your entry into the field will be much easier.

But you can't pick up the ability to write well as you go along. Of the two skills, it is much more important to have training and experience as a writer before attempting technical writing.

SEVEN

Your Own Computer Business: Special Services

So far we have discussed general services for a broad-based market. However, specialization can be very lucrative if you learn skills or acquire computer capability your competition lacks. There may be twenty other secretarial services in your city, but if you are the only one who is equipped to deal with the arcane vocabulary and unique forms used by attorneys, then you are in a position to attract and hold as clients all the law offices in the city.

The following are examples of some special markets and some programs that are available to serve them. The descriptions of these programs are not meant to be endorsements of them. In most cases I have not used the programs myself and can't recommend them. The descriptions are included here only to illustrate what is available.

Farms, Ranches, and Dairies

Do you live in a rural area? Do you know a little or a lot about farming, ranching, or dairy management? The modern agriculturist is sophisticated about technology and knows that computers can help increase crop yields, livestock growth, and dairy production. Although many large farms and ranches already have their own computers, there is a market for computer services in rural areas.

Crop Management System generates reports for any crop on a per-acre or a total-field basis. The program calculates yearly cost comparisons and budget projections, does cost accounting, and keeps income tax records. It will calculate pump-station efficiency and other plant-efficiency factors, and records a history of field problems, either by sections or for a whole farm.

Mixit-2 calculates the least expensive and most nutritious feed blend for a particular type of animal: beef or dairy cattle, swine, poultry, and others. Feeding for maximum growth or productivity is extremely important in stock ranching, and all ranchers recognize the value of exact calculations.

Many agricultural programs are available.

Carol Bjorling lives on a farm in Altona, Illinois. She taught herself to use the Apple IIe and uses it to track crop yields and hog production. "The computer has helped us find out which are our best sows. We are able to keep track of each sow, how many pigs she has had and how she has raised them, and what her genetic strengths are. The workers can't keep track of fifteen black sows and remember which were the good ones. By tagging their ears and keeping records of them on the computer, the workers can come in and say, 'Which ones are the good ones?' "

Carol also used the computer to figure out how the farm would come out under the government's payment-in-kind program in 1983. The country had a surplus of corn, and under this plan the government asked farmers not to plant corn and compensated them not with money, but with bushels of corn, to use up the surplus and still allow the farmers to have corn to sell. The plan was complicated by the government's paying the farmers on the basis of what it considered a normal yield per acre, not what the farmer might actually produce, and, Carol says, "The government kept changing the rules right up until the last day."

A normal yield on Carol's farm is 160 bushels per acre, but the government figure was 138, and they paid only 80 percent of that figure, or about 110 bushels. But when Carol figured the savings in fuel, equipment maintenance, seed, fertilizer, and labor, she found that even if they had a normal year the farm would come out better by taking the payment in kind. Carol used a spreadsheet program, *VisiCalc*, to do her calculations. "From the time we got the computer on February 18 until the deadline in the middle of March, I studied the manual to figure out how we could ask all these 'what if?' questions. We changed the price we might get for the corn, we changed the costs, we changed the number of bushels we could grow." All these factors are variable, and the ease with which a number of combinations could be tried, using the spreadsheet, made the computer invaluable. It turned out to be a drought year and corn yields ranged from thirty to ninety bushels, so Carol's farm profited very well by accepting payment in kind.

Carol also uses the computer for accounting and says it enables her to produce a balance sheet or financial statement quickly at any time, not just at the end of the year, as when they kept their accounts manually.

Carol is now a computer consultant to other farmers.

Churches

Financial management for churches is just as complicated as for any business, since there are individual contributions and expenses for various church activities and charities to keep track of. Important personal records such as births, deaths, weddings, and baptisms must also be recorded. The computer can be a godsend (sorry, I couldn't resist it) for the busy minister and church secretary.

Church Membership is a database program that enables a church to keep track of up to 64,000 members. Records contain names, sexes, birth dates, talents, and financial contributions. It generates printed reports of financial contributions for tax purposes.

Church Membership and Contributions is a similar program that has, in addition, a mailing list and records weddings and baptisms. There is even a program for computerizing scriptural references for sermons.

There are a lot of churches out there, and each one, unless it has its own computer, is a prospect for this special service.

Health Care Professionals

Doctors, dentists, chiropractors, ophthalmologists, optometrists, and veterinarians must keep complex records and are prime candidates for computer services. Often health professionals find it easier to contract out their computer work than to go to the expense and trouble of buying a system. Kaye Ireland told me that one of her best customers is a doctor who had the intention of buying his own system, "but it's so expensive and it takes so much time to learn to use it that he really didn't have the funds or the personnel to do it at that time. So he decided to let me do his work until he was ready. I started typing for him and he was very happy because he was getting his work back the next day and the words were always spelled right. I have a spelling checker on my computer that allows me to make up my own medical-terminology dictionary. At his office, the secretaries were always being interrupted by patients and phone calls so they weren't very accurate. Now he's so happy with this arrangement he's decided not to buy a word processing system after all. He's going to let me do it for him."

Kaye concentrates on word processing: transcribing doctors' patient notes, letters, and medical histories. She has made up a form collection letter tailored to medical practices, for clients the doctors don't want to turn over to collection agencies.

Many programs tailored to medical, dental, and other health professions are available, such as accounting packages, appointment calendars, prescription-form writers, and patient-history programs. *Medirec*, for example, is a program that allows the recording of patient history, symptoms, diagnoses, and treatments. All patients' histories can be searched for common symptoms, diagnoses, or conflicting drug treatments. Reports on individual patients can be printed out listing their past visits, history of symptoms, and so on.

If you plan to specialize in medical transcription, a program is available from Applesoft for learning medical terminology. It is interactive and teaches the student to build a large medical vocabulary through the recognition of roots, prefixes, and suffixes. The program costs only $14, a worthwhile investment for a medical-transcription specialist. You can get it through your Apple dealer or an Apple software catalog.

Chiropractors and a growing number of doctors are aware that nutrition plays a crucial role in the prevention of disease. A number of programs exist for diet analysis and for the diagnosis of nutritional deficiencies. Although I doubt you can make a living from this service alone, it should be a valuable adjunct to any service that caters to health professionals.

Nutritional Assessment is designed to analyze results of various lab tests that assist in the diagnosis, treatment, and monitoring of nutritional deficiencies.

Nutrient Analysis is intended for dieticians and hospital- and rest-home kitchen personnel. It has a built-in data base of nutritional information on 1,000 foods, with room for 3,000 additional user entries. An individual's age and sex are entered and the program gives the optimum intake of nutrients. The program also analyzes individual food items or daily, weekly, or monthly menus for nutritional content.

Law Offices

Attorneys turn out reams of typewritten documents. Many of these documents vary only in small particulars. Wills, contracts, court pleadings, and leases may be 80 percent identical to hundreds of other documents in the same category. Unfortunately, legal forms differ from state to state, and court rules may vary from county to county within states, so there are few programs that offer a library of common legal forms for computers, since most forms (other than federal court forms) are valid only in the state for which they are designed. However, there is a wide-open market for the independent word processor who creates (on disk) a specialized library of legal forms for a given area and therefore is able to offer attorneys an extremely fast typing service. The attorney simply tells the word processor what paragraphs he wants included and what particulars are to be filled in. The computer takes minutes to fill in and print out a document that would take hours to type. Some states allow mimeographed form pleadings to be filed with the court, but even in those states many attorneys still prefer to file original typed documents.

Kristen Hansen, who specializes in word processing for attorneys, has used her computer to compile a library of commonly used paragraphs for each type of legal document, and she can quickly select required provisions and create a customized document using a program called *MailMerge*. Kristen is working her way through law school offering word processing services to law firms. She has been working in the legal field for years. It was a natural choice for her to serve the legal community with her word processing service not only because she is familiar with the forms, the terminology, and the law, but because she had a natural customer base already created for her—the law firms where she had worked. Kristen feels that word processing for attorneys is an excellent way for prospective law students to learn about legal procedures; it is also one of the ways to gain entry to law offices. I also worked in law offices for many years and believe that working continuously with legal forms will supplement law school training.

The two principal on-line data bases for legal research are WestLaw and LEXIS. Subscription to these services is expensive, and LEXIS requires that you use a terminal leased from them. However, a law student might subscribe to either or both of these services and make a handsome living doing legal research, since many law offices do not have computers. The same advantages apply here that were discussed under "Information Search and Retrieval" (see p. 80): because references can be cataloged by so many different classifications, search is not only much faster but more thorough.

There are abundant programs for law offices, from total systems that do everything from keeping a calendar of court appearances to generating monthly billing, to smaller programs that do just one job.

Politicians and Advocacy Groups

The *U.S. Congressional Directory* is the *U.S. Congress Handbook* on disk. It produces mailing lists, labels, and envelopes for all members of Congress, committee and subcommittee members, administrative and legislative aides, office managers, and press secretaries. It includes profiles of each member, including top campaign contributors. Names can be sorted in a variety of ways, including by committee membership, and are updated every year for a $25 fee. You can use this program to sell customized mailing lists, or reports on particular committee makeups, to lobbies and advocacy groups.

The *U.S. Congressional Directory* would supplement a mailing list or information-retrieval service nicely. Think of all the government reports and legislation you can dredge up for special-interest lobbies, consumer groups, and political clubs.

Real Estate Agents and Investors

Realtors are another group whose work can be dramatically simplified and speeded up by the use of computers. Real estate investment and management require complex record keeping plus lengthy and complicated calculations that can be done in seconds on a computer. There are programs that do buy-vs.-rent analysis, loan amortization, escrow accounting, appraising, listings, market value computations, tax-shelter analysis, investment analysis, real estate office management, and income property management. Large realtors already have their own computer systems, but if you have a little knowledge of real estate you can market a number of services to individual investors or small realtors.

Apartment House Manager is a program that keeps records for owners of rental properties. It maintains a master file and status reports for all apartments, maintains rent records, tracks building expenses, generates form letters, and issues monthly and yearly profit-and-loss statements. *The Landlord* is a similar program. In a big city you might make a living entirely from this kind of service; in a smaller city it can be a valuable way to diversify a bookkeeping service.

Sports Groups

Record keeping for almost all sports can be simplified with computer programs. *Swimpak* keeps swim meet records. *Baseball/ Softball Statistics* calculates batting averages and team totals for hits, doubles, home runs, etc. *GolfCap* stores records for up to 500 golfers per disk, 20 scores per golfer. It generates reports by name or by handicap. There are *many* programs for handicapping horse races.

If you have an interest in sports, you can market your services as record keeper for local teams or athletic centers. Sports teams are always looking for sponsors; you could do form letters and mailings for them as well.

I have listed only a few of the possibilities for specialization here, to give an idea of the many jobs the computer can do and how many options there are for exploiting your personal experience and special interests. Many more special programs exist for businesses such as construction and surveying, restaurants, gas stations, jewelers, sporting-goods stores, insurance agents, helicopter operators, and poultry farmers—a random list from one of my software catalogs.

A multitude of possibilities exists for the woman who takes the trouble to look at the options. You need only zero in on an area for which you are suited by experience and inclination; somewhere there is a program that will enable you to use a computer to perform a marketable service for that business.

E I G H T

Telecommuting

To "telecommute" means to substitute electronic communications for physical travel to and from an employer's central workplace. Information is transferred between worker and employer by means of a computer or terminal connected to a phone line or special cable. Radio and satellite communications can also be used, but for our purposes we refer to phone and cable lines.

Telecommuting, like commuting, refers to going to and from a "job," but it can also refer to independent contracting when the contract work is performed for a single company on a regular schedule on a more-or-less permanent basis. The distinction between being an employee and being an independent contractor in such a case makes an important difference in how the worker is paid and the benefits that are available to her (we will examine these differences in detail shortly), but for all other practical purposes the contractor is an employee. As used in this book, *telecommuting* does *not* refer to self-employed people who may use telecommunications to send and receive data; these people are not "commuting."

In most instances, the telecommuter's work site is her home, although some corporations are experimenting with satellite offices in suburban areas. The future may see cooperative neighborhood work centers where employees who live in a neighborhood and work for many different employers may come together to work at equipment collectively supported by the companies they work for.

Who Can Telecommute

It isn't a new practice for employees to do some of their work at home, of course. It is not unusual for a management or professional person to occasionally spend a day working at home to catch up without distractions. What *is* new is that telecommunications and the computer have vastly increased the *amount* of work that can be done at home and have made it possible for some to work at home full-time. More *kinds* of work can be done at home, as well.

The key to this work revolution is the capability of fast transfer of information between office and worker via terminal and telephone. Clerical workers at home terminals can enter data directly into a company mainframe in a matter of seconds, where it becomes immediately available to other employees who may be in the central-office location, or who may themselves be working at a remote work site. The work of programmers, accountants, analysts, and many other professionals requires intense concentration and freedom from distractions, but these people have been prevented from working at home in the past because they required access to a powerful mainframe computer. These people can now access such a computer from their homes.

Any job that is concerned primarily with ideas and information is potentially a telecommuting job. Data entry, word processing, and many secretarial functions—including taking dictation—can be done at home. Engineers, administrators, writers, analysts, accountants, researchers, and many other professionals can also do a great deal of their work at home. Information typed into a terminal twenty miles away can be printed out as a document in the office within minutes. The development of fast, high-resolution telefacsimile devices allows even artwork and blueprints to be sent via telephone and cable.

Telecommuting does not offer as many possibilities and advantages as being self-employed. However, it is a good solution for the woman who wants to work at home but who may not be suited by temperament or inclination to hustling up her own business. It may be an ideal solution for the woman who likes less variety of activity than is required to run a business, or for one who is uncomfortable with the uncertainties of self-employment. Telecommuting is also a good compromise for someone who values her present job and does not want to give it up, but who has a reason to want to work at home. Telecommuting is a liberating option for those with handicaps that prevent them doing the varied activities required of the independent entrepreneur.

Telecommuting agreements with employers can be formal or informal. A person may be hired specifically for a telecommuting job; the requirement to work from a remote site is part of the formal agreement between employer and employee. Very often, however, and particularly for professionals, the arrangement is informal. A person may have been hired officially to work in the office, but by individual arrangement with supervisors she obtains permission to work at home (or some other remote site) at least part-time. In this case it is often the employee who requests the arrangement.

Telecommuters fall into two general categories: professional/management and clerical. Just as in the overall work market, the terms and conditions of employment differ greatly for the two categories, with differences based primarily on that overriding principle of the universe, the Law of Supply and Demand.

Professionals with skills that are in short supply, such as computer programmers and financial analysts, are in a good bargaining position and can just about write their own tickets. They can demand excellent salaries and benefits, often with the option to work at least part-time at home as a condition of their employment. They remain salaried employees with all their benefits retained, and often their home computer or terminal is furnished by the employer.

Clerical workers, such as word processors and data-entry clerks, are plentiful in our present job market, and so the employer writes the ticket. They are usually hired as independent contractors who are not paid salaries but are paid according to what they produce (sometimes called "piecework"), and sometimes they must pay for their own equipment, in many cases leasing it from the employer.

Because conditions of employment differ greatly for the two groups, we will consider them separately.

Professional and Management Telecommuters

To get a salaried telecommuting job with full employee benefits one must be a professional with skills that are in undersupply, according to Dr. Margreth Olson of New York University's Center for Research on Information Systems. Companies are willing to make telecommuting arrangements as a way to attract and retain employees who have valuable skills—the employers' primary motivation for making such arrangements.

Companies report an increase in productivity and better overall performance by telecommuting professionals. Employees say that lack of distractions is one of the major attractions of working at home, and it is this factor that may account for the improved performance. At any rate, everybody's happy.

Telecommuting employees enjoy most of the benefits of working at home previously discussed, although they may not have all the tax benefits. Some deductions are allowed for necessary use of the home in connection with a job, however. The company usually will furnish a terminal or computer and pay for the phone line that connects it to the central workplace.

The option of working at home is not generally offered voluntarily by employers to prospective employees, but such an option can be part of your job negotiations. You need to convince the employer that it is in his best interests to allow you to work at home. (Dr. Olson's study shows that companies are not concerned with the quality of life of their employees, so don't tell them about *your* reasons for wanting to work at home.) Arguments you might offer: studies have shown that professionals working without the distractions of an office environment are more productive; the company saves the overhead cost of space in the office; the ability to access their mainframe computer during off hours will lessen the jam-up and waiting for computer time that plagues so many companies. Depending on how secure you are in your importance to the company, you can imply that unless they let you work at home at least part-time, you will not take the job.

Another way to get a telecommuting job is to convince your present employer to let you work at home. This is what Lisa Walker did.

Lisa is a programmer who graduated from UCLA with a degree in math and computer science. She says, "I started out in accounting, and one of the courses required for accounting was data processing. When I got into it I said, 'Oh, this is it! This is fun. This is ten times better than accounting.' I was one of those whiz kids—to me a computer is a big toy. I love computers."

After graduating Lisa went to work for a firm that provided computer-aided design services to architects. She also married. After about two years, she had a baby. It was then that Lisa talked her employer into letting her work at home. "When I got pregnant, it was planned. I had always assumed they would let me work at home. There was only a two-person programming staff. I was deeply involved with projects and in managing our own computer, a DEC PDP, and if they had cut me off completely it would have been too much for the other programmer to handle. I bought myself a DEC Rainbow [which can be used as a terminal to access the DEC PDP over the phone] without getting a go-ahead from my boss. Then, when I left to have the baby, I told him, 'I have a terminal at home and if you ever have anything for me to do just call and I'll do it.' It was all premeditated. I did it on the safe assumption that I was too valuable to him to turn me down.

"I started working at home one month before the baby was born. I said, 'I've had it! I can't come in anymore.' I was very big. But I wanted to continue to work. It was such a relief to go to part-time. When you're pregnant your mind is so occupied with the coming event that you want to put work aside for a while, but not completely."

For the first year Lisa worked part-time with variable hours. She did not receive any benefits because she no longer worked the required minimum of thirty hours per week. Lisa says, "If I had been putting in thirty hours I would have had paid holidays and other benefits. I did get unemployment and withholding. I was on the payroll, not an independent contractor."

Lisa liked working as a telecommuter better than working in the office. "When I was in the office, I would do a lot of other things besides work on the computer, and that's the kind of work that used to keep me busy full-time, such as getting good prices on computer components and buying things for clients. That's the work that I'm happy not to do anymore. I like to concentrate on the computer work. In the office, even though I was a programmer, my boss would give me a lot of Xeroxing and filing. He'd even ask me to make the coffee if he was having a meeting because I was the low person on the totem pole—I had just been promoted to the technical staff from word processing. I was always the one taking the minutes of the meeting, and I felt like saying, 'Why doesn't someone else do this?'

"Telecommuting part-time worked out better than being employed full-time. It opened up a lot more opportunities for me. I got freelance programming jobs. I got another job teaching computers part-time—I worked only four days a month but they were paying me twenty-five dollars an hour. I have always wanted to teach, but if I had a full-time job there's no way I could ever take a job teaching four days a month. But it was great to get out of the house and do that. I was also planning to start a mail-order software business. I got a resale number from the state of California, which is free, and now, having that number, I can buy software at forty percent off retail and then resell it. My idea was to tap a market that hasn't been tapped yet. I was going to try things out and see what works."

Before things progressed that far, however, Lisa's boss decided to change his business to the development of commercial software. He bought a bigger computer and asked Lisa to come back to work for him in the office. He had no one else able to make the conversion from the old computer to the new one, and he needed her expertise. Lisa asked for and received a substantial raise and the privilege of continuing to work at home at programming, spending three days a week in the office. She still telecommutes part of the time and spends a fair amount of time with her baby.

I asked Lisa how telecommuting mixes with family life. "On the whole my husband likes the arrangement. He gets a variable salary—he's a car salesman. Sometimes he'll have good months and sometimes he has very bad months. He depends on the money I bring in; we need it very much because we just bought a house. Sometimes he gets frustrated because when the baby goes to sleep in the evening I'll jump on the computer. It's my one chance for total concentration, and he complains that I'm always on the computer, that I never pay attention to him. But he doesn't complain too loudly. In fact, when he's home he'll take Wendy for a long walk because he knows I need the time. There was a show on television a while back that claimed computers in the home are ruining families. You do get attached to the computer and spend a lot of time with it, but I don't think it is ruining families."

Lisa was charging her freelance clients fifteen dollars an hour and agrees she was not charging enough. "I was making twelve dollars an hour working for the company, and my boss was charging fifty-five dollars an hour for me. It's so aggravating. You might ask, 'Why did you keep that job at twelve dollars an hour when you can name your own price as a consultant?' It's because I wanted the security of a reliable income. I wanted to balance the job and the freelance work."

Telecommuting has given Lisa freedom and solved a number of problems, allowing her to continue work while she stays at home with her baby. Her job gave her a dependable and predictable income while she built a base of consulting clients that served as a reliable backup to her husband's variable income. Telecommuting has allowed her to drop the work she did not enjoy in the office to concentrate on what she enjoys most— programming. She has established her value to the company as a programmer, and her employer no longer expects her to take notes and make coffee.

Lisa was not charging enough for her services as a consultant, but she had been out of college and working for only two years at the time I interviewed her. But she gained experience and confidence, and she felt secure enough to demand a higher wage when she went back to work full-time for her old company.

Mary Ellen Siudut is a programmer who works for only one company, so, although she gets paid as an independent contractor, she meets our definition of a telecommuter.

Mary Ellen studied programming in college and had already worked as a programmer when she started her family. She says,

"I wanted to continue to gain experience while the children were little, so that when they were all in school I would still be able to enter the field without having to take an entry level job. I also wanted to get out of the house and have some mental stimulation while making enough money to make it worthwhile. If you're paying two dollars an hour for babysitting and you're only making five dollars an hour at your job, it's not worth it.

"I had a lot of different jobs, trying to juggle being a mother and working in the computer field too. I've worked terrible hours, like the four-to-midnight shift, so I could be home with the preschoolers; I've worked two different shifts of two part-time jobs at the same time so that I'd earn enough money but not be away from the kids too much. I tried juggling things so that I worked only a few hours and my mother watched the kids for me. At one time I worked four to twelve; my husband got home at five-thirty, so I'd only have to pay an hour-and-a-half of babysitting, but then I'd be up all night. I was paid awful wages and I wasn't using my best skills at all—I wasn't programming. I worked as a data-entry clerk and the pay was terrible—minimum wage.

"Then I taught computer programming, which was decent pay but I was only working nine hours a week. Anything you do for only a few hours a week normally doesn't pay well. There just aren't any part-time programming jobs if you're a good programmer. They give you all kinds of work and they want you more and more and more.

"I was really strung out while I was working. I was commuting four hours a day when I worked the two part-time jobs at once. I was trying to be Supermom. I think I was the one that suffered more than anybody else."

Mary Ellen saw programming at home as the perfect solution to being able to be at home to raise her children and still be in the computer field. She now makes twenty-five dollars an hour writing programs in Forth (a business-oriented language). She says, "My best pay before was eight-fifty an hour teaching COBOL programming, and after paying for babysitting there wasn't much left. So not only am I making much more money per hour, but there's no babysitting coming out of it."

When I asked Mary Ellen what else she likes about telecommuting, she said, "I feel good about getting mental stimulation. I write real business applications, not just operations. I feel good about being a working person. When someone asks what I do, I feel good about my answer. And I don't have to work too much. Sometimes I work up to fifty hours a week, but normally I work only ten to fifteen hours a week, which is wonderful. During the summer I don't usually have any jobs at all, so I have all the time I need to be a mother. My husband likes the situation. He is extremely helpful. He'll come home and make dinner and clean up after dinner if I need to work. He was very helpful when I was working outside the home, too."

Telecommuting as a technical professional has allowed Mary Ellen to net more than twice as much per hour than she was able to make at part-time jobs. It has cut out commuting time and costs and allowed her to work only as much as she wants to.

Joan Orke, mentioned earlier, is a telecommuting programmer for Honeywell Corporation in Minneapolis. You will remember that Joan's arthritis makes it impossible for her to hold a regular job and limits her to a degree that would make it extremely difficult to do all the things necessary to run her own business from home. For Joan, telecommuting is the solution.

Clerical Telecommuters

The motivation of corporate employers changes when it comes to clerical rather than professional telecommuting. Rather than trying to attract and keep valuable skilled professionals, they are looking for ways to cut costs. The sums required to maintain office space in metropolitan areas are mind-boggling; if a corporation can avoid expanding its facilities by hiring clerks to work at home, it saves significant amounts of money. Dr. Olson's study also found that corporations look for ways to cut costs by eliminating employee benefits—the reason many pay clerical telecommuters as independent contractors rather than as employees.

Banks and insurance companies move massive amounts of information every day, and they were among the first to experiment with telecommuting for data-entry clerks and word processors.

That's unfortunate, because banks and insurance companies are well-known for low salaries and poor attitudes toward their clerical help. Their character does not change when it comes to telecommuting, as we shall see.

Most clerical telecommuting for such institutions involves piecework. The employee is not technically an employee at all but an independent contractor who is paid by a unit of work, or "piece." For a word processor this may be a line of typing or a page of a certain length; for a data-entry clerk it may be a form or a check. There are both advantages and drawbacks to this arrangement. On the positive side, competence is rewarded. If you are fast and efficient, you can do more units per hour and therefore earn more money per hour than a slower co-worker. If you have ever worked where your output was twice that of co-workers paid the same wage, you will appreciate the justice of this system. Another advantage is that a mother working at home with small children who constantly interrupt her may find that keeping track of her time is practically impossible. If she is paid by piece, she can work intermittently and her total output is all that matters. A truly fast typist can earn more money per hour by piecework than she could earn being paid by the hour. There are also the tax advantages of being self-employed: you can deduct the space you use for your work and any other work-related expenses.

On the negative side, an independent contractor who is in every other respect an employee may lose several thousand dollars a year in benefits, because she does not get unemployment or health insurance, paid vacations, sick leave, or retirement. She may also have to rent her equipment from the employer. She does not have any rights as an employee under applicable labor laws. Clerical telecommuters have no bargaining power whatsoever: their skills are in oversupply and the companies can pay what they please. So many women want to work at home that even if an entire telecommuting staff quits to protest low pay, others are eager to take their places.

The benefits of this arrangement to the corporation are enormous. Not only is overhead drastically reduced for these workers, but the companies don't have to pay any benefits, which, again, can amount to several thousand dollars a year per worker. They get much more production for the money they pay for piecework than they do for the same amount of money spent on office help, because an office worker gets paid for the time she doesn't work as well as for the time she does. In a corporate environment this can be a great deal of time indeed. A pieceworker gets paid only when she is producing.

Finally, piecework motivates workers to be more productive, since the more they produce the more they earn, and companies generally report a dramatic increase in productivity and a reduction of error rates by telecommuters. In Professor Olson's study, a few companies who found performance problems attributed them to factors other than the employees or the telecommuting dynamic itself—things such as management attitudes or communications and technical problems. Where these problems did not exist, job performance improved.

Although piecework benefits the corporation far more than the worker, it is not necessarily a bad idea, nor is it necessarily exploitive for corporations to pay workers this way. For one thing, it is the only practical way to have reasonable control over the time/production ratio of a person working out of sight of supervisors. There are some benefits to the worker as well as to the company, as I mentioned earlier. Whether it ends up being exploitive boils down to whether the company pays the independent contractor enough to compensate for the loss of employee benefits. If it does, the pieceworker is way ahead, because she has the tax advantages of being self-employed, does not have to worry about finding work, and can enjoy all the benefits of working at home discussed in chapter 3.

Unfortunately, there are companies who do *not* pay well enough. One of the telecommuters I talked with said that her employer had the attitude that she should not expect to earn as much as she had in the office because "you get to work at home." This has a very familiar smell to it because it is rooted in the same garbage as the ancient rationale "we don't pay women as much because they don't have families to support." Employers can't get away with *that* one anymore, of course, but "you aren't paid as much because you get to work at home" has taken its place. Irrelevance is the core of both rationales. It doesn't matter whether you have a family to support or you "get" to work at home. You have a right to be paid the value of the work you do, period. If someone gives you that "get to work at home" argument, counter with, "How much are you going to pay me for the use of my space at home, since you don't have to pay for my space at the office?" Or, "How much extra are you going to pay me because you 'get' to not provide me any benefits?"

Obviously the potential for exploitation exists, and it's already happening in some quarters. These abuses are why unions and organizations like 9 to 5 (an association of office workers) are very resistant to telecommuting. The Service Employees International Union (SEIU), whose members are clerical and health workers, has gone so far as to call for a legislative ban on telecommuting. Their position is that since serious abuses of people working in the home have occurred in the past (notably in the garment industry), they are likely to occur again, since it is extremely difficult to organize workers who are widely scattered.

Vitriolic statements against telecommuting by purported experts crop up again and again in the press, but they never seem to offer any factual studies or even sound reasoning as evidence, except to mention the garment industry again and again or to make grand generalizations like, "Technology by itself never changed the lives of women." I guess the person who made that statement never heard of the washing machine, the vacuum cleaner, gas stoves, or the automobile. In the case of the garment industry argument, that's like saying automobiles should be banned because a lot of people get killed by them. The answer isn't to ban the automobiles, but to make them safer and remove dangerous drivers from the road. The answer to possible exploitation of telecommuters is not to ban telecommuting, but to start now creating organizations and laws that will protect the telecommuter from abuses.

Because these arguments against telecommuting are so silly, I decided to find out for myself what the situation is from telecommuters in the "worst possible scenario" category— clerical workers doing piecework in the insurance field.

I spoke to three women who work for the Blue Cross/Blue Shield Cottage Keyer program in Washington, D.C. These women all work at home using terminals connected by phone lines to the company's mainframe computer. In this way they enter data coded from insurance claims into the mainframe, where the information is processed. They are required to lease their terminals from the company at $95 for two weeks. They are paid sixteen cents for each claim they enter. Since they are independent contractors they receive no benefits whatsoever—no health insurance, paid vacation, unemployment insurance, retirement, or sick leave.

They are required to do a minimum of 400 claims a day and must work during the hours when the computer is "up"—that is, operating. The time they are allowed to start in the morning varies, depending on who is working in the computer room, but it can be as early as 5:30 A.M. The computer is shut down at 5:00 P.M. Working speed among the three women varied, but all of them were capable of averaging 50 claims an hour, which would allow them to complete their 400 forms in a normal eight-hour day and earn a minimum of $64 a day or $8 an hour. If they are faster, of course, they earn more per hour. However, they are not paid overtime no matter how many hours a day or a week they work. Also, $9.50 a day goes for rental of the terminal, and the rental must be paid whether they work or not, except during extended leave, such as maternity leave. No terminal rent is charged for Saturdays, although they may work on Saturdays. But Monday through Friday, any day they are sick or cannot work they are in the hole $9.50.

Assuming a 400-form output in an eight-hour day, these workers earn about $1,200 a month after the terminal rent is deducted and before taxes. Depending on individual circumstances, net after taxes will probably be somewhere between $850 and $1,050 per month. That still sounds good if you are thinking of wages. But these are not wages, they are contract payments. They do not carry with them the benefits we assume when we hear what people are making. In order to compare those wage rates with what a data-entry clerk working at the company site makes, we must add the value of employee benefits, or there is no true comparison of total value received for work performed.

Donna Griffith, a Cottage Keyer, worked as a data-entry clerk at the company site before she started working at home. She made $614 every two weeks but only worked seven hours a day. When we adjust for a forty-hour week to make an hour-for-hour comparison, her gross would have been $1,543 a month. She received one day a month paid sick leave and one day a month paid vacation—about $123 in benefits. The health insurance provided by the company had a value of at least $75 (probably more, but I'm using very conservative figures in an effort to be fair to the company's side of the case). That brings her income to $1,741, almost half again as much as she's making for the same time now, assuming she works at the reasonable average rate of 50 claims an hour, and the figures she gave me indicate that she does. But that's a conservative figure, since there are values that can't be calculated precisely in dollars, like the security of unemployment insurance and retirement benefits.

It is obvious that, compared to the on-site data-entry clerks, the Cottage Keyers aren't making out very well. I have gone into so much detail primarily to show skeptics how I reached my conclusions, and also to indicate to anyone who is considering piecework as a telecommuter how crucial it is to know exactly what you are receiving and what you are not receiving. The Cottage Keyers I talked to knew they were not getting what they should, but not one of them had worked out on paper precisely how her pay—adjusted for lost benefits—compared to that of keyers in the office. If they had, they might have had more effective arguments when they asked Blue Cross/Blue Shield for a raise. As it is, they were turned down.

However, although two feel they are not paid adequately, all three of the women I talked with are happy with their jobs and are grateful for the opportunity to work at home—an opportunity they believe they would not have had without the Cottage Keyer program. They do differ in whether they feel exploited. They all have good advice and experience to share with women contemplating telecommuting.

Diane Blosse worked for Blue Cross/Blue Shield for thirteen years. When she quit in 1982 she was earning $34,000 a year as a professional-affairs representative. She called on physicians to straighten out problems with claims payments, to explain new procedures, and generally to act as a liaison between physicians and the company. After her first baby she returned to work but didn't like leaving her baby with a sitter, so she quit to become a Cottage Keyer. She now has three children.

Although Diane is making less than half as much as she did

before, she thinks her pay is fair for the work she does. She says, "Basically the job is pretty elementary, and once you learn the keying and the screen, you can do anything you want while you're keying. It's rote work. It's not the most stimulating employment, but it's something I can do at home to bring in income while the kids are little, and we don't have the expenses I had when I had a job. Clothing, going out to lunch every day, babysitting, and I save a lot of time by not commuting. It's perfect—my kids are with me while I'm working, and I can stop to care for them when I need to and I still get my work done.

"If I didn't have this option I would probably still be working at a job. My husband has two children by a previous marriage, so we need an extra income. I don't anticipate doing it permanently, but for right now it's perfect. I don't feel exploited at all. My only complaint is that I feel that work is being sent to me that the keyers in the office don't want to do, the more difficult claims. They take longer to do and so you don't make as much per hour. But my husband reminds me of how much I complained when I was working. I was going to meetings at night, and I was spending a lot of time on the road in my car. There were demands there that I don't have with this job. Doctors as a group are very demanding, and they took a lot out on me. I learned to handle it well, but there were days when I felt mistreated. I wanted to tell them off but I couldn't because of my job. I do really miss the working world, but I don't miss all the ———— that goes with it!

"Being home all the time was a shock at first. I went through a big depression adjusting to it. I still have days when I feel like if I don't get out of the house I'm going to go crazy. I've joined a health club where they have child care, so I can take a break and go there. Or I take a walk with my kids. That's what I like about the job—I can tailor the work to my needs. If I want to start at six A.M. and finish by two, I can.

"I worked for thirteen years and was pretty active, and I don't think I could stay home and not do something besides being a housewife. So this is perfect for me because I want to be home while my kids are little."

Donna Griffith is not entirely satisfied with her situation but feels she has no other options at present. She is the only one of the three I talked with who was doing data entry before she joined the Cottage Keyers. She had been at her job in the office at Blue Cross/Blue Shield for ten years and was frustrated because she "didn't seem to be able to advance." She had other reasons for frustration. "At work, we couldn't even talk. At my age I resented that. They didn't want you to use the phone, and little things like that. I felt like I could be my own boss at home and work the way I want to work. I feel comfortable working at home.

"I didn't consider taking another job because of my age. I'm forty-nine and everything is youth-oriented. It's not easy to find a job after a certain age. I don't have any education beyond high school, and the only experience I've had besides entering insurance claims was work in a cafeteria and as a telephone operator at Blue Cross/Blue Shield. The reason I don't have much experience is that I stayed home when my kids were little. I was in my late thirties when I went to work.

"I think that I'd rather be at home than working in an office. I'm a loner and I don't like to work around people. A lot of people don't like being isolated, but I do. I can talk on the phone or listen to the radio, things we weren't allowed to do at work. I don't know of any other way I could get to work at home, other than what I'm doing now. I don't know how to go about looking for something else to do."

Donna is resentful of the way she is paid and of the way the work is organized. The work comes to the women in batches of 50 claims each. The length of time it takes to do a claim depends on how complicated it is. But instead of mixing up long and short claims so that all batches are more or less equivalent, some batches have all short claims and some have all long ones.

"When they first started this program they were paying the keyers fifteen cents a form, but the forms were all short. Then they started paying a penny more, but now the claims can be more than twice as long. That one cent is not compensating for what you have to do. We're getting only a penny more for all that extra work, and it's not fair. We asked for more money and they claimed we were getting paid too much as it is. They said there isn't anything that can be done about it. There's nothing we can do. I've been a Cottage Keyer for two years and we haven't had a raise."

Donna doesn't think piecework is a good idea for everyone. "I don't think you can do this if you don't have someone to help you. My husband is a government employee and he provides my insurance. If something happens and I can't work, I still have security. A woman who is by herself doesn't have that. So I don't recommend it for single women, or anyone who is ambitious. If I knew of a way to make more money doing this, I would, but I just don't know how to take advantage of being able to operate a computer."

Yvonne Rice is an extremely fast keyer who averages 75 claims an hour. She likes to make $1,000 every two weeks, which she can do by working nine hours a day.

Yvonne had worked at Blue Cross/Blue Shield for seventeen years as a secretary/typist, but when the Cottage Keyer program was started she applied immediately because she "had always wanted to be at home." Her principal reason for wanting to be at home is to be with her two small children.

She earned $18,000 a year as a secretary, and in 1984 she grossed $22,000 as a Cottage Keyer, but of course she did not receive benefits and worked harder and longer hours. On the other hand, she no longer has all the expenses of commuting, babysitting, and clothing—"Here I sit in my bedroom slippers." Since she has never figured all this out exactly, she is not sure how she fares in comparison with her salaried job, but, she says, "I'm working harder than I was before. You can cheat at work, you can take time out for a break, or talk to your friends, but here I don't. I constantly push to work, to make the money. I worked my heart out for three months to get custom-made drapes."

Yvonne, like Donna, feels that she is taken advantage of. "I haven't had a raise for two years. If you call in and complain, they tell us, 'If you don't like it you can quit. We'll find somebody else to do it.' And they can, too. At one time they had a waiting list of two hundred for this program. A lot of women want to work at home. It hurts when they tell you that—I've been with them seventeen years—but I don't want to give up my job. I want the advantages of being at home.

"They don't sympathize with us. We go in there as a group, they consider us complainers. They could make it rough on us—they could just not send us work. See, it scares you. You don't know what your rights are.

"I want the advantages of working at home, so I sit here, I work, and I shut up. They offered us full-time jobs to go back, and I said no. They think I'm making a lot of money. They don't look at how much time I put in. I don't run to the bathroom every five minutes or sit here and talk on the phone to my friends or sit here and smoke all day or take a lunch. But they don't take that into consideration. They're looking at the money I bring home. My taxes aren't taken out, and they don't look at that, either. They don't even remember the ninety-five dollars every two weeks for the terminal. They're figuring if I get a thousand dollars it's all for me to spend, but it's not.

"There are other problems, too. I get claims that aren't made out right and it slows me down. If a claim is wrong, the computer rejects it, and you don't get the money even though you entered it. It's aggravating to sit here all day making money by the piece and lose money because of someone else's mistake. It's frustrating. Another thing—we're supposed to key in four hundred claims a day, but in house [at the company site] they only have to key three hundred.

"My hands and my muscles get tired. I keyed so long one day I thought my arms were going to fall off and my husband had to rub Ben-Gay on me I was so stiff.

"But even with all the problems I don't want to give it up, because I love being at home. If they ever discontinue the Cottage Keyers they're going to have to come with a gun to get the machine out of my house. I want to work at home. I'm not sick as much because I'm not around sickness. I haven't had flu this year, or even a cold.

"If you're going to do this, make sure you get all this ironed out before you sign up. You should tell the company what your expectations are."

Gil Gordon, a telecommuting consultant based in New Jersey, agrees with Yvonne's advice. "There's no doubt the potential for exploitation is there [for clerical telecommuters]. But I think the very same thing happens in an office. The low-paid clerical workers, who tend to be women, are the ones who are more exploitable and more exploited. So I'm not sure how much is telecommuting and how much is tradition. The worst situation is the case where the company, simply as a way to cut payroll costs, takes people who would have been doing the same work and now pays them significantly less money because of the work-at-home arrangement. If that's the case, and particularly if the company has a history of abusive or less-than-enlightened employee relations, then it may just not be the kind of company you want to work for. They would exploit you whether you are telecommuting or not.

"I'd give the same advice I'd give to anybody who is considering any kind of job change: Be clear in your own mind what's important to you, what's on your shopping list. What's the relative importance of working at home and not in an office, of not having to commute, of dressing as you please? For some people the benefits of being at home may outweigh a lower salary. For others it may not come out that way. Make up your personal shopping list, and once you know what's important to you, compare what you have to give up to get that."

Gil warns that one of the things to be alert to in telecommuting is the possible impact on family life. "My guess is that strong marriages will become stronger, weak ones may go over the brink, and those that are on the fence will go one way or the other very quickly. You've got to evaluate your relationship with your spouse and your children, and if for any reason you look forward to getting out of the house in the morning because of what's going on at home, then telecommuting isn't for you."

The three Cottage Keyers I interviewed all have complaints about their jobs, but every one of them said she would not give it up and that telecommuting solves more problems than it creates.

Does Blue Cross/Blue Shield exploit them? It depends on how you interpret the word *exploit*. The women earn less money, when you take benefits into consideration, than they would earn for the same work in-house for the same company, and certainly the company is taking advantage of the demand for these jobs to give the keyers as little money as possible. Blue Cross/Blue Shield can name their own terms because two hundred women are waiting to take over if the present keyers quit. The company benefits from surplus labor and is not responding to the women's complaints. I wouldn't argue if you said the company's attitude and policies are exploitive.

On the other hand, the women say clearly that the advantages outweigh the drawbacks, and they do have other options, including going back to work in the company with full benefits. None of the keyers feels the daily work quota is unreasonable, and the pay is certainly better than that for many regular clerical jobs, even after adjusting for lost benefits. All the keyers can make $8 an hour without strain, and more if they want to work harder. These are far from the sweatshop conditions that critics of telecommuting insist are inevitable.

What the opponents of work-at-home fail to take into consideration is that people are not being forced to work at home, they *want* to work at home. Further, people can't be said to be exploited if they have more advantageous options open to them, yet still consent to exploitative terms. Consent is the key factor.

If you want a clerical telecommuting job, take Gil Gordon's advice and make a shopping list, weigh the benefits against the tradeoffs, and make a responsible choice. If you are in a position where you have no other options than to take a job under exploitive conditions, you may need to (1) upgrade your skills so you have other choices, and/or (2) move someplace where there are more possibilities, and (3) give your support to legislation and organizations that create better terms of employment for telecommuters.

Big business exploits labor whenever it can get away with it, and the Law of Supply and Demand is inexorable if it is not artificially controlled. Clerical telecommuters are not going to get the best terms possible until telecommuting is regulated and telecommuters are organized. Until then, it is up to each of us, individually, to take care of ourselves.

We should do that anyway.

PART III

Running a Computer-Based Business from Home

NINE

Taking the
First Steps

Michaelene Pendleton read the outline of this book in its early stages and said, "You talked me into into starting a home business with a computer. What appeals to me most is running an information retrieval service using on-line database services." Michaelene would enjoy running such a service and is ideally suited to it because she is one of those people who, if she gets interested in something, tends to find out everything there is to know about it. (Just ask her about Aztec civilization sometime.) But Michaelene lives in the same city as I do—Moab, Utah, which has a population of five thousand. To access any of the major data bases requires a long distance phone call. There is virtually no local demand for information retrieval. We have only one industry, besides tourists—a mineral refining plant, which is presently shut down. If it reopens, they might be interested in occasional searches for geological and mineral data, but by no stretch of the imagination could she hope to support herself with local projects.

In order for Michaelene to establish such a business she must reach potential customers in other areas of the country, which means she must advertise. She must pay long distance phone charges in addition to the high costs of accessing the data bases. In order to cover these costs, she must have a high volume of work and charge substantial fees. The primary users of information-retrieval services are large corporations involved in technological design, research, and troubleshooting. She would be extremely disadvantaged by living and working where she cannot make personal calls to sell her services. Although an information retrieval service would suit Michaelene's interests and skills very well, everything else is against it; if she had followed her first impulsive inclination without further study, her endeavor almost surely would have failed.

But Michaelene did further study. Looking for an alternative business, she considered her other interests, skills, and experience (communications, writing, and project management), and, most important, the services Moab needs but does not have. She decided that Moab needs a broad spectrum service that will plan and execute publicity and advertising, write and produce copy for all media, and coordinate projects such as fairs and conferences— all activities in which Michaelene has experience and expertise.

Michaelene bought an inexpensive but adequate microcomputer (a Kaypro 2X) and she has started her business from her home at no additional expense. Because Moab has a depressed economy, she has kept her part-time job while she is building her business; if the business doesn't survive, she'll still have her job. If the business succeeds, she can use her computer to help her in all phases of her operation: word processing for her writing and correspondence, a mailing list program for direct-mail canvassing and advertising, and a modem to send copy directly to a printer's computer and save on typesetting costs. She can buy an accounting program to keep her books and prepare her tax forms. Other special-purpose software can help with project planning and management.

Starting a business in a small city with a depressed economy is a risky undertaking. Michaelene analyzed the needs of our city, assessed her own skills, and set realistic goals with contingency plans in case things don't work out. She couldn't have planned more sensibly.

In order to sell something there must be a market for it and the market must be reasonably accessible. You must have a fair chance against the competition. No major corporation would even think of introducing a new service or product without first studying the market, and it is doubly important for an individual to do so. The giant corporation can survive a bad decision, but an individual may lose her entire investment and not have a second chance, not to mention the damage such a failure may do to her self-confidence and self-esteem. So, it is important to think carefully about starting a home-based business and to make decisions that will give you every chance for success.

Although working at home with computers can eliminate a whole constellation of problems associated with holding a job, working at home has its own set of difficulties. However, if working at home is the right solution for you, it will solve more headaches than it creates, and most of the problems can be worked out with an adaptable attitude and reasonable effort. But to make an informed decision, you need to have an idea of what problems you might come up against, so I have included in these chapters every problem associated with working at home that I could identify from research studies, magazine and newspaper articles, and my interviews with experts in the field and more than thirty women who work at home.

A collection of all the identifiable problems, summarized and presented in one place, is apt to look formidable and perhaps discouraging. But no single individual will encounter all the possible complications or even a major part of them. Further, my interviews with women who work at home bear out strongly that any of these difficulties can be solved with a modicum of ingenuity and determination. I encountered only one woman, Kathryn Hubbell of Eugene, Oregon, who gave up working at home because of a problem (interference from her children); and even then she was not sorry she had tried it, since the experience gave her independence and fulfillment. She simply moved her business into a rented office. All the women I interviewed had encountered problems of one kind or another; none of them was in the least discouraged by these problems and all considered them an inevitable reality of managing a small business.

There are five major points you should evaluate in the first stages of planning a business: what skills you already have or can acquire in a short time; the possible market in your city for the kind of services you want to offer; what you are going to do for money until your business is established; how you can be sure you will like working with computers if you're not already familiar with them; and what demands entrepreneurship will make upon your character.

SKILLS AND EXPERIENCE
ARE YOUR GREATEST ASSETS

What you already know is your single greatest asset and should be a primary factor in choosing your business. If you are already a professional person, then of course you are already well equipped to start your own business, and your choices are simple, unless you want to change fields.

But what if you have no special training? No matter whom you've worked for—lawyers, manufacturers, real estate agents, doctors, retail stores or wholesalers, CPAs, advertising agencies— that experience can be exploited. Even if you were working at the clerical level, you probably know more about how information is processed in that business than the executives do, and any computer-based business is essentially the processing of information. When systems analysts go into a company to set up computer systems, they don't talk to the bosses to find out how work is done; they go to the secretaries and clerks. You're the expert. Software written for specific applications makes the job easier; much of what you need to know to transfer your knowledge to the computer is built right into the program.

For example, if all you've ever done is drive a taxi, you probably know enough about fleet management to sell taxi companies a computer service to keep track of cab maintenance and drivers' earnings, if you can find a program specifically written for that application (and such programs do exist). If you have some programming experience, you can write your own.

Women who married young and chose to stay at home and raise a family may never have had the chance to learn marketable skills. If you are among these women, you will need to invest some time in learning before striking out on your own. Courses at your local college can prepare you to start a business in as little as a year. A typing course is essential, plus dedicated practice until you get *really* good, not just good enough to get by. Enroll in elementary computer courses, but be careful to choose those that are oriented to using software rather than to programming, unless you intend to become a programmer. You will need courses in some areas of specialization, such as bookkeeping and accounting, technical writing, public relations, or whatever your field of interest is.

If your energy and commitment are high, you can prepare yourself in even less time. I grew up thinking it took many years to become well educated in any field because it takes four years to earn a bachelor's degree and many more years for an advanced degree. It wasn't until I actually took some college courses (very late in life) that I discovered that the reason it takes so long to get a degree is that your time is filled up with a lot of courses you don't need, and most courses move at about one-fourth the rate at which you could learn if you were allowed to go at your own pace. Someone famous (I forget who) recently said that there are few topics a reasonably intelligent person can't master in three months by giving it all their time and energy. Although that's an exaggeration, I do agree that many subjects can be learned in much less time than the four years required to get a degree; at least that's my experience as a writer. I am often called on to become extremely knowledgeable extremely fast in order to write something. I can learn more about a given topic in electronics in two or three weeks of independent study than I ever learned in my year of college electronics courses.

Whatever it is you want to do, if you are not already an expert, buy the best books you can find on the subject, talk to knowledgeable people, immerse yourself in the subject, practice, work hard for a few months, and then *do* it. Many people start businesses that way, and most of the women I interviewed for this book are self-taught. *All* the technical writers I know got started this way; it is also how many programmers start. You can do the same thing with database management, bookkeeping, mail order, and a hundred other services. (Not recommended for brain surgery. But you don't do that with a computer anyway.)

MARKET STUDY IS ESSENTIAL

As you have seen, to make sure your business will succeed you must give careful consideration to the market for your services.

In general, if you live in a major city you will need to specialize in order to compete; if you live in a small city you will need to diversify in order to survive.

For example, in a city with many word processing services available, a woman with a legal background (such as Kristen Hansen) has an advantage if she specializes in legal forms and pleadings. However, such a focused market would be ridiculous in a town that has only three lawyers (unless none of them has a secretary). A word processing service in a small city must be prepared to do almost any kind of document.

Big cities have major companies that lease enormous demographic mailing lists, but there is always room for some special focus, such as The National Women's Mailing List, described in chapter 6. You can compile a mailing list of customers for any individual business in a small city or a large one. Larger companies rarely bother with such "small" jobs, but such jobs can be the independent contractor's bread and jam.

Once you have made a tentative decision about the kind of business you want to start, survey the field to ensure that in fact that kind of service is needed. The smaller the city, the more important it is to do this. Personal visits to prospective clients will be more productive than writing letters, since a nonessential letter is easy to shove aside and not answer. Busy people are more likely to answer your questions when you are right there. Explain what you plan to do, and ask if they are likely to use your services. If so, how often? Are they using a similar service now, and if so, are they happy with it? How much are they paying for the service?

Find out whether similar services already exist and, if so, how well they are doing. You might even visit the competition. How you will be received is not predictable. Some may be threatened and hostile toward a new competitor, but if there is plenty of work around, others may welcome you and give you valuable advice. Nina Feldman was surprised that other members of the Professional Association of Secretarial Services were very encouraging and supportive of her when she started her word processing business and even referred their overload customers to her.

GETTING BY WHILE GETTING STARTED

A reality that must be dealt with before you start your business is that as an independent contractor you do not get paid for a job until it is completed. That can be a matter of days, but if it is a big project it can be months. Individuals may pay on delivery of the work, but it is common for corporations to pay thirty or even sixty days after delivery.

At best your income is not entirely predictable. A wage earner receives wages no matter what the economy does, but your income as an independent contractor will fluctuate with economic and seasonal conditions. Your plans must include allowance for these facts, in the form of either a cash reserve or some other source of income to sustain you until your business is well established and dependable as a source of revenue.

The largest single reason small businesses fail is undercapitalization, according to the Small Business Administration. However, one of the greatest advantages of starting a business in your home is that the capital outlay required is minimal—just the cost of your computer system and supplies—and the overhead is virtually nil, usually no more than a business phone and modest advertising. Without the large financial risk that is part of starting a conventional business, your chances for success are excellent.

Still, it takes time to build a business to the point where you can live on the income from it. Some experts recommend that you have enough money saved to support yourself for a year. But there are a number of ways around that rule.

The ideal situation is to live with a partner who has a secure income that will keep the household running while you establish your business. If you aren't so fortunate, you can hold on to your present job until your business can support you. Only one woman I interviewed for this book had a year's living expenses saved when she started. All the others either had supportive husbands or live-in companions, worked at jobs until their businesses would support them, or their businesses supported them right from the first.

Holding a job while you establish a business is a tough way to go, especially if you have children. If you must have a job, one of the best options, because it is so flexible, is to sign up with a temporary agency. If you already have word processing or data-entry skills, you can make $6 to $12 an hour as a "temp," depending on where you live. Your skills don't have to be very good for some of these jobs, so you should not count yourself out if you are just learning and don't have much experience. Working for a temporary agency is an excellent way to sharpen your skills and learn about many different businesses. You will remember that Nina Feldman learned typing while she worked as a "temp."

The greatest advantage of temporary work is that you can work as much or as little as you need to. In many cities you can earn more doing the same work for a temporary agency than you can as a full-time employee. You can work as much as necessary to get the income you need, then as your business grows you can work less. It sometimes takes weeks to find a full-time job, but with temporary work a job is usually available within a week of when you ask for one (and in some cases the next day), so you have a ready financial resource if your business slumps. Demand for temporary workers varies with local economic conditions, however, so check on the availability of temporary work during your planning stages. Assignments can range from half a day to months. Because of its flexibility, temporary work is the perfect complement to self-employment and gives you the emotional and financial security you need to start a business with very little capital.

If you have some savings and the courage to jump in full-time from the start, you should do some careful financial planning. Calculate your monthly expenses and decide how long you can live on the cash you have after allowing $3,000 to $5,000 for your equipment and initial business expenses. Don't forget to allow for some advertising. Have an emergency contingency plan. That is, what are you going to do if you get down to one month's reserve cash and you aren't making enough money yet to support yourself? Be ready, at that time, to ask yourself these questions: Is your business growing at a regular rate so that you can predict that by date X you will be entirely supported by it? If so, you should consider borrowing money to get you through to that point, or earning extra money by working with a temporary agency. Has your business stabilized at a certain point and seems unlikely to grow? Then you must consider (1) whether there are things you can do to accelerate growth, or (2) if you should consider expanding, diversifying, or changing your services, or (3) if you should give it up (rarely necessary!).

GETTING ACQUAINTED WITH COMPUTERS

If you have never used a computer, find out immediately if you are going to enjoy using it. The most comfortable way to learn may be with a knowledgeable friend. Lacking a friend who has a computer, computer literacy courses especially for women offer the most comfortable and supportive environments for novices.

It's probably not a good idea to buy a computer for business applications if you have never laid hands on one, although I know one idiot who did just that—me. But I had absolute confidence that I could learn to use it, and I knew, without any doubt, that it would make me a more productive, efficient writer. Two things were important to this confidence: a writer friend had been working with a computer for several years and testified to the time and trouble it saved him, and my own intensive reading on the subject before I made my decision. But I was already a writer. Under no circumstances should you make irrevocable plans or commitments for an unfamiliar business without first operating a computer long enough to determine that this is, in fact, what you want to do.

If you have computer experience but don't own your own system, it's best to buy one as soon as you are sure you're going to start a business. You'll put yourself under unreasonable stress if you buy your system one day and hang out your shingle the next, so allow yourself some time to become familiar with your new equipment and software before you start your business. How much time you need to learn to run a new system proficiently of course depends on the complexity of the software you will be using. Even though I was a computer novice, I was enough at ease with word processing within a few weeks that I could have taken on simple jobs. For more complex, unfamiliar computer functions you may need several months to become proficient, but individuals vary greatly in how fast they learn. What takes me three months to master, another person might learn in one.

The first decision you must make about buying a system is what kind of software you will need for your business. Unfortunately, good programs often are written for a specific make of computer and may not run on other models. Therefore, before you buy a computer you must know what software you want to use. There is a great deal to learn about software before you buy, so we will deal with that, and with buying a computer, in separate chapters.

If you already own a computer you will need to consider its limitations and what upgrading and new software may be necessary for your business.

DO YOU HAVE WHAT IT TAKES?
IF NOT, YOU CAN GET IT

The women I interviewed agreed that certain qualities of character are extremely important to success in business. But character and success may be a chicken/egg situation, because the demands of entrepreneurship may force you to develop the qualities you need if you didn't have them to begin with. So, strength of character may not be so much a prerequisite as it is one of the earned benefits of going into business for yourself.

Whether you start out with them or earn them along the way, here are the qualities the women I interviewed considered important:

Initiative is perhaps the single most important character trait you must have (or develop) in order to successfully start a business. No one is going to tell you what to do and when to do it; all the decisions are yours.

A reasonable degree of **assertiveness** is required. Selling is a critical element in your business. It isn't a better mousetrap that makes the world beat a path to your door, but marketing, and that takes a go-get-'em personality.

Self-discipline is extremely important. Many self-employed people comment that this is their greatest problem. It's hard to get started when there is no clock to punch; it's hard to stop when work is going well.

Responsibility is another paramount requirement. To succeed you must do your best work all the time. You must deliver what you promise when you promise it. Lost in a big corporation, many people get by with slovenly work. But low standards will destroy a small business.

You must be **willing to take risks,** including the risk of failure.

Another word for this is *courage*. It is hard to walk into a big company and face an executive, perhaps an intimidating burly man with a cigar, and convince him to contract you when your competitor has more experience and a flashy big office downtown. But you've got to be willing to try it, and that takes courage.

Kathryn Hubbell says, "Women have to work harder to get where we want to go, and so we are more afraid to fail. But I think we need to learn to fail and start over. We should take more risks and learn that one or two failures will not determine your whole life. I know men who have gone through several businesses. They say casually, 'A few years ago I had this business but I got tired of it, and then I did something else but I went broke, so I did another thing.' I'm astonished when I hear this. This man is perfectly sane and responsible, but look at his track record. It has nothing to do with the end result sometimes. Or it has something to do with it, but in positive ways. Women need to learn to do that."

Self-confidence also ranks high. Confidence in yourself means being able to claim that you know how to do something you don't really know how to do with the certainty that you can teach yourself to do it before you are caught. This kind of gutsiness separates the tigers from the kitty-cats.

Personality counts. I know one person who has a tough time with customers because he is painfully shy and talks as little as he can, and he makes some people uncomfortable. You have an advantage if you are at ease with people, have an attractive smile, and know how to express yourself with some fluency.

Resiliency helps. In a job you are shielded from company setbacks. Working for yourself, you catch the full brunt of them. You must be able to recover quickly and get on with your work.

I doubt if any one person has every one of these exemplary characteristics. Women are known for having problems with assertiveness and self-confidence. Don't eliminate yourself as a potential entrepreneur because you lack one or even many of the above characteristics. I believe we have the power to change our characters, and I believe this because I have changed my own. At one time I cringed before any male authority figure; I have not only learned to stop cringing, I can fight and win, if I need to. Remember the transformation of Dian Lehmann! All the women I interviewed said that going into business for themselves changed them.

But we don't change by living the same old lives. We need a battleground on which to test ourselves. Going into business for yourself can be the arena you need to develop the qualities of character that will make your entire life richer. The way to learn to take risks is to make yourself take them; self-confidence develops by trying and succeeding; assertiveness is a skill that is strengthened by practice, like a muscle.

The critical factor is determination. If your motivation is high enough, you can grit your teeth and triumph over your weakest link.

A Final Nudge

Starting your own business necessarily involves some risk. If it didn't, no one would be working as an employee. The price of freedom is always a measure of uncertainty, and risk is part of the excitement, after all. People who never take any risks lead very dull lives, yet few people are willing to gamble and start out on their own. They remain in jobs, feeling that they are more secure. The irony is that in a job you are completely at the mercy of your employer. As an independent businessperson your risk is spread over the entire market. You can lose one or even several customers without financial disaster. So, the gamble of independent entrepreneurship is much bigger in people's minds than in reality.

If you think you can handle a little risk, and if you plan carefully, your chances of success are very high. The market for computer services is expanding rapidly. At this stage there is room for many more people, and the opportunities will remain plentiful for a long time to come.

TEN

Now That You're in Business

A typist goes to work and spends almost all her time typing; a hired mechanic spends all her time fixing cars. People who go into business for themselves for the first time are often surprised, and sometimes disappointed, that they spend as much or more of their time on management chores as on the service they are selling. Books must be kept, supplies ordered and picked up, advertising planned and carried out, and sometimes the biggest chunk of time is spent visiting prospective clients.

Your office must be arranged and your time budgeted to allow for these activities. Fortunately, your computer will greatly ease the drudgery of bookkeeping, tax records, and billing chores, and the programs to do them for an individual need not be expensive or complicated.

The fees you charge for your services must also take these overhead costs into account. An easy mistake to make is to undercharge for your services. If you want to net $12.50 an hour you may have to charge $18. Even if you have a very low cash overhead, your time is money. If you spend twenty-five hours a week actually doing word processing, and fifteen hours a week keeping books and calling on clients and various other work-related errands, you must charge for your services so that you are paid for the fifteen hours of management chores as well as the time you spend processing words. You must also pay for your equipment, your phone, your supplies, your license fees, and your taxes.

Checking other similar businesses to find out what they charge will give you an idea where to start. Then, keep a careful record of how you spend your time. To find out your net earnings on an hourly basis, subtract your expenses from your total income and divide the remainder by the number of hours you actually worked.

Someone is bound to suggest that you incorporate, most likely someone who wants to sell you an incorporation kit. The two principal reasons for incorporating are tax advantages and protection of personal assets from lawsuits or bankruptcy of the business. Tax benefits don't start to appear until you are grossing somewhere around $25,000 a year, according to one CPA, and incorporating costs money. In other words, until your income passes a certain level you may actually *lose* money by incorporating. You will also fall into all kinds of record-keeping entanglements.

Lawsuits are something doctors worry about, and bankruptcy is more of a risk in businesses where a large capital investment is required, such as manufacturing. Most things you can do at home are low risk in both these areas.

Some other benefits from incorporating—such as making yourself an employee and giving yourself unemployment insurance and retirement benefits—don't begin to be worth the cost until your gross income is above a certain level. Once your business is going well, check with a CPA to find out if and when you might benefit from incorporating.

As a self-employed person you can put up to $2,000 in an Individual Retirement Account (IRA) each year, and payment of income tax on that amount is deferred until you draw the money out upon retirement. There are other retirement plans available for both individuals and corporations; a CPA can advise you on the best plan for you.

Since self-employed people have no taxes withheld, the IRS will require you to file quarterly estimated tax returns. The forms aren't hard to fill out. The IRS has a toll-free number listed in all phone directories (it is different in each state); call them and ask for a quarterly estimated tax package. If you have any difficulty figuring your quarterly returns, call and ask for assistance.

It's important to keep good records for tax purposes. Your books don't need to be complicated, just a clear record of what you took in and what you paid out, to whom and for what. Be sure to save all receipts and canceled checks. A simple financial program such as *Money Maestro* is a great help. It's a tedious process to type in your checks every month, but at the end of the year the program will figure your total outlay in each category you set up at the beginning of the year, and it's very useful at tax time.

For more details on the specifics of running a home-based business, see *Women Working Home*, published by WWH Press in Norwood, New Jersey. Although this book covers home-based businesses in general, much of the material is relevant to computer-based businesses. The book contains interesting and useful information and commentary by women who run businesses from home. If you can't find it in your bookstore, write: WWH Press, P. O. Box 237BK, Norwood NJ 07648.

Working from Home, by Paul and Sarah Edwards (Tarcher, 1985), is also about running a home-based business, but with different emphases than this book and *Women Working Home*.

Setting Up Your Office

The ideal office for a business in the home is one room set aside and used for nothing else. Not only is it less distracting to work clearly separated from family activities, but a door is both a physical and psychological barrier to interruptions. It also is a psychological aid in separating "work" from "home." If it isn't possible to have a whole room, do everything you can to create a territory that is used for work and nothing else. Screens and movable dividers can be attractive and can be made inexpensively. It may not be comfortable to invite clients to your home if you do not have adequate space or if the muddy family dog and a friendly chocolate-covered three-year-old want to climb into visitors' laps. Children and dogs should not be allowed in the office.

If complete separation of your work space is not possible, appointments with clients can be arranged during nap times or when your children are in school. If worst comes to worst, a helpful neighbor can be called upon to take kids and dog for a walk while you conduct business. Some home businesspeople don't have their clients come to their homes at all; and after all, it's a great convenience for your clients if you go to them.

For most kinds of operations you should have a business phone with a listing in the Yellow Pages. Not only will the listing draw some clients, but a business phone helps establish your professionalism. For the same reason, you should have an answering machine to pick up your calls when you are not home and after business hours.

In another chapter I'll go into some detail about designing your work station for maximum comfort and efficiency. Your general policy should be to give yourself everything you need to make your work easier and to make yourself comfortable and happy while working. Be the best boss you ever had.

Promotion

Promotion is essential to the success of your business, no matter how small. An ad in the Yellow Pages helps attract clients, but usually that is not enough. You must get out there and sell yourself, if you'll pardon the expression.

Your business can be promoted in a number of ways. Joining local clubs and organizations can be an important source of business. Joan Gough is a member of Friends of the Earth; she proposed the idea of putting their membership mailing list on computer disks, and was contracted to do the job. In that case the job came from the organization itself, but most of the time business comes from meeting other members who have need of your service in connection with their work, or who will put you in touch with such people.

Personal calls on possible clients is time-consuming but is also time well invested. Prospective clients will remember meeting and talking with you more easily than they will recall a letter or an ad in the paper. Leave a flyer describing your services and rates in detail, and make it easy for them to remember and contact you by leaving a business card.

Direct mail is expensive, but you can hire a neighborhood kid to leave flyers in doors or on windshields. Unless you are a good graphic designer, pay someone to do a professional-looking job.

A seedy looking flyer makes people doubt your professionalism. (By the way, make sure the kid you hire to distribute them is reliable. A couple of years ago I wondered why I never received our local free advertiser. One day I found out—I saw a kid dumping a bundle of them into a trash dumpster.)

Newspaper ads are also expensive and may or may not be effective. You should choose your paper carefully. Several women have told me that the response was much better from local free advertiser ads than from newspaper ads, with much cheaper rates.

Use your imagination and good sense. An ad for legal word processing will reach more attorneys if you place it in your city's legal newspaper rather than the local daily. Doctors can be reached through medical journals or newsletters. Students are reached by on-campus papers and bulletin boards. Find out which publications reach the select audience that you are after.

Some women have told me that response was good when ads for word processing, intended for college students, were tacked up on bulletin boards in laundromats. What else is there to do while the clothes are washing but read those cards?

Professional Image

Independent contractors working from their homes sometimes complain that their clients do not consider them serious businesspersons. There is a social stigma attached to working from home; you are not considered a "professional."

The problem of not being taken seriously by the business community can be offset to a great extent by your attitude. If you dress and behave like a professional, learn to project confidence and competence, and acquire the little symbols of the business community—such as letterhead stationery, business cards, and a classy attaché case to carry whether you need it or not (you can put your lunch in it)—your clients will be subtly influenced to consider you a serious professional.

Having a room made over into a truly attractive office can help. However, some home entrepreneurs don't have their clients come to their homes at all; they visit clients in their offices or take them to lunch.

Another professional status symbol is the telephone. Unless

you live alone, have a separate phone number for your business and forbid your small children to answer it. That phone should be a business-service phone so that you can have a listing in the Yellow Pages—an important symbol of legitimacy to most people. You can't be at home all the time, but a business phone that rings without being answered during conventional business hours is a sure sign of a less-than-professional operation, so an answering machine is a necessary investment.

Some freelancers report that once clients know you work at home, they tend to call you at night or on weekends. Some people don't mind receiving evening and weekend calls from their clients, but if you do mind, turn off the bell at the end of your workday and let your answering machine pick up the calls—another good reason to have separate phone lines for your business and personal use.

Several women I visited had made up price lists and statements of policy to hand out to all new customers. One had created an instruction sheet to help her word-processing clients edit copy. All felt these printed handouts were important factors in augmenting their professional image and avoiding misunderstandings with their clients.

Technical writing consultant Maxine Wyman has developed a sound psychology for dealing with people who don't want to take her seriously: "When you work in a corporate situation you've got all these other people who may or may not have had contact with technical writers before, and they don't really understand your function or your skills. You have to educate them that 'No, I am not here to input text [on a word processor], I am here because I have better skills as a writer than you do and it's my job to focus on that.' You generally have to go through a process of educating them. Sometimes it's long and sometimes it's short, but you have to work against that attitude. First you must be aware of it and acknowledge that it's occurring, and then you have to figure out how to get around it. You have to communicate what you can do in a way that says to them, 'It will be beneficial to you to take advantage of my skills.' It's part of selling yourself. I hate to see resources wasted, and for someone to attempt to put me in the position of just plain secretary is a total waste of my time and their time. But I can't say, 'That's not what I'm supposed to do,' because that doesn't accomplish anything but raise hostility. You have to sell them the idea and actively demonstrate that you are a resource and can relieve them of work they really don't want to do in the first place. You have to put it this way: 'Look, you have all these responsibilities, and I have these skills and I can take some of these concerns for you. Put it in my hands and you don't have to worry about it.' "

Collecting Debts

Because some businesses, especially big ones, do not take people who work out of their homes very seriously, you will occasionally encounter clients who pay late or not at all.

The problem of slow or nonpaying clients won't be solved completely until the electronic cottage becomes a respected commonplace in the business world. But in the meantime bad debts should not be shrugged off. Most home business receivables are within the limits of small claims court, and small claims are neither expensive nor complicated to file. Lawyers are not allowed in small claims court (although of course you may seek the advice of a lawyer) and procedures are kept simple and inexpensive so that any citizen may have access to justice over matters too small to justify hiring a lawyer. If you sue a client you'll alienate her or him for good, of course, but you would not do business with them again anyway. You're more likely to get your money if you have kept careful records, and the delinquent company will think more carefully about taking advantage of a home-based independent in the future.

If the idea of an individual suing a rich and powerful organization intimidates you, remember that it is troublesome and embarrassing for your deadbeat customer to go to small claims court over a bill they should have paid, and more expensive for them in the long run since they will have to pay your court costs in addition to the original bill if they lose the case. If your claim is legitimate, you are likely to receive a check from the defendant before the matter comes to trial. Going to court is unpleasant and inconvenient for you too, of course, but it may be worth your time to help establish home entrepreneurs as serious professionals.

Beatrice Snow (a pseudonym), who runs a word processing

service from her home in a small Louisiana city, has sued clients in small claims court three times. "The first time I went to court I was scared to death, especially since the man I was suing was on the city council. But that's what made me mad. He was a public official who didn't pay his bills, and I thought he ought to be embarrassed. It never went to court. As soon as he was served with the complaint, he paid up. The most important thing about that experience, though, was what it did for my self-respect. By suing him I was saying, to myself as well as to him, that I'm not someone who can be pushed around; I'm not just someone who "does typing" in her home, I'm a professional and expect to be treated like one, which means you pay my bill. I had a lot more confidence after that.

"Another guy I sued didn't pay up when served with the complaint and didn't show up in court. I won a judgment against him but I never tried to collect. He was just a flaky individual and I figured it was more trouble than it was worth to collect. There have been a couple of times when people didn't pay me and I haven't pressed the issue; those were the times when I knew I hadn't delivered what I promised. You have to be honest with yourself about what kind of work you are delivering. In any business there are occasions when things just go wrong, or there is poor communication between you and your customer. I wish, though, that people would give me a chance to make it right and not just go away mad and refuse to pay. Maybe it's up to me to call them and ask what went wrong—I'm still working on that one. But when I know I'm right, I sue. The best thing about working for myself is that it has made me tough. If you're going to survive as a businessperson you have to learn to stand up for yourself."

ELEVEN

The Importance of Networking

I don't know where I got the idea, but I grew up with the notion that the only way to get ahead honorably is on merit alone; that cultivating contacts and using one's connections in high places to advance oneself is something well-bred people simply don't do. Naturally I considered myself well-bred—whatever that means. Perhaps the naïve movies of the forties and fifties—the source of most of my values—were to blame.

But in the real world merit frequently isn't enough. Who you know and whether they like you (or owe you a favor) are often important elements in getting a job or a contract. It took me a long time to learn that lesson, but it probably wouldn't have done me any good earlier, since women who reached young adulthood in the fifties were raised to think of other women as rivals, if not enemies. In general we didn't even talk to one another about things that matter, much less help one another professionally. That's why Betty Freidan's book *The Feminine Mystique* (published in the sixties) was such a bombshell. It was the first time many of us understood that our career problems were social and political and not due to some defect in ourselves. Friedan told us we were not alone, as many of us believed we were.

Fortunately for the woman who enters the work force or the

business world today, women have learned to help and encourage one another. Powerful networks exist to advance women in their careers, and some are now emerging to help women who are in business for themselves, and some specifically created to serve women in computing.

Contacts made through networks can help your business in many ways. Network members who work for the companies from which you are soliciting business can steer work your way. Women in businesses like yours who are well established may no longer want the small jobs that you will welcome when you're just starting out. They will be willing to pass them along to you as a service to their clients and as a help to you.

But the advantages don't stop there. Advice is available when you encounter a problem you don't know how to solve. Women with more experience can advise you on what to charge, how to handle a difficult client, or how to accomplish tasks you haven't done before. They can tell you which computer repair services are best and what software is good for a particular job. They can advise you on what type of advertising works best in your area.

Just as important as their advice is the moral support they offer. Kathryn Hubbell thinks it is particularly important for single mothers to do anything they can to be around people who will support and encourage them. "People who work at home and who are also tied down with children can become very isolated professionally. It's important to join a businesswomen's association or network. In Eugene [Oregon] we have a local businesswomen's group, the Alliance for Career Advancement, which is specifically designed for women to network and help one another in business. It's been an amazing source of energy and strength for me. I also belong to Women in Communications, a national group. It's kept up my professional training and kept me in touch with other women doing what I'm doing [public relations].

"I make sure I stay in touch with people who share my problems, even if I can only meet for a cup of tea or phone in the middle of the day. I need the contact desperately; I found I can't carry that emotional load without it. I discovered I had a lot of limits when it came to running a family and a home plus running a business. I needed people more than I ever had."

Networks provide you with the company of people who, because they have similar goals, understand who you are and what you are doing. You'll get encouragement, role models, and potential friendships. These women are likely to help you in times of trouble, and you'll have somewhere to turn for help with your work when you are sick or overloaded or out of town.

Join every relevant group you can afford to join. Remember that for women who work at home, this is also a way to keep from being too isolated.

Here are a few suggestions:

National Alliance of Homebased Businesswomen (NAHB)
P.O. Box 95
Norwood NJ 07648

Established in 1980, NAHB exists to encourage personal, professional, and economic growth among women who work from, or wish to work from, their homes. The NAHB provides a support network of professional contacts for their members and, through various publications, forums for the exchange of information and support. A directory of members enables you to contact other women in your area who work at home. A number of chapters across the country hold meetings you can attend. A quarterly newsletter has news of members' achievements, information about resources, ideas for business, and helpful items about running a business.

NAHB should be a high priority on your list of networks to join. Their book, *Women Working Home*, is full of useful information, encouragement, and advice. If your local bookstore doesn't have it, you can order from WWH Press, P.O. Box 237BK, Norwood NJ 07648. *Women Working Home* is updated periodically, so write for the price of the current edition.

Membership in NAHB is $30. Send a check with a brief description of your business or the business you are planning.

National Association of Women Business Owners
645 North Michigan Ave.
Chicago IL 60611
(312) 951-9110

This organization welcomes women who run businesses from

home and offers local and national newsletters, regular local monthly meetings, annual national conventions, political involvement, educational seminars and workshops, problem-solving and referrals, and, of course, networking with women who have similar interests.

National Association for the Cottage Industry
P.O. Box 14460
Chicago IL 60614
(312) 472-8116

This is an association for people who run all kinds of businesses from their homes, and differs from NAHB in that membership is open to men as well as women. This organization is very active in watchdogging legislative action that discriminates against work-at-homers. Members receive a quarterly newsletter, *Cottage Connection.*

The association serves as a clearinghouse for information about home businesses; conducts forums to discuss common problems and experiences; sponsors regional conferences, co-sponsored by the U.S. Small Business Administration, with speakers and seminars on such topics as marketing, insurance, record keeping, dealing with isolation, microcomputers, and how to run specific kinds of businesses such as secretarial services and mailing lists; and sponsors Cottage Fairs to showcase home businesses and promote public awareness of work-at-home opportunities.

Individual membership is $45.

Mind Your Own Business at Home
P.O. Box 14850
Chicago IL 60614
(312) 472-8116

This is not an association but a newsletter published by Coralee Smith Kern, who is the founder, executive director, and driving force behind the National Association for the Cottage Industry. In 1983 Kern was selected the Women in Business Advocate of the Year by the U.S. Small Business Administration. Kern also owns Maid-To-Order, a maid service that she runs from her home. In her newsletter Kern reports on "information, proposals, surveys, studies, propaganda, and miscellaneous wisdom being issued by government agencies, corporations, universities, and private experts to assist the businessperson and the home worker."

Subscriptions are $24 a year. A sample copy is $5.

Association for Women in Computing
c/o Dorthy Firsching
4905 Americana Drive
Annandale VA 22003

This group is a professional organization dedicated to helping women advance in their careers and to giving women technical and emotional support. Many members are independent contractors who work from their homes. Through their San Francisco Bay Area chapter I received the names of several women whom I contacted in the course of researching this book. AWC has more than two thousand members and is growing. Their newsletter has plenty of useful information, and there are national conferences as well as local ones. There are chapters in many cities, and they sponsor local conferences and seminars.

Membership is $30 a year, and may be worth the money if you need to network specifically with other women who work with computers.

Women in Information Processing
Lock Box 39173
Washington DC 20016

WIP, established in 1979, helps its members achieve career goals in a variety of ways. Seminars keep members abreast of new developments in business and technology (which move very fast in the world of information processing). Members give one another advice and support, both in career opportunities and on-the-job problem solving. Membership is more than four thousand and includes women who work at home. There are local chapters called *forums* in many cities. Membership is $45. Membership includes a subscription to *Forumnet*, a national newsletter. However, the issues I have received so far include only a calendar of events in each city and profiles of accomplished members. For useful information it doesn't compare to the Association for Women in Computing newsletter.

I have not been happy with my experiences with this organization. However, I live too far from any major city to belong to a forum, so I have had experience only with the international office in Washington, D.C. The attitudes of the administration in Washington need not necessarily affect how the local forums are run, and you might enjoy and profit from your membership.

Women in Communications, Inc. (WICI)
P.O. Box 9561
Austin TX 78766
(512) 345-8922

WICI serves women in all of the communications professions: public relations, journalism, etc., and has twelve thousand members and more than 150 chapters. WICI promotes the advancement of women in all fields of communications; works for First Amendment rights and responsibilities of communicators; recognizes distinguished professional achievements with a variety of awards; and promotes high professional standards throughout the communications industry. The organization publishes a membership directory, political-issues alerts and legislative memos, a five-year job and salary survey, and other specialized publications on careers in communications.

This is a very dynamic organization that can be of great value if you need contacts in the media or in public relations.

Directory of Women's Media
Women's Institute for Freedom of the Press
3306 Ross Place, N.W.
Washington DC 20008
(202) 966-7783

This publication is an invaluable aid for women who work in public relations, advertising, or the media. The directory lists women's groups and individual women who are concerned with periodicals, publishers, news services, columns, radio, TV, video, cable, film, music, art, theater, graphics, writers' groups, public relations, news services, columns, radio, TV, video, cable, film, music, art, theater, graphics, writers' groups, public relations, speakers' bureaus, media organizations, bookstores, library collections, directories, and catalogs. If your home business involves working with the media you will want to be listed, and of course the directory is a great resource for contacts.

The directory is updated yearly; write for the current price.

The National Women's Mailing List
The Women's Information Exchange
1195 Valencia St.
San Francisco CA 94110
(415) 824-6800

This listing is not directly relevant to working at home but is valuable if you want to hear from—or find—people who are active in women's interests and issues. The list is absolutely voluntary—no one can put you on the list but you. They do not buy lists from magazines or other organizations. It costs nothing to be put on the list, although they ask for a voluntary donation of $3.50 for expenses.

When you fill out the form to be put on the mailing list, indicate your principal interests so that you receive mailings from people and organizations concerned with those interests. You can restrict your participation. That is, you can authorize your name to be given to anyone who wants it, or you can specify that women's organizations, political candidates, or individual women only may have your name.

One of the first mailings I received after I put myself on this list was from the National Women's Health Network, which I didn't even know existed. They monitor legislation, drug companies, and the medical profession and serve as advocates for women's interests. The network can offer advice and information to individuals on many health issues, and their newsletter contains news of health issues and reports on medical research relevant to women. I was glad to discover them, since health is one of my major interests, and this contact alone was worth my $3.50 donation.

Computers are one of the categories of special interests on the mailing list. If your business involves promotion, marketing, politics, or public relations, then you are also a potential customer for selected categories of the NWML. They will send you their price list on request.

For those who offer word processing and related services:

Independent Professional Typists Network (IPTN)
12 Chicory Way
Irvine CA 92715

"IPTN members are encouraged to participate in a network-ing process to enhance professional knowledge and personal growth. IPTN serves as a forum and gives members the oppor-tunity to share experiences and insights." This network pub-lishes a newsletter covering everything of interest to anyone who runs a word processing business at home. One issue included an article about coping with toddlers while trying to work. IPTN sponsors conventions and workshops and encourages the forma-tion of local chapters. The founder of this organization, Peggy Glenn, is the author of *Word Processing Profits at Home.*

Professional Association of Secretarial Services (P.A.S.S.)
c/o Secre-Help
2200 E. 104th Ave. #103
Northglenn CO 80233

P.A.S.S. is another networking organization for mutual help and the sharing of information among people who run secretar-ial services, including many who operate from their homes.

Nina Feldman (her business is described in chapter 4) states that P.A.S.S. members have given her an enormous amount of support. Nina has trouble asserting herself when customers say to her, "Why did this take so long? Why do you charge so much?" There are people who will say such things no matter how little you charge or how fast you do the work, but even though Nina knows this she has trouble asserting her own worth. She finds that her friends in P.A.S.S. give her the support she needs, saying as often as they have to, "Stand up for your-self! Charge what you're worth!" Nina states that many P.A.S.S. members started working at home but now have big offices and staffs in downtown San Francisco and other Northern California cities. She finds it helps her to assert herself when she knows she charges less than they do.

In all things, she says, P.A.S.S. members have been totally supportive and helpful and often refer overload business to her or customers who move from their areas to Nina's (Oakland). One such referral turned out to be a major client. Referrals also come when a member is sick or goes on vacation. This system works both ways, of course—it's nice to know there are people who can be called on in an emergency to take care of your customers so that they aren't alienated when you can't accept their work—and whatever feelings of competition that exist are outweighed by the benefits of cooperation. Networking has made an enormous difference to Nina, and she thinks support of this kind is important to anyone who is going it alone.

Nina also belongs to the Independent Professional Typists Network and the National Association of Homebased Businesswomen, but says that of the three organizations P.A.S S. has been the most valuable.

Displaced Homemakers Network, Inc.
1531 Pennsylvania Ave. S.E.
Washington DC 20003
(202) 547-6606

Displaced homemakers are former career homemakers who have lost their source of economic support through divorce, separation, widowhood, ineligibility for public assistance, or disability of their spouses. The Displaced Homemakers Network is a national nonprofit organization that works to increase options for economic self-sufficiency among displaced homemakers by providing counseling, workshops, skills training, and job-placement assistance. In some areas they provide computer-skills training.

The DHN can be a valuable source of peer support and nurturance during the difficult transition from years of homemaking back to the job market. If there is no listing for the Displaced Homemakers Network in your area, contact the national headquarters at the above address.

Computer User Groups

These are your single most important source of help with computer problems and information about computers and software. You'll find out what software is available free; sometimes copies are distributed at meetings. If you join a group just for owners of your particular brand of computer, you'll receive help in troubleshooting problems with hardware or software. Almost anything you want to ask can be answered by someone in a user group, since such groups often include one or more very experienced people. These groups are a great way to learn about computers and new developments and to make business contacts. You'll also find out which dealers in town give the best services and support. Check with computer dealers in your area for the names of local groups. News of user groups is found in a variety of computer periodicals, including *InfoWorld*. Lists of user groups sometimes appear in computer directories of various kinds, and by the time you read this someone may have put out a directory just for user groups, as there are undoubtedly thousands of thm by now—every ciy large enough to support a computer store invariably has a local user group.

Telecommunications Networks

Sandy Emerson is concerned about the isolation of women who work at home with computers. "A computer without a modem is an isolated entity. It's just you and your computer and whatever you're doing. If women get isolated at home with computers, that will be too bad. But if computers are viewed as windows, because of their communications capability, then that will preserve the gains that women have made in viewing one another as allies."

Computers equipped with modems are indeed windows, and there are certain special groups for whom the computer may be a crucial link to the world, rather than a means of isolation.

Severely disabled or chronically ill people may not be able to leave their homes. Access via a computer and modem to a telecommunications network such as The Source or CompuServe, where someone can be found to "talk" to at any time of the day or night, can substantially brighten the lives of shut-ins. The same is true for those who live in geographically isolated areas, if they have a phone line and can afford the long-distance charges to access the nearest connect number.

Some people do not function well in personal relationships; the on-line services are an important outlet for them. Witness Dorothy (a pseudonym):

"I don't get along with anybody very well. I have a horrible life history and it left me explosive and unstable. I'm not trying to make excuses but I'm over forty now and I'm tired of trying to change. I just decided to withdraw and the hell with it. I'm a caretaker at a small ranch [in Wyoming], which works out well for me because I'm alone nine months of the year and the physical exertion of outdoor work is a great healer. I'm too nervous to use a computer for work, but I bought an Apple to learn something new and keep my mind occupied in the evening. I love it for the contact it gives me with people, through CompuServe. That's ironic, isn't it? I spend a lot of time on line. The best thing about it for me is that I can choose who I want to 'talk' to, and at any point if things don't go right I can just ignore any further communication from that person. There are some creeps on that system just like anywhere else, but there are lots of nice folks too. It's the whole world on a computer screen, really.

"I can sign on and off anytime I want. It's great to get up at two in the morning when you can't sleep and go on CompuServe and there they are—all these people and all these things to do. I thought at first it wouldn't be like a real relationship but it is. You find yourself very emotionally involved. The same kind of games go on between people that happen in 'real time,' conflict and humor and anything else you can think of. But the bottom line is you can back out anytime you want, which is what you can't always do in real life, at least not as easily. You can even change your name and come back as somebody else and they won't know they're talking to the same person.

"On the SIGs [special-interest groups] you leave messages for each other, just like a bulletin board. You can read all the messages or just those addressed to you, and you can also leave private messages if you want. There is a very dynamic feel to it, not at all like a message on paper. You can also have real-time communication on the CB simulator, although that's mostly dominated by kids. (Real-time means you are both present on the system at the same time, rather than leaving messages to be picked up later.) But you can make an appointment with somebody and meet them on CB. If that person lives in New York and you live in Los Angeles, it's a local call for each of you even though you are talking across three thousand miles.

"I get a lot of sustenance out of this contact. To a normal person it might seem warped, but I am an emotionally disabled person. For me it is a lifesaver, maybe a mind saver. The only trouble is that when you discover this world and open it up, it can be a terrible addiction. Especially if you have to pay long-distance charges to connect. You can go broke, and it's very hard to keep under control. My phone bill was over three hundred dollars the first month I was hooked up. You should be wary of that."

I'll second Dorothy's warning because I did the same thing. I live in a remote area of Utah where very few people share my interests. CompuServe gave me access to unlimited numbers of people with similar interests through the special-interest groups. (The Source can do the same thing, but it is more expensive.)

Through CompuServe's Work-at-Home SIG, I contacted two of the women who are profiled in this book. From other members I received valuable information. I first heard of BIPED, a nonprofit corporation that trains disabled people to work at home with computers, on the Work-at-Home SIG. Legislation that affects work-at-homers and problems of insurance, liability, and taxes are discussed on this SIG, as well as the comparative merits and defects of various computer systems. A SIG offers support, too. If you have a problem or a triumph, you'll get help or celebration, respectively, from SIG members.

There are SIGs dedicated to particular brands of computers. If you have problems with the computer or your software, a note on your SIG bulletin board can be read by *thousands* of other users—an answer is usually quickly offered.

Through the Literary SIG, I was able to find someone who had a copy of a poem I hadn't seen for thirty years. The poem is obscure and anonymous and has never been anthologized, to my knowledge, yet I had a response to my query within forty-eight hours of posting a notice on the Literary SIG bulletin board. There resulted a warm and entertaining exchange with a stranger in Canada. That's the sort of odd and valuable connection these services can make for you.

Another notice on the Literary SIG bulletin board announced the founding of a writers' union, giving the address in New York and describing some of the issues they intend to tackle. Such information might not have come to my attention otherwise.

There are SIGs devoted to the outdoors (Outdoor SIGers are

the friendliest, chattiest people on the system, I think), music, medicine, cars, games, cooking, flying, and all sorts of other topics. New special-interest groups are constantly forming; you can approach CompuServe with an idea and form your own.

I also second Dorothy's observation that there are occasional creeps on the system. The best way to get rid of them is to ignore them. They become bored and go away if they get no reaction. I would add that people will present themselves as experts who are not, and I caution you to examine critically any advice you receive—get a second and a third opinion. If someone is always visible on the bulletin board, giving advice to everybody, ask yourself why he is spending his time this way. The Work-at-Home SIG has its share of this sort of person, but this is a minor problem considering the number of truly knowledgeable and helpful people you find there. My solution has been to communicate with individuals by private rather than public messages, which is always your option. Sometimes I want to post a public message—"Does anybody know. . . ?" I ignore answers from people whom I have already identified as undesirable, and use the private message mode to continue a dialogue with other respondents. If I continue the conversation with public messages, the others keep butting in.

A major problem with these services is that because of the expense of telephone access for those in outlying areas, they are practical only for people living in cities with local access numbers. Even then, CompuServe charges $6 an hour, which doesn't sound like much until you find out how much time it takes to do *anything* on line. Alternatives to AT&T, such as MCI, Sprint, Telenet, and Tymnet, are also not available in many outlying areas, but will save money for those who live in the areas they serve. Information on what communications networks are available to you will be provided when you sign up with The Source or CompuServe.

Fortunately, in the next few years some alternatives to telephone hookups will become available to the public. We have come to regard telephones as the only option for two-way communications, but they're not. Users groups may cooperate to buy satellite services to transmit messages to anyone who has a receiver; receivers are going to get cheaper. On-line services

such as The Source or Dialog, if they're smart, will launch their
own satellites to eliminate the high phone tariffs that stand
between them and their customers, and consequently they'll get
more business. Police and fire departments are already using
radio signals to connect terminals in their vehicles to computers
back at the station. Another option being explored is the use of
the cable through which you receive your pay TV. It's not
complicated to adapt it to two-way communication. How or
when all these options are going to be exploited for home
computerists is not yet clear, but the demand for a solution
already exists and will escalate as the need for telecommunication services grows. Telecommunications will continue to be the
boom technology of the next decade.

One way to save money on long distance telephone charges is
to write your messages off line (that is, before you connect with
your on-line service) and upload them once you are on line
(*upload* means to transfer data from your computer's memory
or disk to the computer at the other end of the line). Your
communications-software manual will tell you how; it is important to buy a program that allows you to do this.

You can sign up for The Source or CompuServe at most
computer dealers. The Source has a $100 sign-up fee and charges
more per hour than CompuServe, and subscribers tell me there
is little difference between the two companies otherwise. They
also tell me that The Source is harder to use, but this may
change, since both services are constantly being upgraded. Do
some investigation on your own before you make a choice.

Computer Bulletin Boards

Commercial on-line services are expensive, and that means they
are not accessible to everybody. Much less noticed by the public,
but thriving, are the noncommercial computer bulletin boards.
Some charge a membership fee before you can access them,
but most don't.

Computer bulletin boards are usually run by individuals who
donate a computer and a phone line and their time to set up a
board—usually referred to as a CBBS (computer bulletin board

system). Why would anyone do that? The pleasure and satisfaction of sharing; the rewards of networking; exchange of information; a sense of community; the new friendships that evolve; entertainment; or political idealism. These people are akin to the breed that in the sixties founded free clinics, held free concerts, and opened free stores.

Many operators of computerized bulletin boards are political idealists who believe that whoever controls information controls the country, and that this power rightfully belongs to the common person. The control of information is related, of course, to political and economic power; and the more people know, the more power they have to control their destinies.

In this sense the people's computer networks are a political movement. When alternative computer-communications paths like those mentioned earlier are available to everyone, it will become almost impossible to control the dissemination of information, because so many people will have the means to broadcast from their own homes.

Another important thing to understand is this: our relationships with most communications media are passive. We can't talk back to TVs and radios, and we don't have any choice in what those media send to us other than to change channels or turn them off. Even our use of the telephone is limited—we do not pick up the telephone and call a stranger since we have no way of finding out if the person on the other end of a line wants to talk to us. We can buy or build a ham radio but we are limited by a number of factors that control who we can talk to, how far away they are, and when they are available.

The people's computer networks give us, for the first time, two-way communications with strangers all over the country who share our interests. A key factor in this new freedom is the computer bulletin board as a place to meet and a forum where everyone has an equal voice. A second key factor is that, unlike telephone, radio, or TV communications, you don't have to be "on line" at the same time as the other person. You can access the system at any time, over any distance, and trade information with people who share your concerns and interests, because that information is stored for as long as it is useful and can be retrieved at any time by anyone who wants it. There are hundreds of these free meeting places, perhaps thousands by now (nobody has a way to count them accurately), and somewhere there is one that has something for you. *Nobody who has a computer and a modem need ever be alone.*

In my adult lifetime I have seen the lives of women change because of communication. When women began talking to one another they realized that often their problems were political rather than personal, and they began to seek political solutions. This work is still going on, of course. But more recently I have seen networking for women grow so that women are now making inroads where they could not before—and this is mainly a function of communication. With the information already in my files I can contact thousands of women, selected by any number of criteria, through networks with which they have voluntarily affiliated themselves. By so doing they have tacitly promised help and support to other women like themselves. What a conrast to women's lives only a generation past!

But my main point is this: If organizational networks have done wonders for women, imagine what computer networks can do. Today, if I want to reach all the members of, say, the National Association of Homebased Businesswomen, I would have to (1) put a notice in their newsletter or (2) get their membership list and send each member a letter (expensive). But suppose I found out that some legislation unfavorable to work-at-homers was coming up three days from now? There is no way I could mobilize NAHB in that length of time. But if members had a computer bulletin board, I could put a notice on it in a matter of minutes. Any member accessing the bulletin board within the next three days would see the message and could call or wire her representative. She could telephone noncomputing members of her local chapter to forward the message; and if the day does come when every home has a computer (I think it will), even that step won't be necessary.

Computer networks give us access to information, and *information is power.*

The potential of CBBS networks is vast, and we haven't yet even begun to tap it. Partly because so many people aren't even aware that they exist—they don't advertise, since most are not commercial enterprises, and they are usually ignored by computer magazines. It will take some time to discover all the ways in which these networks can be used for everyone's benefit and for them to gain the recognition and use they deserve.

CBBSs already exist for people who are interested in such topics as genealogy, kinky sex, astronomy, games, medicine, and science fiction. These are meaningful associations for individuals who live far from others who share their special interests. But these assocations are superficial compared with what could be: How about a CBBS for cancer patients and their families, where information and support could be shared? What of the Navajo geologist who takes a fascinating job she loves, but who may have to work far away from her home, isolated from her own people and culture? Couldn't a CBBS for Navajos help her find contacts in whatever state she is in? What about the handicapped? Forums on local, state, and national and political issues? Grass-roots organizing? The sharing of information by farmers, or horse breeders, or cultivators of rare orchids? These are just a few suggestions of what CBBSs can offer; but for these things to happen the CBBS must stay in the public domain, because of course anything that is commercialized (including systems like CompuServe and The Source) must cater to the majority—and the money—in order to survive. Most of the time, the minority is ignored, no matter how important that minority might be. Each *individual* is important, and should be provided for, but our commercial system often does not permit it. We, the people of the United States, in order to form a more perfect union, must create these connections: commercial enterprises must be kept out of it. To be a people's resource, it must remain a people's movement.

It is important for women to be aware of the potential of CBBS networks and to learn about them and to participate *now*. This phenomenon is new and dynamic and not yet set in cement. The pattern with movements, however, is that they soon begin to stratify and an elite becomes entrenched. When the inevitable issues arise over the licensing of CBBSs and access to satellite communications, women and minorities must be present to ensure that their interests are served along with eveyone else's, or they're going to be disenfranchised. Again.

CBBSs come and go and it's hard to keep track of them. One way to find out what is available in your area is to check listings of CBBSs on The Source or CompuServe. You can ask about them at a local user's group (an excellent source of bulletin boards in your own area) or computer store. If you find just one, once you access it you will find the phone numbers of others.

The Complete Handbook of Personal Computer Communication, by Alfred Glossbrenner (St. Martin's Press, 1983), has some very good information on CBBSs.

If you want to start your own CBBS, some programs are available to help you. Check a software catalog for your brand of computer. If you are interested in programming, a book called *How to Create Your Own Computer Bulletin Board*, by Lary L. Myers, is available from Tab Books, Inc., Blue Ridge Summit PA 17214. But be forewarned—it's not for beginners. Free bulletin-board programs are available from existing CBBSs and clubs.

If you are excited about networking through telecommunications, buy *The Network Nation*, by Starr Rosanne Hiltz and Murray Turoff (Addison-Wesley). This is a thorough, thoughtful book that explores in depth many of the possibilities of human communications via computers.

Discussing computer networking is all well and good, but what about the people who need information but don't have computers and aren't likely to buy them? What about migrant farm workers, the unemployed, or those whose incomes are too low to afford computers? What about those who haven't enough use for them to justify the purchase? In spite of all I've said about CBBSs being a people's forum, don't we end up, once again, with the information (power) in the hands of those who have the money?

These questions bring us to the Community Memory Project.

I have been worrying about egalitarian access to computers only for about a year, but computer-oriented people who have social consciences have been pondering the problem since the early seventies, trying to figure out ways to make computers work for all people, not just for those with money.

One such group is the Community Memory Project in Berkeley, California. They hope to make computers accessible to anyone who has a quarter. Their idea is to make coin-operated computer terminals to install in public places, like vending machines or public telephones. They plan to put terminals in libraries, bookstores, cafes, perhaps even on street corners. Anyone who has a quarter can drop it into the slot and leave a message, or search for one, in a data base. Each data base would serve just one community, with up to twenty terminals distributed at strategic places in the area, to allow a free two-way interchange of information and opinion unrestricted by any authority—governmental or commercial—and which is so cheap as to be virtually free.

Messages can be labeled with key words or phrases, and can be recalled by others who are interested in the topic and who search the data base using the same key words: "For Sale," "House for Rent," "House Wanted," "Lost Dog," or "Gun for Hire." Any number of people can participate in political forums labeled by topic: "Ecology," "Impeach Mayor Jones," "Nudism Now." Movies, restaurants, plays, and books can be commented on, and opposing views and reviews can be added to the original messages, with no limits on length or subject matter.

Central to the philosophy of the Community Memory Project is the idea of the urban "virtual village"—a community of people linked by common interests and communication. Anyone who lives in a city knows how easy it is to live three doors away from somebody for five years and never speak to them. You might be missing a vital connection. Through the medium of the Community Memory terminal, however, you will probably find each other if you have an interest in common.

Containing the network within a certain geographical area is also important if attempts to rent a house or find a lost dog are to have a reasonable chance of success.

With this system the same benefits accrue as with the CBBSs, but with two very important differences. A CBBS, to be useful, must be limited to one general topic, and most of the time interaction will be solely through the bulletin board, since a majority of the people will be geographically remote from one another. The Community Memory Project will be geographically *limited*, making personal contact practical and thus opening up many additional possibilities, such as finding an apartment to rent or a car to buy. Local topics such as city council elections, who's the best doctor in town, or which is the best restaurant are of practical interest to all. And because unlike CBBSs, the user base is limited, the topic range can be broad.

The idea has great potential for networking on a local level. Women will be high on the list of those who can benefit. For example, exchange babysitting cooperatives will be easier to administer. It will be easier for women to help one another find jobs, housing, and friends, and to form groups based on common interests (maybe even a women's computer-users group—to date I haven't heard of one).

Several women are involved with the Community Memory Project (called CM or CMP by the people who work there). One of them is Sandy Emerson, who worked at CM for two and a half years before she quit to become a full-time writer. "I joined the project at a time when they hadn't answered their mail for two years. I did everything: I published their magazine, I was the mouthpiece for the project to the outside world, I wrote some pamphlets, and I started using a computer terminal connected to U.C. Berkeley in order to set type for the *Journal of Community Communications*. That was fun. I love the editor and the typesetting programs, and that seemed worth doing. I came to the CMP because my friends were working on it, and it seemed a lot more interesting to me than the public-health job I had. I had a degree in public health and was working for a federal health planning agency and it was just awful—very bureaucratic.

"In the health profession I had been involved with women's clinics and I was teaching self-help, birth control, and abortion counseling. The CM struck me as an information self-help project. In the community clinics medical knowledge was brought down to a consumer level, and in CM information technology and communications were brought down to the consumer level. To use the public terminal you will not have to learn a special language, and spacing is not important—either lower case or upper case is all right. All the ways in which computers are traditionally unforgiving are gradually changing.

"We're trying as hard as we can to build networking into the way the system is deployed and the way the system interacts with the user. Certainly The Source and the CBBSs show that people will put up with all kinds of awkward software to use an electronic bulletin board. They really like it. Dow Jones [the financial on-line information service] has recently been forced by subscribers to add a bulletin board.

"Our concern is, which people are going to use CM? Are we just going to reach the same general slice of the population as The Source? We'll have to see. Our idea is that people will not only use the system, but they will run it themselves. They will begin to acquire the equipment themselves. It's supposed to have a way for almost any kind of computer terminal to hook in. Neighborhood associations are supposed to arise that run the different clumps of terminals. There are several different levels of self-management that will be explored."

Nobody claims the Community Memory idea is without problems. There is the potential for scams and slander, and the problem of how to design an indestructible computer terminal, and of how to pay for the system. But the idea is so good that it seems destined to happen. Three pilot "nodes" (CMP's term for the computer and its cluster of terminals) have been in action in Berkeley since 1984. Public response has been enthusiastic, with more than six thousand messages recorded in about eight months.

For more information on the Community Memory Project, write:

Community Memory Project
916 Parker St.
Berkeley CA 94710
(415) 841-1114

For information on how other groups are planning to make computers work for everyone, write:

Public Interest Communications Association
318 17th Ave.
Seattle WA 98122
(206) 329-1804

The Computer Services Collective
Applied Science Building
UC Santa Cruz
Santa Cruz CA 95064

The Journal of Community Communications
Village Design
P.O. Box 996
Berkeley CA 94701

T W E L V E

Work and Family Life in the Home: A Challenge in Choreography

Working with Children

It can be difficult to work at home with children not yet in school. Small children are strongly bonded to their mothers and need constant contact. They can't be expected to understand, much less obey, a rule that they can't disturb Mommy for an hour while she works.

Mothers working at home with children is a controversial issue with unions and academics. Proponents of women working at home state unequivocally that children benefit from having their mothers at home and that child-care expenses can be eliminated. Those who are against women working at home argue that those benefits are a myth, that work for pay and children do not mix, and that women who try it give it up in short order. Both arguments are simplistic, and few seem to have asked the women who actually work at home with their children.

My own interviews with many work-at-home mothers clearly indicate that successfully mixing motherhood and working at home depends on many factors, including the type of work being done; the size of the home and the ability of the mother to isolate her workspace; the temperament of both mother and children; the ability of the mother to set firm limits on her time and space and to enforce these with her children; the availability and willingness of the father or other family members to care for the children while the mother works; and the nature of the work itself—whether it can be done at night or during school hours, or if it must be done during hours determined by factors other than the mother's convenience.

For some women who have small children, the only solution to the problem of interruptions is to pay for child care until the children are old enough to go to school. Chris England had a live-in helper for the first year and now has her toddler in nursery school. Carol Bjorling also has live-in help.

But if your business is such that it doesn't matter what hours you work, work can be scheduled during naps, after bedtime at night, or early in the morning before the children wake up. The Blue Cross/Blue Shield Cottage Keyers I talked to do data entry that does not require much concentration, and these women manage very well with small children playing in the same room with them. Cottage Keyer Diane Blosse says, "I have an office in an extra bedroom and my children stay with me while I'm working and I'm right there with them. My baby doesn't walk yet and she crawls around and hangs on my legs. My work doesn't require a lot of thinking, and I don't really make many mistakes at it. I stop and take a break when I need to care for them, and I still get my work done." Diane was a professional-affairs representative for Blue Cross/Blue Shield before she became a Cottage Keyer, so she makes far less money now, but when I asked her if it was worth the loss of income to be at home with her kids, she said, "Absolutely."

Cottage Keyer Yvonne Rice has two children, ages four and eight at the time I interviewed her. Yvonne has her kids at home while she works but makes them understand that she is working at a job just the same as she was when she left the house. They are expected to help out and care for themselves to whatever degree they are able. Yvonne started the program when her daughter was one year old, and took her through toilet training with the potty right beside Yvonne's desk. Yvonne chose to work at home mainly because she wanted to be with her children. It would defeat her purpose to hire help or send them to a babysitter, but she says it is hard to balance work with mother-hood. Nevertheless, she loves being at home and says on the whole it has worked out well.

Programmer Mary Ellen Siudut has four children, ages ten, eight, four, and three at the time I interviewed her, and can't have her children around while she's working because program-ming takes intense concentration. She has solved the problem by being very disciplined and structured in her work. She says, "The first year I was under a lot of pressure because I felt I had to work all the time, that it was always hanging over me. I think that's one of the disadvantages of working at home. But this year I've been able to teach myself to work on a schedule. I establish in my mind particular hours I am going to work. I try to block out time so I get my work done, but when the children come off the school bus I can stop and be with them for a while to talk about school, and then send them off to play so I can go back to work. It works wonderfully if you can say, 'Now I'm going to stop' if the children get restless. You come downstairs and read them a story and make yourself a cup of tea. My husband comes home at five and he will make dinner if I need to continue to work.

"I don't think my children really feel that Mommy works. If I'm upstairs, I'm here, in their minds. I don't think it matters to them, it's just like I'm vacuuming or cleaning. If they really need me, I'm available, but I don't allow them to come up for every little problem. I just tell them they can't do that, I'm working now."

But Mary Ellen does not work full-time, and her husband is supportive and helpful. Mary Ellen states that these two facts make a big difference. Women who are single parents and/or who work full-time may find that they must have help at least part-time. Cooperative babysitting groups exist in some areas. Find out about such groups and utilize them. Under such pro-grams, mothers trade babysitting services so that they avoid the financial drain of child-care costs. Household chores or recre-ation with your own children can be scheduled during the hours you are tending someone else's children, minimizing the time you "pay" for your own children's care. Friends and relatives may be willing to babysit for a consideration other than money.

As we have seen, working at home with children works for

some and not for others. There are as many different circumstances as there are individuals, and just as many ways of
coping—or not coping—with problems. But I could find only
one mother who gave up working at home because her children
interfered with her work.

Kathryn Hubbell, of Eugene, Oregon, started a public relations agency in her home because she wanted to be accessible to
her children. But after a few months she moved into a rented
office, partly because she was not able to keep her kids from
interfering with her work. She says, "Kids don't know how to
act around an office environment. It's hard for young children
to understand that you are not available to them if you're sitting
in that chair by the desk talking on the phone. They don't make
that discrimination in their minds very well. You might be
talking to a client on the phone and there's laughing or screaming or yelling in the background."

Lisa Walker is a programmer—work that requires intense
concentration; she said this about working at home with a
baby: "It's a challenge to work at home with a small baby. At
first it was very difficult because the baby didn't have a schedule.
I was new at being a mother and it was easier to handle the
computer than it was the baby. But now she's on a schedule
and I plan my work around her. When I know she's happy in
the morning, then I get on the computer and work. When she's
unhappy and it's time for her nap, I spend time with her and
put her to sleep.

"I always have her in the same room with me while I'm
working. There's a playpen and she'll spend some time in that.
She's walking now and she's a handful, but the whole house is
baby-proofed. The only problem is that sometimes she likes to
bang on the keyboard, so I have to push her away. When she
was very little I used to work with her on my lap, and I would
work with one hand. But then she got too old for that and
started trying to grab the flashing red lights on my disk drives.
Now she's content in the playpen or wandering around. I have
to get up and get her a new toy every now and then.

"There's no period where I can sit for more than two hours at
a time. It's more a matter of working for an hour, get up for half
an hour, work another hour. But programming is a sedentary

job, so it's good to get up and move around. The only problem it presents is that when you're programming, you can get so deeply into a problem that you reach a level of concentration that you hate to break when the baby needs you, and that is very frustrating. You're just about to solve a problem and the baby starts screaming."

Nevertheless, Lisa is very happy working at home with her baby and thinks it is the perfect solution for her as a new mother. Lisa has taken pains to make things work—she has baby-proofed her house, she adapts her work to the baby's schedule, and, even more important, she has the right temperament. She accepts the fact that she will be interrupted and adapts herself to that reality. She works at finding ways to cope. Lisa is also blessed with a happy baby. If her baby were more temperamental or hyperactive, the plan might not work so well. Lisa's husband also helps out with the baby when he is home.

So many factors affect how successfully you can work at home with children that it is impossible to predict what will happen until you try it. If you find you can't cope with having the children around while you're working, chances are some ingenuity and adaptability will result in a solution of some kind, such as changing the hours you work, recruiting a neighbor, relative, or friend as a babysitter, or finding an exchange babysitting group. All but one of the women I talked with feel that benefits of working at home are worth the trouble involved.

Linda Oshins, of Columbus, Ohio, went further than anyone else I interviewed in expressing enthusiasm for mixing computer work and children. Linda started her systems analysis and consulting business at home; her husband, Joe, also works with computers. Linda has a son, Jake, who is in high school. She says, "All of us play on the computer together, and work on it together, and there's a very rich exchange of knowledge. It's a wonderful thing for kids. If I had to choose just one thing that's very critical, it's to get a kid a computer as early as you can.

"My son was ten when we got our first computer, and he's fourteen now, a freshman in high school. He is able to do more different types of things than my husband and I do. Joe and I use the computer in an actual work situation, while Jake has the luxury of using it as a theoretical tool. He can program in assembly language, and is teaching himself C [a computer language], and he is going to be the best programmer of the three of us. I use him a lot in my actual work and so does Joe. We ask him to figure out ahead of time the debug routines for our programs; he saves us hours of time.

"My husband started the Ohio State University Computer Camp for kids, and my son volunteers to work there in the summertime. He has more knowledge of microcomputers than any of the staff, since their backgrounds are in mainframes and minicomputers and formal education in systems that are not related to the IBM microcomputer. So, my son wrote all the useful routines that ran the camp last year, when he was thirteen.

"The computer is a social tool as well. There are always three boys in my house in front of the screen programming together, silly things like making a G the size of a piece of paper so you can type out *GO TEAM* and get a banner. And we play that way together as a family. We said that over Christmas we weren't going to work for four days solid, but we got together and wrote programs for fun.

"These experiences have made Jake a different kind of teenager. He knows something, and we recognize that, and that's a big part of his sense of self-worth. He can say at the dinner table, about computers, 'Did you know that this does this?' And we can say, 'No, we didn't, we'll try it out tomorrow.' It makes us very close; it's a great family experience. We've had so much fun in every way."

The Importance of Structure and Self-Discipline

I don't know about you, but the only reason I used to get to work on time was that if I didn't, I would get fired. Who's going to fire you for goofing off when you're the boss?

Many work-at-homers find it very easy to form bad habits. A few people complain that they let their grooming habits deteriorate: they don't get dressed in the morning, forget to comb their hair, and tend to gain weight. A screenwriter who works from his suburban ranch house in California says it took him three years to learn to pass by the refrigerator without stopping every time.

And then there are cats. As everyone knows, cats are sent here by the devil to keep us from doing our work. Purring, they settle on our laps and prevent us from getting up to go where we really ought to go. They seduce us into sitting in the garden. If all else fails, they curl up and go to sleep on the very piece of paper we need to work with, and if we try to lift them off, they pull the old Limp Trick. I have never met a cat person who could muster up the temerity to move a cat in this condition, and as far as I know there is no solution to this problem.

Other home-based businesspeople say that the worst trap is that because they work at home they tend to overwork. This is a common problem for the self-employed no matter where they are based; but working at home, with the equipment and paperwork always within easy reach, makes it even easier to fall into the trap. This tendency to overwork with computers is widespread and can become pathological. The computer nerd, famous in the folklore of the industry, spends almost all his waking hours at the computer. He is almost always male, poor at human relationships, and often brilliant. Not quite as bad, but still in a lot of trouble, are men and women who spend so much time at their computers that they create computer "widows" and "widowers." Their marriages develop severe problems or crumble altogether. The problem is so widespread that some marriage counselors now specialize in this syndrome.

Working too much and developing bad habits are two problems that may be related to having spent most of our lives letting other people dictate our working conditions. If we don't have a rigid nine-to-five structure to work within, we don't get to work when we should, and we don't quit when we should, either. If our job does not depend upon presenting a good appearance, we are not motivated to pull ourselves together in the morning. We all depend to some extent on other people to keep us tidied up and in line. With certain maddening exceptions like Bella Abzug and my aunt Alma, we all seem to be blobs of oatmeal that don't know what shape to take if no one puts us in a bowl.

So, working at home requires that you find a way to impose a structure that normally would come with a job. I have tremendous problems with self-discipline and structure because as a woman and as an employee I have been conditioned all my life to do what other people tell me to do. If no one tells me to do something, I tend to do nothing—literally. I can sit and stare at a wall longer than anyone I know.

I have found a few devices that help. One of them is to dedicate one room in my home as an office and commit myself to the rule that when I enter it, I work; when I leave, I quit. I don't take a manuscript out to the living room to edit. I don't bring a book I am reading into my office. For a while I rented an office downtown and that worked best of all, but it nullified some of the financial advantages of working at home.

Another device I use is a kitchen timer. It's like punching a clock. As long as that timer ticks, I work; when the bell rings, I quit, do some stretches, get a cup of tea, and peer out the window to see if anything is going on in the neighborhood that requires my attention; then I set the timer again and go back to work. It helps me keep track of my time on projects billed by the hour, but its main purpose is to give me a structure to work in, because without it I don't work. That the system works is evidenced by the book you now hold in your hand.

Ways can be found to trick your own character (or lack of it). Isolate your workspace; work by the clock just as you do at a job; form a habit of getting dressed and ready for work just as if you had to go downtown; invent your own method. Whatever works.

Staying in Touch

The self-employed person who works at home must interact with clients, arrange for advertising and publicity, and make contacts to assure future business. You will meet new people all the time, and therefore your personal contacts may be greater in number and variety than they would be if you had an office job. There will be periods of time when you are working alone, so the total number of hours you spend with other people will be less, but many people who work at home say this is an advantage rather than a problem. Working alone allows them to concentrate better and work more efficiently.

Telecommuting is another matter. Isolation may be a major drawback of telecommuting, where most of the worker's tasks are performed at the terminal and there is little reason to have contact with other people. My interviews with Blue Cross/Blue Shield data entry clerks who work at home confirm this. One of the problems encountered by corporations that have pilot telecommuting programs is that some employees do not like working at home. The reason most frequently given is isolation. People like to spend their workday among other people. They miss the socializing.

However, even when the nature of your work forces you to work alone much of the time, isolation can be offset by joining professional organizations, computer users' groups, women's groups, political clubs, the PTA, and church committees. You can take university continuing education classes—the ones that are fun and sociable, like folk dancing or art—or find a dance or exercise class, perhaps even join a gym, or participate in your community-theater productions. The time for this will come from those ten to twenty hours a week you are saving by not commuting. Remember too that now your business hours are flexible. You can play tennis every morning at ten if you want to! All these activities not only bring you together with people who have interests in common with yours, but result in possible contacts for new business. They may be more satisfying, too, than taking coffee with your neighbor, because they all involve learning something new or being of service to your community or developing a skill, perhaps even all of these at once.

Telecommuter Diane Blosse had a hard time adjusting to the isolation of working at home, but she now belongs to a health club that has a child-care service and takes her lunch hour there every day. Joan Orke goes in to the office at least once a week and maintains daily contact with her co-workers by telephone.

For some people, computers may solve problems of isolation rather than create them. Shut-ins are among the most enthusiastic users of electronic bulletin boards. Telecommunications allow them to make contact with many people, and some might have very few contacts otherwise. In the chapter on networking you'll find many suggestions for staying in touch.

THIRTEEN

Computers and Your Health

Vision

Many people who have no previous problems with their eyes develop vision-related distress after working with computer VDTs (video display terminals, or, translated into real people language, computer screens). Complaints include headaches, blurred vision, eyestrain, changes in color perception, and irritated or burning eyes. The problem is a serious one, since the percentage of workers reporting problems precipitated by VDT use runs as high as 91 percent (percentages vary from one report to another. The *lowest* I could find was 54 percent).

Considerable controversy exists over why VDTs precipitate eye problems in people who either had no prior complaints or whose prior eye problems had stabilized. Unions and other workers' advocacy groups claim that the fault lies in the VDTs themselves, and demand that manufacturers improve their equipment to reduce eye stress. Manufacturers claim that the problem lies in ergonomics (the design of the work station) and in people's work habits and disclaim any responsibility.

The American Council on Science and Health surveyed the studies on health problems associated with VDTs and concluded that most eye problems are the result of poor work habits and badly arranged work stations, which supports the position of the manufacturers.

People like myself who have developed severe eyestrain as a result of working long hours at the computer, despite good work habits and well-designed work stations, are resistant to this argument and tend to believe the problem must be entirely in the VDTs. Both arguments are simplistic, each position being based on insufficient information, and, like most such arguments, each is partially right and partially wrong. My own history of VDT-associated eyestrain is typical of what many people are experiencing, and by examining it we can see how complex the problem is and determine some guidelines on how it can be avoided.

I began having trouble within a year after getting my first computer. I had already read advice that people who wear glasses should get a pair with the focal length adjusted for work at a computer, so I did that. But I still had problems. Most noticeable was that I could not watch television or a movie on the same day I had been working at the computer, nor could I tolerate being out in the sun. I got uncomfortable buzzy feelings in my head and vague symptoms I am still hard pressed to describe. Not knowing what else to do, I limited my work at the computer to two or three hours a day and gave up movies and TV.

Then, in 1984, pressing to meet a deadline, I began to ignore signs of visual fatigue and kept working long past when I knew my eyes were tired. I developed a severe case of eyestrain. I couldn't look at the VDT or read. As soon as I finished my manuscript, I rested my eyes. They seemed to recover very, very slowly. After a month, my eyes felt better and I could read, so I tried to return to work at the computer. Within twenty minutes my eyes were just as bad as they had been when I quit. Therefore, I was convinced that the cause of the problem was the VDT itself. The evidence seemed overwhelming.

But even when I did not work at the computer, I was not recovering as I thought I should. I went to see my optometrist, who told me, "You should recover from eyestrain overnight in most cases." He seemed to feel the discussion was closed, so I left. His statement frightened me. I decided that I probably needed to consult an ophthalmologist, and was half-convinced that something serious had happened to my eyes. Since I had no money and no health insurance, I could do nothing but wait. Another month went by.

Then a friend sent me two pamphlets, "VDTs and Vision" and "Visual Hygiene," published by the Optometric Extension Program Foundation, Inc. (OEP), an organization "devoted to continuing education and research in vision." From these pamphlets I learned that:

- What I had been experiencing is called *sustained nearpoint visual stress*; that such stress is relatively new because of the changes in our work and recreation during the last fifty years; that our vision was not designed for constant nearpoint work and that many vision problems are the result of failure to adapt properly to nearpoint work conditions.
- Continuous nearpoint visual stress can result in permanent as well as temporary adaptive changes, including nearsightedness, astigmatism, suppressed vision in one eye, and poor eye "teaming."
- Visual stress can produce physical fatigue, irritability, short attention span, loss of efficiency, and high error rates in all activities, not just work, and therefore can dramatically affect the quality of one's life.
- Working with computers is more stressful than other nearpoint work because "jobs which formerly allowed physical movement and opportunities to look away from near work now require extended, tiring concentration on a VDT image." Glare, reflections on the screen, poor lighting, scrolling screens, improper contrast, and flickering and/or fuzzy images compound the problem.
- Nearpoint visual stress can be reduced by proper workstation design, stress-relieving lenses, and vision training.
- "Behavioral optometrists" are specialists within the field of optometry who are knowledgeable about visual stress; they use more extensive, specialized vision testing than do ordinary optometrists, are alert to the need for good workstation design and can help analyze work-station problems, and are qualified to give special vision training to teach you to move your eyes together as a team, and to track and scan properly.

(I am grateful for the OEP for permission to paraphrase extensively from their literature, and to Thomas Lecoq of the OEP for his many helpful suggestions on this chapter.)

I found an optometrist who does vision training in a nearby city. His tests showed that (1) one of my distance lenses was not the proper prescription, creating stress on that eye; (2) I had suppressed vision in one eye; (3) my eyes did not work together in many situations; (4) my eyes were taking an abnormally long time to change focus from near to far vision; and (5) I had poor tracking ability—that is, I could not follow a moving object without very jerky movements of my eyes. These deteriorations in my vision had taken place so gradually that I had adjusted to them and was completely unconscious of them! He told me that these problems were not caused by the computer, but were preexisting. His opinion was that it was the problems I already had that made me unable to cope with nearpoint visual stress, not the stress itself that caused the problems. Stated in general terms, people may have vision problems that go unnoticed until the stress of working with a computer aggravates them to a critical point. Then can we say that computers do not "cause" vision problems? This may be semantic hair-splitting, because the fact remains that many people do not experience vision problems until they begin working with computers.

The optometrist did not think that looking directly at a light source, which is what you are doing with a VDT, was a significant factor, as long as brightness and contrast were properly adjusted. But just as our eyes were not designed for constant nearpoint work, they were not designed to look directly at a source of light, either, so with a bit of layman's arrogance, I insisted that light was a likely factor, since my personal experience was that light aggravated my condition. Confirming my suspicions in this line, computer manufacturers are trying to develop non-light-emitting display screens that are economically feasible. They are doing that because whether they acknowledge it publically or not, they believe the light-emitting screens are causing problems. One solution—liquid crystal display screens— are being marketed as I write this—the same technology as the LCD display on your wristwatch. However, the OEP informs me that evidence suggests that LCDs will probably eliminate only about 10 percent of complaints. Several low-light technologies are being explored but as yet are too expensive to be marketed successfully.

My optometrist prescribed simple exercises for me that I could do at home, and within a week my eyestrain was substantially relieved, although not gone. I could work again! Encouraged, I carefully observed myself at work. I found that I had formed the habit of staring fixedly at the screen all the time I was typing, even when I didn't need to see what was on the screen. I retrained myself to look at the screen only when necessary. This also allowed my eyes to change focus often, from near-near to medium-near vision. This change of habit cut my screen time by about two-thirds when typing original copy, although the process of editing still requires me to look at the screen almost constantly and results in a great deal more stress. The optometrist advised me never to work for more than forty-five minutes without taking a break; I have reduced this to half an hour, and less when I edit.

I bought an antiglare filter for my screen, which was already supposed to be low-glare. The filter made a noticeable difference. The physical aspects of my work station were already well designed, so I had no problem with that.

However, a substantial problem remained: my sensitivity to light. I remembered that vitamin A is essential to eye health, so I started taking a very high dose. In twenty-four hours my eyes were dramatically better, and have remained so ever since. I estimate the improvement of my sensitivity to light to be about 70 percent; there remains some sensitivity; I still can't watch TV, although I adjusted the brightness downward. However, I can work much longer at the computer every day, although not as much as I think I should be able to. It seems likely that I was suffering from a vitamin A deficiency. Because vitamin A can be toxic when too much is accumulated in the body, after a week I reduced the dosage to 50,000 I.U. daily, and later I reduced it again to 25,000 I.U., which is generally considered a safe level for prolonged use.

Early in our discussions my optometrist said to me, "If the problem is the VDTs themselves, then why do many people use VDTs all day every day and never develop any problems?" I was very resistant to that argument because at the time I had done everything possible to relieve the stress—or so I thought. My progress to this point had me almost convinced that his argument was correct. But the following summer I worked for three months at a computer with a black-and-white screen that has a much higher resolution than the one I had at home. (*High resolution* means the image is sharper.) I found that I could work at this terminal seven or eight hours a day with only minor eye fatigue, while at home I could work only three or four hours a day without eyestrain. Recently, I bought an Atari ST computer with a display modeled after the one I used that summer—it has a black-and-white screen with high resolution and low flicker. I can now work more hours a day without extreme discomfort. This is a clue that my intolerance of TV may be due to its high flicker rather than the light.

These experiences have convinced me that much of the trouble may indeed be in the design of the VDTs themselves. The answer to my optometrist's question may be that the people who don't have trouble have no pre-existing maladaptions of their vision. But that doesn't mean that the design of the displays has nothing to do with eye problems associated with VDT use—as my experience certainly indicates. It only means that people with good vision are able to tolerate poor conditions. The rest of us can't—and remember that the statistics say that's 50 to 90 percent of us.

My experience also shows that there is a lot to know and to educate the public about if we are to work at VDTs without problems. When I told Thomas Lecoq of the OEP about my experience with vitamin A, he informed me that some optometrists are considering the value of vitamin A in relation to visual stress triggered by working at VDTs, but this information certainly isn't available to the public yet.

Although many people experience no problems whatsoever working at a VDT, the vision problems that do exist are serious and widespread, and every computer user needs to be informed and to exercise a great deal of care in how she sets up her work station and forms her work habits. I have told my story at such length because I want to make the point clear that many different factors contribute to vision problems at the computer. As stated earlier, the arguments of the various workervs.-manufacturer factions are simplistic—they seem to want to reduce the issue to a single cause, when in fact the problem is complex and multifaceted.

Based on a number of studies, my own experience, and the recommendations of the OEP, here are some guidelines to protect your vision when you are operating your computer:

Display screen. Buy a high quality, high resolution monitor for your computer. If a display comes with the computer you buy, make sure it is top quality (see guidelines on pp. 220–223). The surface of a display becomes electrically charged and gathers dust very quickly. Clean it every day before you start to work. Adjust screen brightness and contrast for maximum comfort; adjustments will be necessary with changing light conditions in the room. Arrange your work station so that no reflections fall on the screen, and it has no glare. Even if your monitor is characterized as "low glare," an add-on glare filter may substantially reduce glare. Your display should be about 20 degrees below eye level and mounted on a tilt/swivel base so that you can adjust it to your comfort.

Room lighting. Do not face windows or light sources while you are working. Arrange light fixtures so that they do not create glare or reflections on the screen. Lamps and overhead fixtures may have to be hooded or baffled. The OEP literature says that room light should be three times brighter than screen background, and screen characters ten times brighter than screen background. They don't give the faintest clue as to how you judge this, so you must give it your best guess. Thomas Lecoq suggests using a photographic spot light meter.

Work habits. Arrange your keyboard, copy, and screen so that they are about equal distance from the eyes. The keyboard should be arranged so that your wrist and lower arm are parallel to the floor. I recommend a detachable keyboard so that your position can be changed to avoid physical as well as visual fatigue. If you use a straight chair, it should have comfortable, adjustable back support and be of a height that allows your feet to be flat on the floor and your thighs to be parallel to the floor. I have a chaise, which allows me to work with my legs extended parallel to the floor; this is very comfortable for long hours of work and gives excellent back support. My detachable keyboard rests comfortably on my lap. While working, look at the keyboard or elsewhere in the room as much as you can. Do not develop the habit of staring fixedly at the screen. Take frequent breaks and look at objects at a distance.

Vitamin supplementation. If you find your eyes becoming hypersensitive to light, try a vitamin A supplement.

Vision. If you wear glasses, it is imperative that you get a special pair with focal length adjusted to your working distance from the screen. Working distance will vary with the size of your screen and the size of the characters on the screen, and with personal comfort and preference. I work 28 inches from a 12-inch screen, which I now think is too close. When I go to a new prescription I will increase the distance to 36 inches. I am a farsighted person, however, and these distances may be entirely inappropriate for nearsighted or normal vision. You have to work out your own optimal conditions, preferably after consultation with a behavioral (or vision-training) optometrist. If you do not already wear glasses, you may still benefit from "stress relieving" lenses just for work.

Optometrist Michael Luby of Grand Junction, Colorado, tells me that one signal of developing problems to watch for is difficulty in shifting focus from near to far vision. If it takes several seconds to adjust from looking at the computer screen to something across the room, your visual system may be tightening up on you. He suggests that you do the "calendar rock" during your breaks to help keep your eyes flexible and limber. The calendar rock: focus your eyes for a few seconds on something close, like reading material, then look across the room at a calendar or clock for another few seconds. Repeat this movement for a minute or more.

I was so stunned to discover that I had so many vision problems of which I was unconscious, and which were not corrected in any way by my glasses, that I recommend that *everyone* who plans to use a computer visit an optometrist who does vision training (or a behavioral optometrist) for complete vision testing. An ophthalmologist or ordinary optometrist will not do; neither uses vision training to improve eye adaptation and performance.

With early discovery of latent problems that may be aggravated by computer use, and correction of them to whatever extent possible with appropriate exercises, you may save yourself considerable discomfort and in some cases irreversible progression of nearsightedness or astigmatism. Check the optometrists listed in the Yellow Pages for *behavioral optometrist* or *vision training*. If that yields no results, write to the OEP for a list of their members in your area (their address is given on p. 191).

What About our Kids?

Optometrist Michael Luby specializes in vision training for children. I asked him how parents can protect their children from computer-related eye problems. He told me that children's vision systems are so flexible that they can mask problems for years by compensating in some way. For example, if they can't turn their eyes inward and "team" them properly, they can compensate by focusing harder. This may go on for years before it creates noticeable problems, but by that time they have formed a deepseated unconscious habit of using their eyes improperly, and this can be corrected only with vision training. For this reason, Michael recommends that all children be thoroughly tested by a vision-training specialist before they begin school, then regularly thereafter at least every two years, but preferably yearly. School tests are not adequate to catch these kinds of problems.

Michael further recommends that when your children work at the computer you should make sure they take frequent breaks. Watch for squinting, red eyes, rubbing of the eyes, headaches, and tilting the head to one side while reading. They should not move their heads while reading the computer screen; if they do, it means their eyes are not moving properly. They should not move their lips or sit too close to the screen. If your child has trouble reading, the problem may be in her eyes, not in her mental ability.

What About Radiation?

In 1979, four women who worked at VDTs in a Canadian newspaper office had babies with birth defects. High incidences of problem pregnancies and birth defects associated with VDT work have been reported several other times. These reports have caused considerable alarm.

Public concern about radiation from VDTs is apparently without factual support. VDTs emit no more radiation than TV sets, and radiation levels of both are set by law well below levels that can cause health problems—levels that are determined by government agencies. What that statement means to you depends on how much confidence you have in government agencies.

The American Council on Science and Health states that many different types of birth defects have been reported, suggesting that the problems do not have a common cause. A number of government agencies, both Canadian and American, have reviewed these incidents in detail and have found no reason to believe that VDTs have any relation to the pregnancy and birth problems, but the public has been stirred up, and fear, once planted, dies hard.

The trouble lies in the way information is presented. The incidence of cancer is very high in this country. If four people who work in an office got cancer, we would not run around saying, "Typewriters cause cancer!" Computers are new and, like all new technologies, are viewed with a suspicion that borders on paranoia. A few doomsday opportunists, most of whom know little about computers, make themselves media stars by blaming computers for everything from the breakup of the American family to the exploitation of labor, as if the American family was in great shape and labor was not exploited until computers came along.

Although it is not *common* for cancer to cluster, it is not statistically improbable, either. The same is true for birth defects and pregnancy problems. Depending on how you define *birth defects*, between 2 and 6 percent of all babies are born with them; and what the isolated reports on clusters of birth defects supposedly associated with VDTs also fail to mention is that there has been an alarming rise in the incidence of birth defects in populations that have virtually nothing to do with computers, such as Navajos living near toxic waste disposal sites. Precise figures on the number of pregnancies that end in miscarriage are not possible, since many are not reported, but informed estimates say anywhere from 15 to 20 percent. It makes statistical sense that problem pregnancies and/or birth defects will occasionally cluster, and it is very clear that environmental factors not connected with VDTs have a significant role. The fact that VDTs happen to be in the same place is of no factual relevance at all unless and until someone proves that such clustering never occurs where there are *no* VDTs, or that such clustering occurs more frequently where there are VDTs than elsewhere, and/or that VDTs emit unsafe levels of harmful radiation—at this time a matter of controversy.

Cathode ray tubes (used both in TVs and VDTs) do emit ultraviolet and X-radiation. There is considerable debate over how much radiation is safe, particularly in the case of X-radiation, since its effects are cumulative. Most CRTs emit X-radiation far below government standards, but the reports of pregnancy problems associated with VDTs are raising questions about that standard.

Because of public concern and the oddity of the clustering of birth defects and pregnancy problems, the National Institute of Occupational Safety and Health [NIOSH] announced it would undertake a study of six thousand pregnancies. Unfortunately that study was abandoned. Until a controlled study is done, it would make sense for pregnant women to be cautious, but not paranoid, about working long hours at close range with computers.

Where to Get Information

For information on the conservative side you can write to the American Council on Science and Health, 47 Maple Street, Summit NJ 07901.

For information biased on the side of workers, 9 to 5, an organization of office workers, also keeps an eye on these issues. 9 to 5 has offices in many cities, but for information you should write to:

9 to 5
1224 Huron Road
Cleveland OH 44115
(216) 566-9308

An informative booklet titled "The Hazards of VDTs" is available from the Ontario Public Service Employees Union, 1901 Yonge St., Toronto, Ontario M4S 2Z5, Canada, for $2.00.

For the most sensible information on vision and VDTs, and for help in locating a behavioral optometrist, write the Optometric Extension Program, 2912 South Daimier St., Santa Ana CA 92705. Enclose a self-addressed, stamped envelope. You can also call them at (800) 423-4111, or (714) 250-8070 in California.

If you are interested enough in vision and VDTs to read a 273-page report, send $15 to the National Academy Press, 2101 Constitution Ave. N.W., Washington DC 20318, and they will send you the National Academy of Science report "Video Displays, Work, and Vision."

PART IV
Nuts and Bolts

F O U R T E E N

How to Learn About Computers

Learning about computers is not hard, but people seem to conspire to make it hard. Teachers, writers of instruction manuals, and writers of books often seem to think that the more detailed their explanations, the easier they will be to understand. But most of the time they just cover up the forest with a lot of trees.

Computer educators make a more serious mistake: they don't seem to make a distinction between the needs of the person who wants to become a technician or programmer and the needs of the person who simply wants to learn to *use* a computer. *The unspoken assumptions of computer writers and educators often give novices the impression that they must become technological experts in order to operate a computer—and this is not the case at all.* You don't have to be a mechanic to drive a car, and you don't have to understand digital electronics or programming to operate a computer. That's the most important thing to remember when choosing your resources for learning about computers. I believe that many people who are curious about computers are driven away when they enroll in a computer science class and find themselves plunged into programming in the first session, before they even have time to understand fully the difference between hardware and software. There are computer literacy classes, in which they simply introduce people to computers and what they can do, explain how to operate them, explore equipment options, and give the students a chance to become familiar with various kinds of software, without going into electronic design and programming. Currently, however, there are too few such classes.

If you keep in mind that you needn't be an engineer or a programmer to use a computer effectively, you can ignore 80 percent of the available educational material, thereby making selection much easier and assuring that you will not be plunged into technical details that are overwhelming to beginners and useless to all but experts.

Fortunately, there are many different ways to learn about computers, so you can make choices that suit your style. You may also be limited by where you live. I taught myself to use my computer by using the manuals provided by the manufacturer, reading books and computer magazines, and, in times of catastrophe and panic, calling a knowledgeable friend long distance. Mostly I learned by fooling around and finding the right answer by accident. Moab does not have a computer store, the usual HELP! resource of most computer owners. I never once had the assistance of a real live person showing me how to do things. For a while I belonged to an Osborne user group, and I have occasionally traveled 265 miles (one way) to attend meetings! Because I think a user group is one of the most valuable educational resources for the new computer user, I consider them first.

User Groups

The easiest and most pleasant way to learn about computers is to join a user group. User groups are associations of people who own computers, usually of a particular brand. They meet at regular intervals to exchange information and to brainstorm problems. Computer dealers often know about user groups in your area for the brands of computers they carry, or you can write to the manufacturers.

User groups have several advantages over classes. Once necessary business is dispensed with, the meetings are usually unstructured, with people grouping themselves according to their specific interests and problems of the moment. In a class the instructor decides the subject for discussion, and even if you are not particularly interested in the history of computers you will hear about it anyway if the course syllabus calls for it. But a user group responds to whatever questions and needs its members bring with them to the meeting. No time is wasted over irrelevancies (unless they are entertaining!). Also, there is no instructor, no competition for grades or performance, and the atmosphere is informal and relaxed. These differences tend to make the user-group meeting both intense—because anything discussed is almost surely someone's immediate problem—and fun—because of the spontaneous and informal atmosphere.

The advantages don't stop there. When you ask your dealer questions about your computer, you are always aware that you are taking up the time of a person who is in business to make money. No matter how much she assures you that she is happy to help you with your questions, you know perfectly well there is a limit. But a user group consists of others like yourself who are in a process of discovery. They are not there to make money but to exchange information, and the atmosphere is egalitarian. Since you are all learning, no one will make you feel stupid. (Sometimes there is a resident "expert" who likes to flaunt his expertise. You will know him because he never asks for advice or information, only gives it. Don't be put off; use him. It fills his need.)

Members of a user group exchange phone numbers (or a membership roster is provided) so that they can call one another for information and advice or just to talk computer talk. You always have a resource, and no matter what time of day it is, someone on the list will probably be available. If you rely on your dealer as a resource, if he can't answer a question you are stuck. But in a user group, if Paul doesn't know, Jane might.

Another benefit: even when you don't have a problem to discuss, listening to someone else's problems at a user-group meeting acquaints you with problems that might occur in the future—and you'll know the solution before the problem occurs.

Unfortunately, user groups are often composed mostly of men—I was one of only two women in my Osborne group. Do not allow this to discourage you from joining one. If you find yourself the only woman in your group, your discomfort will probably disappear when you discover how genuinely friendly and helpful computer buffs are (as a rule).

If you don't yet own a computer, join a user group anyway. I would be very surprised if you were told you couldn't join because you don't own a computer. Computer owners are extremely partisan about their particular brands and will delight in trying to convince you to buy the model they own. But since they have nothing to gain in hiding the system's weaknesses, they will tell you the problems they have had as well; it's a great way to evaluate a particular model before you buy it.

Perhaps the single most important service of the user group is the support it can give to novices. In the group you will find many others who are just as confused as you are. You will find out that you are not stupid or dense, that other clever and intelligent people have just as much difficulty as you do working through the resistance to what at first seems to be an overwhelming volume of new information, and to new ways of thinking about work. The volume of things to remember and fit together is intimidating at first, then you learn to slow down and take things a step at a time, and to call someone when you get stuck, someone who understands completely how you feel.

Magazines

Magazines are my favorite source of information about computers and everything related to them. Periodicals are usually the *only* source of up-to-date information on computers. Computer technology develops at amazing speed, so books on the subject may be out-of-date by the time they reach the bookstores (it often takes a year from the time an author turns in her manuscript to the day the book appears on a bookstore shelf—and sometimes longer).

Magazine articles also focus on a specific topic and treat it in much more depth than is possible in books that cover more general topics. For instance, I have been contemplating the purchase of a hard disk drive on which to build a rather large data base, but I don't know much about them. A search through my books turned up very little. Hard disk drives are given a paragraph, if they are mentioned at all. In addition, development in the industry has accelerated in the last year, which hasn't been incorporated into the latest books. And lo! Along comes my new issue of *Popular Computing* with a detailed article on hard disk drives, telling me everything I want to know.

Many magazines are directed to personal computer users, and their articles range from strictly elementary materials to detailed surveys of sophisticated software. Some popular computing magazines assume that their readers are at different levels of expertise and try to publish something for every level. I like that because I am always challenged to move up a level.

Among the most valuable services provided by computing magazines are the comparison-shopper features that appear regularly. A magazine may feature an annual personal computer survey, another on printers, word processing software, or almost any other area in which there are many competing brands. Particularly valuable are the software evaluations. Since prices and the market constantly change and products are continually upgraded, these features are enormously helpful when you are shopping. The articles compare prices and features of all the brands.

Of equal value are detailed educational articles about various computer peripherals and the "how does it work" features. If you are going to buy a modem and want to know all you can about it before you shop, you are almost sure to find a thorough explanation printed within the last six months in one of the many popular computing magazines.

Personal Computing is a general interest computer magazine. *Family Computing* is a good magazine for beginners, especially if you have children. It doesn't cover any topic in much depth, but it is written in a way that novices can understand. A few other general computer magazines are published, but the most useful are the magazines for specific brands of computers. When you buy your computer you can find out about these magazines from your dealer—she may even carry them in her store. Most large newsstands and bookstores stock a considerable variety. These highly specific magazines may be the most valuable source material you can read, since everything in them pertains to your computer and is potentially of use to you. Magazines published by national users groups for a particular brand are also very useful.

Many magazines publish occasional supplements that deal in

depth with a particular topic—all the software they have reviewed in the last year, or a comparison-shopping guide to portable computers, for instance. These guides can be very useful, so when you see one that appeals to you, grab it immediately—they go fast and don't stay in print long.

An important tip about reading the magazines and their supplements: even the articles for novices will contain unfamiliar terminology. You may have trouble remembering the difference betwen RAM and ROM, although you have read the definitions a dozen times. If the article makes sense to you otherwise, don't worry about it. You will assimilate terminology slowly and imperceptibly. You needn't understand everything in an article to get something out of it. Gradually you will realize you understand more and more, and gradually you will find yourself reading more-advanced articles, still muttering to yourself that you don't understand half of it.

Books

If you wander into your neighborhood bookstore you are likely to find that the section for books on computers is larger than those for cook books or books on auto mechanics or gardening. A lot of junk is being put out because it can be sold, so be wary.

Many books appear and disappear within a few weeks. The competition is stiff, and the bad book with the flashly cover and big advertising budget may sell better than the good book by the self-publisher who can't afford advertising or extensive distribution. I have often looked at a book that I recognized to be good, and then because of a cash flow problem or general indecisiveness I left it behind. A week later it would be gone, never to appear again, so my recommendation is that if you see a computer book that truly appeals to you, write a bad check if you have to, (just kidding!) but buy it *now*.

Because of the very short shelf life of so many computer books, it is hard to list books that will still be available in the future. A few, however, are classics and should be around for a while, and they are listed at the end of this chapter.

Go to the bookstore with specific questions in mind that you want answered. If you can't understand your *WordStar* manual and want a better book, then simply look for titles with *WordStar* in them. "I think I'll buy a book about computers" isn't enough. You can go crazy that way. Pick an area you want to know about, such as *programming in BASIC, word processing,* or *how to turn on your IBM PC.* Remember, you don't have to be an engineer, so immediately eliminate those books that make you feel like you do.

Next, plan for enough time to stand in the bookstore and read the first chapter of any book you are interested in. By the time you have finished the first chapter you should know something you didn't know before, understand it clearly (or be convinced you can with a rereading), and, most important, you should be excited because you learned something you've been wanting to know. You should be eager to go on to the next chapter. If you feel frustrated and annoyed, don't assume you're dense. It's probably the book; go on to the next one.

Computer buffs talk to one another at the computer sections in bookstores. I have a friend who has a rich social life based around his daily hour or two in his favorite store. Such browsers may be able to direct you to just the book you need.

The ideal place to shop for computer books is a large bookstore in a university town, or the student bookstore. The B. Dalton Bookseller chain stocks a great variety of computer books. Computer dealers sometimes carry a good selection of books about the systems and software they carry. Many books are advertised in the computing magazines, and the reviews that these magazines publish may help you in your selection.

You will probably need to read only one or two general books about computers to learn enough to get started. The most helpful books for the novice are those that help you learn to use a major program—in most cases you will need such a book to supplement the terrible manual that comes with the program. But other than one general introductory book on computers (like this one!) and a book or books on the specific software you own, you can learn most of what you need to know by reading the appropriate magazines, visiting users' groups or a helpful dealer, and reading your owner's manuals. When you need another book, you'll know.

You will find quite a few books recommended throughout this book. *Personal Computing* has a regular book-review section; you will discover books there that might not be in your bookstore and read an assessment of their worth as well, although reviewers can be somewhat arbitrary and harsh in their judgments.

Here are a few books I haven't mentioned elsewhere:

The Prentice-Hall Standard Glossary of Computer Terminology, by Robert A. Edmunds (Prentice-Hall, 1984). A good computer dictionary will make your life a lot easier and learning faster. There are quite a few dictionaries on the market but unfortunately many of them are poor. When I shopped for a dictionary I tested each one by looking up three common terms that I know well. I was shocked to discover how many definitions were garbled, incomplete, imprecise, or absent altogether. The Prentice-Hall glossary is not perfect, but, balancing factors such as clarity, completeness, and price, it came out on top in my survey.

DON'T! (Or How to Care for Your Computer), by Rodney Zaks, (Sybex, 1984). This is the only book I have found that deals exclusively with how to *prevent* computer breakdowns by avoiding the conditions that cause them. I wish I had found the book earlier. The computer dealers forget to tell you about the hazards of cold, dust, disturbances in line voltage, and many other conditions that will damage your equipment. This book is directed mainly to commercial computer users, but most of the material is applicable to home computers as well.

If you want to understand more about the impact of computers on our work, our lives, and our society, the following books will be useful:

The Telematic Society (previously published as *The Wired Society*), by James Martin (Prentice-Hall, 1981), is a preview of the future effects of computers and telecommunications, with an emphasis on their benefits to the individual.

The Third Wave, by Alvin Toffler (William Morrow, 1981), gives the large view of the future as affected by the shift from a manufacturing economy to an information-based economy. This book will help you understand what the computer revolution means to the society as a whole.

The Second Self, by Sherry Turkle (Simon & Schuster, 1984). Written by a PhD. sociologist, and reads like it sometimes, this is nevertheless a fascinating book about how people relate to computers, with a large section of the book devoted to accounts of children interacting with computers. This is the highlight of the book and reminds us once again that children are far wiser and more sophisticated in their thinking than we give them credit for. Highly recommended.

The Electronic Cottage: Everyday Living with Your Personal Computer in the 1980s, by Joseph Deken (William Morrow, 1981). The title is misleading because Deken does not write about working at home with a computer, which is what the term *electronic cottage* has come to imply. He discusses what computers can do, with the emphasis on individual applications in the home rather than business applications. But what Deken does, he does very well. He explains computers in detail and in terms of their functions in a way that is meaningful to the person who is going to use a computer in her home.

Dealers

Anyone who sells computers should show you how to use one (within reasonable limits). It is to the salesperson's advantage to do so—if she can get you enthused, she may sell you a computer. Also, service is an important part of a dealer's responsibility. Anyone who buys a computer for the first time needs lots of help and advice. Personal computers are designed to be as simple to operate as possible, but complexity can be reduced only to a certain limit. Computers perform complicated, powerful functions, after all, and a reasonable amount of skill and training is required to utilize them effectively.

Manufacturers attempt to provide complete documentation for their machines, but these manuals are usually badly written and so detailed that the sheer volume of facts is intimidating. The new computer owner needs and deserves some personal help in learning to use her machine. At present, that person is the dealer who sold her the computer; and both the manufacturer and the customer expect the dealer to serve as educator as well as merchant. This isn't a fair demand, but it is a situation we are all forced to accept until (1) manufacturers realize it is their duty to provide some free training by their own personnel for each new customer, and/or (2) enough smart people realize there is a good living to be made as home-computer tutors. These people will come to your home, help you set up your station, and teach you the rudiments of operation for a moderate fee. They will be available by phone for consultation, perhaps at a monthly service rate. The computer consultants I know of at present cater to businesses or to the user who has special program needs, and charge more than the average person can afford.

Computer dealers are beginning to fill a need that schools are ignoring—the need to teach people to use software. Some give seminars on the use of a particular program, such as *VisiCalc*, or a general approach to word processing. Unfortunately, these seminars are sometimes expensive, but may be worth the money if you need to learn to use a complicated program like *dBase II*.

Computer Centers

A relatively new phenomenon, which I hope will grow, is the computer center, where machines can be rented by the hour. I imagine they will become for adults what electronic-game arcades are for kids. But of course kids will visit these centers too. The fun part of computer centers is that you may find yourself being kibitzed by a nine-year-old who will clearly and enthusiastically explain something that your computer dealer only made more difficult.

If there isn't a friendly kid available, staff members will assist and teach you. You can stay as long or as short a time as you like, limited only by your schedule and your budget. You can visit anytime the store is open and expect to meet other people who are interested in learning about computers and who will eagerly and generously share information. And you can try out a variety of computers.

Tutorials

A variety of tutorials are published in a variety of media: casette tapes, disks, and video tapes. Some computer manufacturers now provide tutorials with their machines. Tutorials guide you step by step through the operation of a computer and/or its software. Their value is that when you make a mistake, you receive an instant explanation of what went wrong, and you are guided down the correct path. Your software dealer should be able to tell you what tutorials are available for your system; they are not widely advertised.

Television

Check your TV listings to see if *The Personal Computer Show* is aired in your area. This is an excellent way to introduce yourself to a whole spectrum of ideas about computers. The advertising is at least as educational as the show itself, because the ads are for computers and related products and services and will describe and demonstrate new products. *High Tech Times* is another to watch, although it is not confined solely to computers.

In some cities computer classes are available on the public education channel. I expect that more and more about computers is going to show up on TV, so check it out.

Classes

Before enrolling in a computer class be sure you know what topics will be covered and if they meet your needs. Ask how many different kinds of machines you will have an opportunity to use and if you will have a chance to try out various software packages. Find out how much emphasis will be placed on programming and the technicalities of electronic processes.

College classes still tend to be structured for technicians and programmers, but in the last year there has been a proliferation of classes given by computer consultants and dealers that are limited to teaching the use of certain popular software programs or a particular brand of computer. These are the most useful classes to the novice.

It is well documented that women have trouble learning technology in a male-dominated environment, and the dropout rate for women is high. A number of programs have developed to counter that problem, and there may be one in your area. The Women's Computer Literacy Project in San Francisco offers seminars for women only and has been phenomenally successful. Polly Taylor, whom you met earlier, is a graduate. After taking their seminar she went right out and started her own business. The Women's Computer Literacy Project is expanding to give seminars in major cities across the country. You can write to them at 1195 Valencia St., San Francisco CA 94110.

San Francisco State University offers a course titled "Computers Without Fear" for both men and women who feel they can't compete with the technology aces. There may be similar courses at one of your local schools. The EQUALS program and the Math/Science Network are expanding fast; check universities to see if either of these organizations have branches there. They may be able to guide you to women-oriented classes.

Documentation

Detailed instruction manuals, often referred to as *documentation*, come with your computer and the software you buy. So many of these manuals are so badly written that the situation is a joke in the computer industry.

Nonetheless, with some patience and a sense of the absurd, you can sit down with your computer and the manual and teach yourself everything you need to know. If you come across something you just can't understand, somewhere, on the other end of a telephone, is someone who can explain it to you. It may be your dealer, a person employed by the computer or software manufacturer who does nothing but answer questions over the phone, or a member of your users' group.

You can't break your computer by pressing the wrong key. Sometimes you can bumble so badly that you may ruin your software or your document disk, but if you take the sound advice to make backup copies of *everything* before you even *think* of using it, there is no mistake that is irreparable.

Bumbling around on your own is really the best way to become familiar with your machine and to gain confidence. By making miqtakes again and again, and finding out that nothing terrible happens, you break through your initial resistance and learn a lot, too.

The most important factor that affects your learning process is your attitude. There is nothing difficult about computer technology; there is just so much to know that it looks and feels overwhelming if you look at it all at once. The trick is to slow down and take it one step at a time, and find out who the people are who will answer questions willingly and with clarity. As women, most of us have been conditioned to be resistant to knowledge that involves math, technology, mechanics, and science, but this conditioning can be overcome with patience, and eventually it will crumble altogether. Making contact with other women who are learning about computers should be immeasurably helpful and supportive. Chapter 11, which discusses networking, includes a list of organizations that will put you in contact with women who have similar interests to yours.

But even if you live where there are no such resources, you can teach yourself. Others have learned this way, and you can, too.

FIFTEEN

Hardware Primer I: The Computer

Most personal computers are marketed as attractively packaged units usually including a display screen, a keyboard, and at least one disk drive. In many people's minds the word *computer* refers to this integrated unit. However, technically, a computer is only the hardware elements that do calculations and process information. The devices by which the computer communicates with the operator and other machines are *peripheral devices*, often referred to simply as *peripherals*. This distinction is useful to remember because considering peripherals separately from computers allows more options in buying a system. You can "mix and match" various devices: the display screen that comes with your computer is not necessarily the one you are required to use; disk drives may be added or replaced.

This chapter explains the elements of the computer itself. Peripherals are explained in chapter 16.

RAM

RAM stands for *random access memory*, which simply means that the computer operator can put information into memory and take information out. When the computer is turned off, everything in RAM is lost. That is why your computer must have a storage medium such as a tape or disk to store data on if you want to keep it permanently, or at least until the next time you want to work on it.

You also load your programs into RAM whenever you want to work with them. The bigger and more complex the program, the more RAM space you need, so RAM size is an important factor to consider when choosing your computer. RAM capacity is expressed in terms of kilobytes, symbolized by the letter K. Although *kilo* means 1,000, when you're talking about computers a kilobyte is 1,024 bytes. A byte is a configuration of bits, usually eight, and a bit is one unit of binary information. But you don't have to remember all that. Just remember that the number of K tells you the amount of information that can be held in RAM. You must know how much RAM your computer has to know if it will run your programs. All computer manufacturers will tell you how much RAM they provide, and all programs will tell you how much RAM they require. Just make sure the computer RAM is equal to, and preferably larger than, the RAM requirement of any program you want to run.

Many microcomputers on the market are sold with a minimum amount of RAM to get you started, and are then expandable by adding extra memory "boards" later. These computers are intended for people who want an inexpensive computer to learn on, or who don't want to do more than play a few simple games or run some very elementary programs. If they find they are hooked and want to expand to more capability, they can. For those people such systems fill a real need, but I am assuming you are reading this book because you want a computer to do serious work for you, and that calls for certain minimum requirements in several areas. For RAM, I would suggest that you settle for nothing less than 64K to start with. Even the cheapest personal computers in the workhorse category on the market currently offer that much RAM. (The amount of RAM in a computer is a function of what type of microprocessor it has; we will get to that shortly.) If you start with less RAM and have to expand it later, you may end up paying much more than it would have cost you to buy 64K of RAM in the first place.

Buying minimal RAM with the intention of expanding it later is an option you may have to consider if your finances are tight, but it should be a last resort, and be *sure* the system is expandable.

ROM

ROM (*read only memory*) is the "permanent" memory in your computer. I put *permanent* in quotes because some ROMs can be altered by the user. The read-only memory is permanent in the sense that nothing in ROM is lost when the computer is turned off. In some computers ROM holds the operating system, and many computers now have applications programs stored in ROM, an excellent plan that I hope becomes more popular.

While the amount of RAM is a very important factor in your choice of computer, the amount of ROM is not—it will always be adequate for any particular system.

The Microprocessor, or CPU

CPU stands for *central processing unit*. It executes instructions, controls operations, and performs the built-in logic and arithmetic functions of the microcomputer. Although it is often referred to as the "brain" of the computer, the CPU does nothing on its own and must receive instructions from a higher authority: the operating system and the software. The CPU is more akin to the central nervous system, which receives messages from the brain, performs automatic functions, and distributes instructions to the working parts of the body.

The CPU is a microprocessor, which is a lot of processing circuitry on one tiny silicon chip. A number of different kinds of microprocessors are in use for computers, and the kind of microprocessor is almost always designated in the specifications you read in reviews and product literature. You don't need to know the differences between each because the differences show up in performance described in other terms that are easier to compare.

However, you should know the difference between the two most common *types* of microprocessors, 8-bit and 16-bit, because this is an important distinction. *Bit* is a contraction of *binary digit*, which is one item of digital information—a 0 or a 1. The terms *8-bit* and *16-bit* refer to the number of bits a microprocessor can handle at once ("in parallel"). You can see that a 16-bit microprocessor ought to be able to handle information much, much faster than an 8-bit machine because it handles twice as much information at one time, but in practice it doesn't always work out that way, because the speed of processing depends on other design factors as well. That's why the IBM PC, which has a 16-bit microprocessor, performs more slowly than some 8-bit machines on certain benchmark tests. Most of the 16-bit machines on the market as I write this are not "true" 16-bit computers; other architectural design factors limit their ability to utilize fully the potential power of their 16-bit microprocessors.

At this stage in the evolution of computer design, a 16-bit machine does not have enough speed and memory advantages to justify the extra cost for the person who is going to use it for a home business and who has a limited budget. Some of the 16-bit machines are indeed faster than 8-bit computers, and some offer "windowing," which allows access to more than one file at a time (a great convenience), but these are luxuries, not necessities. The main advantage of 16-bit machines is that they allow for much larger RAM (random access memory), thus allowing the use of much larger and more powerful programs than has been possible on the 8-bit machines, which until recently have been limited to 64K of memory. The 16-bit microcomputers usually have anything from 128K to 640K RAM (although theoretically they can have up to 16 million bytes, architectural limitations keep them from reaching that potential). That's a great deal more memory than the conventional 8-bit machines, but even this advantage is a temporary one, since ways have now been found to increase memory in 8-bit machines.

The 16-bit microcomputers are a more recent development than the 8-bit machines and are much more expensive. Unless you have reason to want a program that requires a very large memory, an 8-bit machine will be adequate and will cost you much less. People trying to sell you a 16-bit machine will tell you that (1) 8-bit machines are obsolete and (2) no one is writing new software for them. It is not true that 8-bit computers are obsolete: Japanese computer manufacturers have recently developed a high-speed, large-memory, low-cost 8-bit system standard called MSX that is already popular in Europe and that will soon be introduced in the United States. As for the second objection, no one needs to write new software for 8-bit computers because there is a wealth of excellent software already available and that will continue to be available far into the future.

I ignored the 16-bit computers and kept cranking along on my junky old 8-bit Osborne 1 until the Atari STs became available. These computers, like Apple's Macintosh and Commodore's Amiga, are based on the Motorola 68000, a *32-bit* microprocessor. (Currently, 32-bit CPUs are limited by the computer's architecture in the same way that 16-bit machines are; that is, they are functionally only 16-bit machines in some operations just as the 16-bit computers are functionally only 8-bit machines in some operations.) However, the Atari STs are selling for less than most 8-bit suitable-for-business computers and for about half the price of their closest cousin, the Amiga. The 520ST sells for about $800 (including display screen and disk drive) and comes with 512K of RAM. Both STs come with a package of features usually found only on computers costing two to four times as much. They are high-performance low-cost machines and I enthusiastically recommend them as well-suited for home businesses. Compare them feature for feature with the famous IBM PC and with the Amiga and the Macintosh, then compare the price.

I believe the Atari STs will define the standard for inexpensive microcomputers for some time to come, and in order to compete, Atari's rivals will have to come out with computers of comparable performance and value. Such machines may be on the market by the time you read this, but use the STs as standards against which to measure other computers.

Clock Speed

The clock synchronizes the computer's operations, and the higher the frequency of the clock, the faster the machine can process data and instructions. "Higher frequency" means more cycles per second.

Since few people are aware of the clock and its central role in determining the speed of the computer, many hardware reviews in magazines omit mention of it. But the clock speed is definitely something you should ask about and compare among computers. Speeds have increased from 1 megahertz (1 million cycles per second) a few years ago to 12 megahertz today, and 25 MHz is on the horizon. Most microcomputers have clock speeds between 2 and 8 megahertz.

Unfortunately, there are many other factors that affect how fast a computer processes information, and the clock speed is not an absolute indicator—it tells you how fast the micropro-cessor *could* run, not how fast it *does* run. It *is* an upper limit, however. A computer with a clock speed of 8 MHz may in fact only run at 4 MHz because of design limitations. But a computer with a 2 MHz clock can never run faster than 2 MHz no matter how well it is designed. When all other factors are equal, choose the computer with the higher clock speed.

Operating System

If the applications program is your chief administrator, the operating system is office manager. It is the go-between, or interface, between your applications program and the computer, passing along each command to the appropriate part of the computer, and coordinating work.

The operating system may be permanently programmed in-side your computer, or it may be on a disk that you will have to load like any other program when you start up your machine. Although it is somewhat more convenient to have it residing in the computer's internal memory (ROM), whether or not it does isn't a significant factor in choosing your machine.

What *is* significant, however, is that all applications pro-grams are operating-system dependent, meaning that a pro-gram written for one operating system won't run on another operating system unless it is modified. So, the particular operat-ing system is a significant factor in your choice of computers because it will determine what software you can use. (The most successful and popular programs may be available in several versions for different operating systems, however.)

If there were only one standard operating system, and one way to format disks, you would be able to run any program on any computer, and read and write on any disk of a compatible size. But this is the planet earth and it is run by a bunch of noodles—us. So we have many different operating systems for computers. The situation is analogous to having to buy records made especially for your own kind of record player, and not being able to play them on anyone else's phonograph unless it is the same brand as yours.

All operating systems work well for their own machines. It would be silly to say that any one system is better than all others—they all have strengths and weaknesses. You will hear that CP/M and MS-DOS come the closest to being industry standards because they are the operating systems of choice for more different computers than any others—CP/M for 8-bit machines and MS-DOS for 16-bit. Perhaps the best thing about these operating systems is that a lot of software is available for them, both commercial and, in the case of CP/M, public domain (free). Some of the free software is very good. You can find out what free software for CP/M is available from CP/M user groups or user groups for brands of computers that use CP/M.

CP/M-86 is a version of CP/M for 16-bit machines. However, the current *standard* for 16-bit machines is MS-DOS, due to the irrational belief of many computer manufacturers that in order to survive they must make their machines compatible with the IBM PC. However, Apple, Tandy (Radio Shack), Commodore, and others have their own proprietary operating systems— meaning no other brand can use the same operating system.

The operating system is the single most important factor in determining compatibility with other computers, if you have a need for such compatibility.

I/O Ports

Input/output ports are connecting interfaces (plugs, sort of) that allow the computer to communicate with other devices such as modems, printers, and external monitors.

Unfortunately, different devices require different kinds of ports, so you must be sure that the computer you buy has all the I/Os you are going to need. If you buy a portable with a very small screen you may want to use an external monitor whenever possible; be sure the portable has a video (or monitor) port. If you think you may want to add another disk drive at a later date, be sure it can be done without major modifications. Anything you want to add must have a place to connect to. Think carefully now and try to anticipate your future needs.

The most common interface for printers and modems is the RS232C serial port. The RS232C simply refers to an industry standard, and *serial* refers to the way data is sent, one bit at a time. Data can also be sent parallel, or 8 bits at a time. Any computer you buy should have at least one serial port (but preferably two) and one parallel port.

Color, Graphics, Sound

There are some applications for which you may need color, graphics, or sound capabilities. These features may be essential to commercial artists and designers, or for creators of games and educational programs for children, or fine-arts artists experimenting with computers as generators of design or environments (I have walked through an artist's construction of angel hair and colored lights that responded to the disturbance my body created in photoelectric beams. It was all controlled with a computer). Marketing presentations may require color charts and graphs, or you may want to use the computer as an aid in teaching or writing music. Color, graphics, and/or sound may be essential for any of these applications.

Unless you have a real need for such features, however, it is better to buy a computer without them. Color graphics and games require different kinds of capabilities in a computer and its peripherals than common business applications require, and sometimes these are mutually exclusive. A printer that does a beautiful job on graphics, for instance, will usually not give you the best quality printing on correspondence and manuscripts. If you have a fantasy of buying a computer that will be a workhorse for you and an entertainment/education center for your children, for the most part you are going to be disappointed. Most games and educational software require all three features— color, graphics, and sound. Unless you need color for your business purposes, you will not want to spend extra hundreds of dollars for a high quality color monitor so that your children can play games. Not all computers handle graphics; again, if you don't need that capability for your business applications there is no sense in paying extra for it. In general, the operating systems that are good for games are not good for business programs and vice versa. You may be better off to buy two computers: one for your business and a small games computer that can hook up to your color TV for the kids. Dramatic exceptions to this rule are the Atari STs, which are so cheap that, for far less than you would pay for most 16-bit computers, you can buy a system with a monochrome monitor for your business use, and add a color monitor for graphics and games. The Ataris handle both business and games applications well. So does the Amiga, but the difference is—the price!

SIXTEEN

Hardware Primer II: Peripheral Devices

You will recall that any device that enables your computer to communicate with the outside world is called a *peripheral*. Peripherals include keyboards, display screens, disk drives, modems, printers, and anything else you might add to your system to enhance its communication capability.

A microcomputer normally comes equipped with several peripheral devices—such as a display screen, a keyboard, and at least one disk drive. Other peripherals are normally purchased separately—printers and modems, for example.

For the sake of completeness, the assumption in this chapter is that each peripheral is being considered as an add-on device, and compatibility with the computer is discussed. When the device is built in, of course these discussions do not apply. But when considering what computer to buy, you should evaluate the built-in peripherals just as carefully as if you were buying them separately.

If you like a particular computer but a peripheral device is not satisfactory, you can usually add one that is more to your liking. For example, if the computer has a poor-quality display screen, you can buy a separate external monitor. Computers with only one disk drive usually have the capacity to add another drive. Such adaptations add to the cost of your system, of course, and it is wise to look further; perhaps there is a system that has everything you want without the expense of add-ons.

Mass Storage

There are three main types of permanent data-storage media: floppy disks, cassette tapes, and hard disks.

Cassette tapes are attractive because they are cheap, and because you can often use a cassette player you already own and avoid the expense of purchasing one for your computer. Cassette players are often provided or recommended with the less-expensive computers, particularly the game computers. Cassette tapes are not suitable for business applications, however, mainly because they are too slow. Because of the way floppy disks are configured, your computer can go straight to the exact place where a bit of data is stored (called *random access*). On an ordinary cassette tape, the computer must search through every bit of tape preceding the data you want (called *linear access*), and while it searches, you wait. This situation may change in the next few years, however. As I write this there are a few new types of tape cassettes on the market (new to the popular market, not to the computer industry) that are very fast compared to ordinary cassettes. They are perpetual-forward-type tapes—like the 8-track continuous-loop cassettes used for musical recordings—and they soon may be common and affordable. These tapes can be distinguished from regular cassette tapes because they are called *streaming tape cartridges*. These tapes can hold massive amounts of data, making them attractive in spite of their linear access. Their most suitable use is as backup storage for hard disks.

The most common storage medium in use right now is the floppy disk, called floppy because it bends. These come in 5¼-inch and 8-inch diameters, and a new type that varies between 3-inch and 3½-inch, depending on the manufacturer. What size disk you use depends on the size of the disk drive in your computer. Floppy disks are changing very fast as the industry finds ways to pack more and more data on one disk. How much data one disk will hold is described in terms of density—single, double, or quad—and whether it is single or double-sided. A double-density disk will hold approximately twice as much as a single-density disk, and a quad-density disk will hold four times as much as a single-density disk. A double-sided disk will hold twice as much as a single-sided disk and is used in disk drives that can access both sides.

Under development are isotropic 5¼-inch floppy disks that can hold 5 megabytes per side—or roughly 15 times more than a quad-density disk. In practical terms the capacity is 1,000 to 2,000 pages of single-spaced text per disk!

Disk drives are also rated by density. A single-density disk drive will not read a double- or quad-density disk, although you can read down—that is, a quad-density drive will read a single-density disk. A single-sided disk drive will read only a single-sided disk; a double-sided disk drive will read both sides of a double-sided disk (as well as a single-sided disk). You buy the type of disk that is compatible with your drives.

In general, the more density the better, and double-sided disks are better than single-sided, because the more storage on one disk, the less time you spend changing disks back and forth. When I bought my Osborne 1, the only drives available for it were single density, and the Osborne uses 5¼-inch disks. These disks hold about 35 double-spaced pages of copy, which seemed ample to me when it was only theory. In practice I found it was not enough, and I upgraded my computer to double density so I could get 70 or more pages on a disk—much more convenient when you are working with book-length material. Recently I bought a new computer with quad-density double-sided 3½-inch disks. Each disk holds 720K, or 8 times more than my original 5¼-inch disks—smaller disks do not mean less storage! Ways are continually being found to increase density. 8-inch disks can hold up to about 700K, but most microcomputers come equipped with 5¼-inch drives and 8-inch drives must be added on. I believe that 3½-inch disk drives will become more popular because, in addition to their high storage capacity, their small size makes them easy to handle and store.

Although floppy disks are faster and more reliable than cassette tapes, they are prone to failure from any number of environmental factors, such as oil from your hands, dust, cold, and electromagnetic disturbances of various kinds. It is frustrating and depressing when you have recorded hours, perhaps days, of work on a disk, and it crashes (fails) so that you cannot retrieve the data. At present the best protection against such catastrophes is to make duplicate copies (commonly called *backups*) of all your disks. Every piece of documentation you receive with your computer and your programs will advise you to form this habit, and it is advice you should certainly heed. But best of all would be a medium where such catastrophes didn't happen. This is another area where 3½-inch disks shine—they come in protective cartridges and are far less prone to contamination and failure than floppies (which come in envelopes with holes in them).

Hard disks, sometimes called *Winchester disks*, are based on an entirely different principle from floppies, and hold vast quantities of data. They are very tempting to buy because they are faster and much more convenient. However, they are expensive (although they are getting cheaper all the time) and have two main flaws: there is no quick and easy way to make backup copies of your data, and they are extremely delicate, so that when they crash, you have real troubles. Manufacturers are working very hard to overcome these problems, however, and by the time you read this, technology advances may have improved their reliability. But I caution you to investigate thoroughly before you buy a hard disk. Talk with people who own them and read articles about them in the current computer magazines. There is no question that when the wrinkles get ironed out they will be the best means of mass storage that is also affordable.

All but the very cheap personal computers come with a data-storage device built in. Usually this is a 5¼-inch or 3½-inch disk drive; some personal computers have built-in hard disks in addition to a floppy-disk drive. If it would be valuable to have disks that are interchangeable between various computers, buy a computer with 5¼-inch disk drives—several programs exist that allow computers with different disk formats to read from and write to each other's disks. For business applications, two disk drives are essential unless you have a hard disk.

Monitor, Display, Video Display

All these terms refer to the same thing.

A monitor is anything that allows you to see what you are doing on the computer. It can be a built-in screen, or an external screen that is connected to your computer through a special "port," or your TV set. If your computer does not have a screen built in, you will have to select an external monitor.

Because eyestrain is so common among computer users, the monitor is an important consideration in the choice of a system, whether as an integrated part of the computer or purchased separately. The screen should have sharp, clear images, adjustable brightness and contrast, and a nonglare screen. There should be no distortion at the edges and corners of the screen, no halos around letters and images, and no flickering. As you move the cursor (see p. 223) across the screen, no trail of light should follow it. Lines of text should be straight and even.

Screen sizes range from 5-inch to about 25-inch (measured diagonally, like a TV); a 12-inch screen is a good choice for anyone who must be at the terminal for hours every day. If you buy a portable computer with a tiny screen, you can add on a separate large-screen monitor—but be sure the computer has a place to connect it (called a *video port*).

Monochrome (single color) monitors show white, green, or amber images against a dark background. Amber displays seem to be growing in popularity; be sure to try out all three colors to determine which you feel most comfortable with. (If the computer comes with its own monitor, you may not have a choice.)

Monochrome displays are the best choice for someone who has no need of color, since monochromes are much cheaper and have better resolution (sharpness) than low-priced color displays. To get high resolution on a color monitor, you must pay two to four times more than for a monochrome, and of course there is no sense in doing that if you have no need of a color display. This price difference is one of the reasons it is usually not practical to use the same computer for both games and business applications. Monochrome displays sell for as little as $100, with most falling in the $150 to $250 range.

If you have a need to create color graphics, or if you are going to tutor children using educational software, you will need a color monitor. With color, the choices become slightly more complicated. Color monitors are of two types: composite-video and RGB.

Composite-video monitors use the same principle as your TV, which is a simpler technology than RGB, and so these are cheaper, but their resolution is inferior. They are not a good choice for prolonged work at the terminal, although they are quite adequate for games. The retail price ranges from $300 to $400.

RGBs (RGB is short for red-green-blue) have crisper images and some have a wide range of subtle and beautiful colors. Unfortunately, prices start at about $400 and can go as high as several thousand dollars. Most color monitors support at least 16 colors; the top-tech RGBs can give literally millions of color gradations. RGBs are of no use if your computer cannot utilize their capabilities. A 16-color monitor won't do you any good if your computer will only handle 8. Make sure your computer supports RGB color monitors before buying one.

A number of variables affect the resolution of a monitor. One of these is bandwidth, or the rate at which the monitor can accept data from the computer. Bandwidth is expressed in megahertz, or MHz. The low bandwidth of most TVs makes them unsuitable for prolonged use as computer monitors. Although their resolution is adequate for pictures, they cannot give clear alphanumeric display. When selecting a monitor, you should know at what rate your computer sends data to the monitor. There is no point in paying for a 25-MHz monitor if your computer transmits at 12 MHz. If you can't find this information in your computer manual, ask your dealer or call the manufacturer.

Another variable affecting resolution is the pixel density on your screen. Pixels (short for picture elements) are the little dots of light that make up the image. The closer together they are, the more solid the picture and the sharper the image on the screen. The number of pixels on a screen is expressed by two numbers, the horizontal and vertical pixels—some as low as 165 x 126, others as high as 1,280 x 1,024. In general, more is better. It would make sense to rate pixels by density, or the number of pixels per square inch. If you want to compare the pixel density of a 12-inch monitor and a 9-inch, you have to do some involved mathematics, because the number of pixels is given for the entire screen. An easier way to compare pixel density is by dot pitch, or how close together the dots are. A dot pitch of less than .4mm indicates a high-resolution screen, from .4 to .6mm is medium resolution, and over .6mm is low resolution. You may have to call the manufacturer to get this information; the specification sheets on monitors do not always specify the dot pitch.

My experience is that the resolution of a computer is an important factor in preventing eyestrain, and I strongly recommend that you buy a computer with a high-resolution display.

The best monochrome monitor I have seen on a low-cost computer is the one that comes with the Atari ST. It is black-and-white with 640 x 400 resolution.

Video-display technology is such that the more you get from the monitor, whether it is a wide range of colors and/or high resolution, the more memory in the computer it needs to do its work. For this and the other reasons stated above, if you buy a monitor separately from your computer, it is important to be sure that your computer will support the monitor's capabilities.

Keyboard

Computer keyboards differ from typewriter keyboards because they have special keys to control features that typewriters do not have. For example, a little mark called a cursor appears on the computer screen to tell you exactly where you are working. There must be something on the keyboard that allows you to move the cursor around the screen to where you want it. This is usually done with arrow keys (there are four keys with an arrow for each direction).

The most important key is the control key. When the control key is depressed, a number of letter keys on the keyboard change function and become command keys. In *WordStar*, for example, holding the control key down while you type the letter Y will delete an entire line of text (the line where the cursor is at the moment). The control key is similar to the shift key on a typewriter except that instead of converting letters to capitals it changes letters to commands. All computer keyboards have this key.

Most computer keyboards have number keys in the standard typewriter locations, but also have a numeric keypad on the right side of the keyboard for serious number crunching. If you intend to work often with numbers and are accustomed to a calculator keyboard, be sure your computer includes this feature.

Progammable function keys allow you to program one key to represent a whole series of instructions when it is used with the control key. For example, there is a command I use frequently when transferring files from one disk to another: $B: = A:^*.^*[v]$. Don't worry about what it means, just notice that it contains eleven keystrokes, not counting the shift for the *, $:$, and $]$. By programming a function key, I can write this command with two strokes—the control key and the function key. Very convenient. Much longer instructions can also be programmed under one key. An added benefit of this function is that you don't have to memorize long instructions that are as hard to remember as chemistry formulas.

Programmable function keys are not included with all computers. Although you may not see an immediate use for them when you first start computing, later they will be quite a convenience, and I suggest you consider this feature a highly desirable one.

If you listen to the experts about the importance of a detachable keyboard, you'll save time and trouble by eliminating, from the start, a slew of computers with attached keyboards. Many physical problems associated with computer work have been traced to work-station design. When the user must always work in a certain position she is more likely to develop eyestrain and backaches. A detached keyboard with a flexible extension cord allows you to work in any position you like and to vary your distance from the screen. Consider the possibilities a detached keyboard opens up, such as working in bed. This is such an important feature that I wouldn't consider buying any computer with an attached keyboard.

Since the keyboard is the sole physical interface between you and the computer, it should be tried for fit and comfort as carefully as you try a pair of walking shoes. Anyone who types knows how important touch is, and how much it differs from one typewriter to another. Touch is often adjustable on typewriter keyboards; on computer keyboards it is not (so far). It's advisable to spend some time typing on the keyboard of any computer you consider buying to find out if it has the right feel for you. Some keyboards have keys that tend to stick; others have oddly shaped keys that are difficult to get used to.

So, the rule is: *Try it before you buy it.*

Printers

There are several different types of printers, but the most common types used with personal computers are dot matrix and letter quality.

Dot matrix printers form letters by combining many tiny dots to form the shape of a character. The dots are made either by little rods that are pushed against an inked ribbon, or by tiny jets of quick-drying ink blown through holes to the paper. Because the rods or the holes are in a head that does not have to move to bring characters into position to be printed, these printers are very fast. Also, the dots can be activated in any combination, allowing many more configurations than just letters, numbers, and symbols; these are the printers that do all the fancy graphics so often featured on the covers of computer magazines.

Letter quality printers use some form of print ball or wheel. Some are the "golf ball" type such as the ball used on Selectric typewriters, but most are "daisy wheels," which are disk-shaped, with the characters on the end of little petals—thus the name *daisy wheel*. A third type is the "thimble," which is a daisy wheel with the petals bent at right angles to the disk. On each of these variations, the whole wheel must turn to bring each character to the right place for impact; consequently, these printers are much slower than the dot-matrix type. However, they also produce much more attractive print, usually indistinguishable from typewritten copy, which is why they are called *letter quality*. They cost more than dot-matrix printers and are not useful for anything more than very primitive graphics, since they are limited to the number of characters and symbols that fit on one print wheel.

Your first decision about a printer, then, is whether you want dot matrix or letter quality. (Letter quality printers are sometimes referred to generally as daisy wheel printers, but that is slightly inaccurate since not all letter quality printers are daisy-wheel printers.)

When speed, low price, and/or graphics capability are high priority factors, the choice is dot matrix. When producing high quality copy that looks like it came from a typewriter is the primary consideration, you need a letter quality printer.

The perfect printer would be a dot matrix that produces letter-quality copy, but so far no one has been able to overcome fully the limitations inherent in dot matrix technology. Many people are trying, and they come closer and closer, but ultimately, no letter made up of dots—no matter how fine and densely spaced—can quite equal the clean, sharp lines from the integrated characters of impact wheels. I hope someone makes a liar of me soon, because letter quality printers are slow, expensive, and cannot form any but the crudest sort of graphics—yet, that's the kind you must buy if your most important need is professional looking "typewritten" copy.

Which type of printer you buy will depend on the requirements of your particular business applications. If you must do graphics then of course you must buy a dot-matrix printer. But if you will use your printer primarily for business correspondence, manuscripts, and reports, and have no need for graphics, you should buy the letter-quality printer.

After the primary choice of type, the important considerations in choosing a printer are:

Speed. The speed of printers is designated by the number of characters they will print per second (written as *cps*). Dot matrix printers are much faster than letter quality, printing from 30 to several hundred cps, the majority being in the 100 to 200 cps range. Letter-quality printers start at about 15 cps and reach a maximum of about 60. If that sounds very slow in comparison to dot matrix, consider: when I'm in my very best form, I can type ten double-spaced pages per hour. My 55-cps letter-quality printer turns out 90 to 100 pages. I'm happy.

Buy the fastest printer you can afford. It will make a difference when you are busy. Speed is one of the most important comparisons to make between printers that may otherwise be similar.

Paper feed. Paper is fed to the printer in one of two ways. The first is by roller (friction) feed, which is exactly the same method used in a typewriter. This is the best way to feed individual sheets of paper.

On tractor feed printers you use continuous fanfold paper with holes on each side. The holes fit over sprockets on wheels on the tractor device, and each time there is a "line feed" the wheels move the paper forward a line. After printing, the sides of the paper with the holes in them can be torn off. High quality paper is available that is so finely perforated you can only tell it is fanfold paper by looking very closely at the edges.

My recommendation is that you buy a printer that has both mechanisms. You can't appreciate the speed and convenience of a tractor feed until you have used one, but there will be times when you need to slip a special sheet of paper in the roller and print something on it, and without roller feed you just can't do it.

Type styles. Most letter quality printers have a good selection of typefaces to choose from. You can buy several fonts and change them easily, but to change type styles within a document you have to stop the printer and change fonts manually.

Type styles on dot-matrix printers are controlled by software, and it is very easy to have several styles within one document. Some "dot addressable" printers allow you to design your own symbols and letters using special software. This is also the type of dot matrix you should buy for the highest possible quality graphics and print.

Variable character and line spacing, superscript, subscript, boldface, underscore, strikeover, and alternate pitch are features that are available on both types of printer. Be sure you have software that supports these features or they won't do you any good.

Ribbons. Ribbons for printers come in the same formats as ribbons for typewriters: in cartridges or spools, fabric or film. Film cartridges are tops for quality and ease of installation, but of course they cost more. When printers require ribbons available only from the printer manufacturer, they are likely to be very expensive. When looking at printers, always ask about ribbon costs (when comparing, be sure you also ask for the number of impressions per ribbon, as they may vary in length). Prices vary significantly.

Compatibility. Not all printers will operate with all computers. Be sure the printer you buy is guaranteed to run with your computer. Some computers require that a separate printer-interface card be installed internally; all will require a cable to connect the printer to your computer's appropriate port or interface. Many problems arise because different manufacturers wire the RS232 port in a variety of ways, so that a printer with an

RS232 connection will not necessarily communicate correctly through a particular computer's RS232 port. These problems can usually be solved by changing the configuration of the connecting *cable*, but many dealers don't know how to do this. For this reason, (1) don't assume that a printer will work with your computer just because it is "RS232 compatible," and (2) don't buy the printer unless you have a money-back guarantee that the dealer will get it working for you.

Your printer's features must be supported by your computer and its software. It is a good idea to buy a popular, standard printer because it is likely to be one of those supported by your computer—check for sure before you buy. If you want to do graphics, particularly color, you may save yourself a lot of grief by buying a printer designed specifically to work with the computer you own.

Word processing features also must be supported by your software—things such as variable spacing, superscript, boldface, strikeover, and underscoring.

Print buffers and spoolers. My *WordStar* program allows me to write or edit one file while another is printing if the second file is on the same disk as the file being printed, but the writing is slowed down considerably. I have found it less nerve-racking to turn over my computer to the printer and go have a cup of tea while a file is printing out. One man in my Osborne-users' group prints so much that he bought a second Osborne solely to run his printer, and it is in use all the time. However, that seems an extreme measure. Part of your dealer's demonstration should include how easily and quickly work can be done on the computer while it is sending files to the printer.

Print buffers and print spoolers are devices that speed things up by managing the information sent to the printer; they free your computer to do other work while a file is being printed; but I suggest you wait to buy such devices until you have had your computer and printer for a while and know exactly what your needs are.

Modems

A modem is essential to communicate from one computer to another over a telephone line. A modem is a device that trans-

lates the digital electrical signals from your computer into audio
signals that can be transmitted over your phone line. The modem
at the other end of the line will translate the message back into
digital signals. This process is called *modulating* and *de-
modulating*, and *modem* is an acronym of these two words.

Some computers are now being made with communications
capability already built in, and I foresee a day when almost all
computers will be so equipped. If the computer you buy has
such capability you should consider it a sizable advantage, but
only if you *need* it, since it will add to the cost of your basic
system. On the other hand, a separate modem will probably
cost you between $200 and $600, so calculate accordingly.

Modems transmit data at varying rates called baud rates.
Baud rate is not technically defined as the number of bits
transmitted per second, but in practice that's how it works out.
You don't need to remember what *baud* means, but you do
need to remember that the higher the baud rate, the faster
information is transmitted—an important consideration if you
pay long-distance charges to transmit data or access one of the
on-line (accessible by telephone) services such as CompuServe.

The two standard baud rates for personal-computer modems
are 300 and 1200. The 300-baud modems are cheaper, but if you
foresee making any significant use of long-distance access, I
urge you to spend the extra $200 or so to buy a 1200-baud
modem. It sends and receives data four times faster than the
more common 300-baud type and therefore will cut your phone
charges by 75 percent. You will save the extra cost very quickly.
You will also save money on the charges made by on-line
services. Although they normally charge you higher rates for
1200-baud access—in the case of CompuServe, the charge for
1200-baud is twice the rate for 300-baud—since you transmit
four times faster you cut costs by half by using the 1200-baud
system.

Some computers allow you to give your modem commands
directly from the keyboard. Others do not and require a communications program to complete your kit. One of the best
programs available is a public-domain program called *MODEM
7*; *public domain* means you don't have to pay for the program,
except perhaps the cost of the disk it comes on. You can get a
copy from anyone who has it, and almost any users' group is

bound to come up with one for you. You just have to make sure it is a version adapted for your particular make of computer. *MODEM7* can also be downloaded from CompuServe or The Source.

Another choice you need to make when buying a modem is whether you want an acoustic coupler or direct-connect type. The acoustic coupler is a device on which you place the telephone handset. It receives and sends signals by the same routes used to recieve and send voice. The direct-connect type plugs into a modular phone jack and no telephone is used at all. It transmits a cleaner signal and there is less chance of problems in transmission and reception. This type is more expensive. Lastly, the better modems are "intelligent." They can be programmed to do a number of things automatically: they can place a call and transmit data at some future time designated by you; they can answer calls and accept data the same way; routines you perform often—such as dialing numbers and entering access codes—can be programmed to be done automatically. Of course, you pay more for an intelligent modem.

S E V E N T E E N

A Strategy for Buying Hardware

The process of selecting a computer system can be made simple if you take the time to carefully define your needs before you begin to shop.

There are four primary decisions you need to make before you start shopping. The first and most important decision is what you want to use the computer for (which really means what software you want to run on it); the second is whether your computer must be able to use the same disks and programs as another computer—for example, a computer owned by one of your clients or a friend; the third is what specific features you would like the computer to have; and the fourth is how much money you can spend.

WHAT ARE YOU GOING TO USE THE COMPUTER FOR?

The first step in intelligent computer shopping is to make a list of everything you think you might do with your computer. Are you going to do word processing? Accounting? Inventory? Apartment management? Cost analysis? Information retrieval from on-line database services? Communication with other computers? Programming? Games and educational software?

Although you don't want to buy more power than you need, be careful not to define your needs too narrowly, because it will be cheaper, generally, to buy the capability you need now than to have to add on in the future, or worse, to find out that you can't do something you want to do without buying an entirely different system. Maybe you want to do only word processing now, but ask yourself what you might be doing three years hence. Anticipating your needs now and buying a system that already has the capabilities, or that can have them added economically, will save you money and grief later.

The next step is to become familiar with the programs available to do the jobs you have listed, using the guidelines set out in chapters 18, 19, and 20, which deal with software. In other words, shop for your software first—but don't buy yet. Pick the top three programs you like for each job, so that you are not locked in—you may want to make tradeoffs between a program you like and a computer you like. The program you like best may not run on the computer you like best, so if you have a few backup choices you will have a better chance of matching a good program with a good computer.

DO YOU NEED COMPATIBILITY?

Your second step is to decide whether you need a computer that is compatible with other systems owned by your friends and/or potential customers. If your friend, partner, husband, customer, or boss has a computer and it is important to be able to share programs and run disks interchangeably, you must buy a compatible computer, which will narrow your field of choices considerably and make decisions a lot simpler. Often the easiest thing to do is to buy exactly the same model. However, some of the newer computers are compatible with several other machines, so you may be able to buy a different brand that is not only compatible with the computer you want to work with, but that has more features and more computing power. Most notable in this category are the IBM PC compatibles, the ones with MS-DOS operating systems. Once you have determined which brands are compatible with the computer(s) you must work with, you can still apply all the other strategies in this chapter to narrow down the field to a final choice.

WHAT FEATURES DO YOU WANT?

The list of jobs you want your computer to do, your choice of software, and your compatibility needs will determine most of the features you need in your computer and its peripherals. For example, if you have decided to design educational programs for children, you will need color and probably sound capabilities. If you are going to do word processing for hire, you will need a letter-quality printer rather than the dot matrix type.

By making a list of the jobs you want to do and choosing a tentative list of programs you want to buy, many of the features you need are selected for you automatically—my principal reason for recommending this strategy.

At the end of this chapter is a list of questions that, if you have followed the two suggestions above, will help you pin down the features that are essential to you. Those left are optionals. Copy these questions and your answers, or take this book with you when you shop, so that you can refer to them whenever you are tempted off the track by a computer that sings and blows bubbles in eighteen colors but won't hold more than ten words at a time in its memory. (It is *imperative* that you leave your eight-year-old at home while shopping for a computer.) Also, for the sake of your budget, it is as important to determine what you *don't* need as well as what you *do* need.

Compatibility

What if you had to buy a different radio for each station you want to listen to? Suppose every car sold had to have its own special gasoline—or every camera used a unique kind of film that would not work on any other camera. What a cry of outrage from consumers there would be! We would be furious; we would say this way of doing things was impractical and unworkable, if not absolutely crazy.

Yet, until very recently, programs written for one computer would not run on another, and this is still true for most programs. In most cases disks that contain data can be read only by the machine on which they were written. In some cases, once you buy a computer you must buy only the printer manufactured by that company, because no other printer will work with that machine; the same is true for some other peripherals. These three things—programs, disks, and peripherals—are dependent on hardware features of the individual computer.

This situation came about partly because the computer industry evolved according to the Topsy Principle: it just grew, without standards and without coordination, for the most part. Another part of the blame lies with greedy entrepreneurs who tried to create captive customers: once you buy an Acme Ace computer, to be sure your add-ons will work you must buy other Acme Ace products. Once you have invested a great deal of money in programs and peripherals for the Acme Ace, if you want to buy a new computer you have to buy another Acme or lose that investment, since nothing you own will work with any other brand of computer.

Fortunately, it has at last occurred to the computer industry that a certain amount of standardization is in its own best interests. Standardization allows components and software from one system to work with other systems, and that's what is meant by the term *compatibility*.

For instance, a small company has a better chance of competing with a large one if its computer will run the same software. Software developers are most interested in high-volume markets and concentrate their programming efforts on serving the needs of big names and big sellers like Apple, Tandy, and IBM, while ignoring computers that don't have huge sales potentials. But the small companies need quality software for their products, too. The solution? They design their machines to run the same programs as the industry leaders.

The introduction of the IBM PC set off an industry earthquake, and many IBM PC compatibles are on the market. The idea was that IBM is so big and so powerful in the marketplace that there were bound to be hundreds of programs written for their machine. To compete with IBM, the smaller companies have designed computers that are cheaper, have more features, and will run the same software as the IBM PC. To a large extent they have succeeded, but unfortunately they have also created headaches for the consumer because some of the software written for the IBM PC will run on the IBM compatibles and some won't. A critical element in IBM's design is copyrighted and can't be copied. If programmers writing their programs for the IBM avoid addressing that element directly, their programs will run well on other machines with IBM-compatible operating systems (MS-DOS). Some do and some don't. If you buy one of the IBM

PC compatibles, don't buy any program written for the IBM unless you have a guarantee in writing that you can return the program if it won't run correctly on your machine.

Compatibility is an important consideration for anyone who has a need for her computer to interact with other computers. There are two main areas of compatiblity to be concerned about: software and disk format.

Software. If it is important for you to be able to run the same programs as someone you are associated with (by this I mean actually using the same disks), the safest thing to do is to buy the same make and model of computer. Programs written for a particular operating system are not always interchangeable between machines using that operating system. If a program written for a particular computer addresses specific hardware properties of that machine, it will not work on another computer, even though it may have the same operating system. Sometimes software is not even interchangeable between different models made by the same company! Apple computers are well known for this incompatibility.

Disk format. Formatting is a function of the way in which the operating system locates data on the disk. Two computers with the same operating system may still be incompatible if they format disks differently. It is important to understand that a disk containing data only (not programs) can be read by any computer, with any operating system, if it is read under the same program which wrote it (in many cases even by different programs) and if the disk format of the reading computer is the same as the computer which wrote the disk. More and more computers now have the ability to read and write a variety of disk formats so that data can be exchanged between many different computers. There are also programs that can add this ability to a computer that was not originally designed that way.

Even if there is no disk compatibility, data can be exchanged easily by telephone and modem, since most data is encoded the same way. The easiest method, however, is simply to take a disk from one machine and insert it in another.

You must decide how important each form of compatibility is to you. Program compatibility is the trickiest of the two; data transfer between machines can always be worked out one way or another. If you don't mind buying your own versions of programs so that you can work in tandem with another computer, then you only need to buy a computer that reads and writes the same disk format, or learn to transfer data by telephone.

Expandability

If finances require that you start with a minimal system, be sure you buy one that can be expanded to meet your future needs, or you may have to buy a whole new system in a couple of years. Your computer should have at least one but preferably two serial ports and a parallel port. Various peripheral equipment may require either type and you should be prepared with both. Printers use both serial and parallel ports. Extra disk drives will require a parallel port. (Some computers allow you to add a disk drive by hooking it up internally.)

If you are considering a computer with less than 64K RAM, ask if additional memory is an option for your model. Some manufacturers now provide for the addition of a second operating system—for instance, some Apple models are equipped with the Apple operating system when you buy the computer, with an option to add CP/M. This expandability allows you to take advantage of a wealth of business software written for CP/M, while still enjoying the games and educational software written for the Apple system.

The Dimension 68000 allows expansion to use five different operating systems. Such a machine is ideal for someone who wants to do freelance consulting or programming and must be able to work on a variety of different computers. There are drawbacks to such machines, however. Expense is one of them, and "emulators" are notoriously slow.

Worksheet

Use the following worksheet to make preliminary decisions about your computer system. Many of these items will be determined by the software you choose. Some items will be decided by your compatibility needs, and some are simply reasonable minimum requirements for any business system. Where you don't have any answer, you have some flexibility in your choices. Refer to chapters 15 and 16 to refresh your memory on technical details.

COMPUTER:

Maximum price _____

Operating system, based on software choices and compatibility needs _____

Minimum RAM, based on largest software requirement. Recommended minimum, 64K _____

Color?_____ Graphics?_____ Sound?_____

Mass storage. Recommended: 5¼-inch or 3½-inch disks; a hard disk if budget allows it _____

Disk drives. Recommended: two double-density _____

Number of RS232 ports. Recommended minimum, 2 _____

Parallel ports. Recommended minimum, 1 _____

PRINTER:

Maximum price _____ color required _____

Type (dot matrix or letter-quality) _____

Paper feed. Recommended: both roller and tractor feed

_____

MODEM:

Maximum price _____

Type (acoustic coupler or direct connect). Recommended: direct connect _____

Baud rate (300 or 1200). Recommended: 1200 baud _____

Price

You can save yourself a lot of wasted time and energy if you analyze carefully, before you start to shop, exactly how much you can spend. The upper limit of your affordable investment will screen out whole classes of computers and peripherals before you even begin. What's comforting is that more expensive is not necessarily better. You may get fancier, you may get faster and more powerful, but what good is all that if you don't need it in the first place? A hard-disk drive, with its capacity of thousands of pages, is hardly a sensible investment for a student who is going to use a computer only for writing term papers. A letter-quality printer may be a waste of money for someone who wants only to print out computations for her own files. A 16-bit microprocessor may double or quadruple the RAM you have available to work with, but a reporter who uses it to write news stories that are never over a thousand words long is throwing her money away. (Ironically, 32-bit computers give you very large RAMs but some cost less than 16-bit machines.)

Following is a budget worksheet that will help you figure out what you can spend on each element of your computer system. Next are some general points to consider when shopping, and a discussion of ways to compare prices between computers. Finally, there is a shopping checklist for comparing various models of the components of your computer system. Photocopy this checklist and fill out one for each brand you consider. In this way you will have an organized way to compare features.

Budget

Start with the total amount you feel you can spend for a system. Then apportion the money according to the rough guidelines given below. For $2000 you can buy a good basic computer and an adequate modem and dot-matrix printer. For $3000 you can buy the same basic good computer plus a 300/1200-baud modem and a high quality printer. If you are willing to shop for used equipment you will save a great deal of money initially.

Total budget for entire system _____

COMPUTER. Allow $800 to $4000. For less than $2000 you can buy a good 8-bit computer, perfectly adequate for most business requirements, that has the following minimum features: 64K RAM, 2 double-density disk drives, 1 parallel and 2 RS232 ports, and a 12-inch monochrome monitor. The price goes up as you add things like good color and graphics capabilities, more RAM, a built-in modem, and hard disk drive. For about $1000 you can buy a 32-bit computer (the Atari 520ST) with 512K RAM, two double-sided double-density disk drives, 1 parallel and 1 serial port, and a 12-inch monochrome monitor. Prices of 16-bit computers vary greatly; allow a minimum of $2300 for 128K RAM, two disk drives, serial and parallel ports, and 12-inch monitor. _____

Printer. Allow $400 to $600 for simple dot matrix, to $2000 or more for sophisticated color graphics. Allow $1000 to $2000 for letter quality. _____

Modem. Allow $175 to $600, depending on baud rate and extra features, and whether you buy mail-order or from a dealer. The ADC Smart Duck has both 300 and 1200 baud and is an excellent buy at about $170 (mail order direct from manufacturer).

SOME GENERAL CONSIDERATIONS

The computer industry is notorious for releasing products before all the kinks are worked out. They rush their creations to market before they are thoroughly tested, in the hope of being the first with a computer with new or unusual capabilities. During the first two years a product is on the market all the bugs show up, and it usually takes that long to correct them, or, if the computer isn't going to make it, to drop out of the market.

Computer companies are also appearing and disappearing like fireflies. Therefore, it's a good general rule not to buy a computer from a company that has been in business fewer than five years, nor a computer that has been on the market less than two.

Another consideration is service. If you live in a large city there will be easy access to repair centers for any major brand, but if you live in a remote area, service can be a real problem (I ship my Osbornes from Utah to Berkeley for repair). Don't buy until you find out what your repair and service resources are.

Dealer support means that the dealer is willing to help you with any problems that come up (within reason). Check out the dealer's local reputation before you buy from her.

Computer manufacturers make it tough to compare prices because each defines base unit differently. One basic computer may seem like a bargain because it sells for $1,000 less than another that looks the same. But when you get it home you may discover that it has only 32K memory, one disk drive, a 7-inch screen, and that there is not very much you can do with it for business applications.

One way to beat this system is to get a price quotation on a certain configuration from each computer dealer, regardless of what they call a "base unit." My suggestion for this configuration is: 64K RAM for an 8-bit system, 128K for a 16-bit system, or 256K for a 32-bit system; two double density disk drives; a 12-inch monochrome screen; and one parallel and two serial ports. Comparisons still won't be easy because one computer may have more RAM even in its base unit; another may have a hard disk built in; and another may have an add-on memory option that another doesn't have. You will have to make adjustments for these things, but if you start with the configuration recommended, your shopping will at least be somewhat less confusing.

If you follow my suggestion you will quickly discover that the most famous and popular computers usually are not the best buys. Before you make any decision, I suggest you consider the Ataris, the IBM-PC compatibles (*not* the IBM PC—it is overpriced), and the Kaypros. These are not the fanciest nor even the best machines on the market, but each model in these lines is a good buy in its class, and will give you something solid to compare with. If, in spite of advice to the contrary, you are thinking of buying an IBM PC, at least do not do so until you have compared it feature for feature and price for price with the Tandy Model 1000 and other IBM compatibles.

A very appealing option—if you have a need or desire to carry your computer around with you and use it in libraries, on planes, in motels, at companies you are visiting, in restaurants, or under trees in a national park—are the lap (or notebook) computers. Some weigh as little as 4 pounds. Most have LCD displays, which cannot be read easily in certain kinds of light, their one major drawback. These systems can be configured so that they will do many things a full-size microcomputer will do, but you will pay more for the same capability. If you need the convenience of true portability, however, they are well worth the extra money.

Computer Shopping Checklist

Make several photocopies of this list and fill out one for each system you are considering.

Model _____

Manufacturer _____

How long in business? _____

How long has this model been on the market? (recommended: 2 years) _____

Repair service available locally? _____

Is the dealer willing to teach use of computer and give telephone support? _____

Base unit price _____

Price for unit that includes the following minimums: two disk drives, 64K RAM, two RS232 ports, and 12-inch monochrome monitor _____

Free software included with purchase of machine:

_____

_____

(If any of this software is what you were going to buy anyway, deduct the value of that program from the price of the computer for purposes of comparing price/value received with other computers.)

RAM _____K Expandable? _____ Built-in modem? _____

Graphics? _____ Color? _____ Sound? _____

Disk drives: Density _____ Double- or single-sided? _____

Hard disk option? _____

Microprocessor _____ 8- or 16-bit _____

Clock speed _____MHz Operating system _____

Additional operating systems available? _____

Monitor: Size _____ Color _____

(If monitor is smaller than 12 inches, add $200 to price of computer for purpose of price/value received comparison with other computers, since you will probably want to buy a 12-inch external monitor.)

Monitor resolution (recommended dot pitch, .4mm) _____
(Compare all monitors to the black-and-white Atari ST as a high standard)

Keyboard (how you like the touch and layout) _____
Programmable function keys? _____
Built-in modem? _____ (If yes, subtract $300 from price of computer for 300 baud, or $500 for 1200 baud, for purposes of price/value received comparison with other computers.)

Is the documentation easy to read and understand? _____

Special features and subjective reaction to dealer demonstration:

_____
_____
_____

Printer Shopping Checklist

Model _____
Manufacturer _____
How long in business? _____
How long has this model been on the market (recommended: 2 years)? _____
Service available locally? _____
Price _____
Type (dot matrix or letter-quality): _____
Speed _____cps
Paper feed (roller and/or tractor) _____
All features fully supported by computer? (Check with the *computer* dealer for this as well as the printer dealer.)

_____

If dot matrix: Color? _____ How many? _____
Dot-addressable? (for highest quality graphics) _____
Is the documentation easy to read and understand? _____
Special features and subjective reactions:

_____
_____

Modem Shopping Checklist

Model _____
Manufacturer _____
How long in business? _____
Service available locally? _____
Price _____
Baud rate _____
Type (acoustic coupler or direct connect) _____
Special features and subjective reactions:

_____
_____
_____

External Monitor Shopping List

(You will need an external monitor only if your computer does not come with its own monitor, or if the built-in monitor it comes with is smaller than 12 inches.)

Model _____ Manufacturer _____
How long in business? _____
How long has this model been on the market? _____
Is service available locally? _____ (Note: Monitors have very low failure rates.)
Size, measured diagonally _____
Ajustable brightness?_____ Adjustable contrast? _____
Nonglare screen? _____
Bandwidth?_____MHz. (The higher the better, except that it won't do any good to buy a monitor with a bandwidth higher than your computer can transmit).
Pixel density? _____per square inch, or dot pitch _____mm. (Recommended dot pitch is .4 mm or less. If this information is not available, compare total pixels for 12-inch screen. The more pixels, the better the resolution.)
If monochrome, color of display _____
If color: type (composite-video or RGB) _____

Number of colors _____ (Don't pay for more colors than your computer can transmit.)

Special features and subjective reactions: _____

_____

_____

_____

Where to Buy a Computer System

COMPUTER STORES

Computer stores come in all sizes and vary greatly in the products and services they offer. Many will give discounts on the computers they sell, but on the whole you will pay more than you would at a discount department store or from a mail-order house. The strongest argument for buying from a store that specializes in computers is the support it gives, with knowledgeable information, advice, and repair service. Also, chances are that salespersons in a computer store will know more about the computers they sell than will those in department stores. You need as knowledgeable a person as you can find to answer your questions while shopping. Also, once you buy your computer, you are going to need someone you can call for help when the computer goes *toot* when you think it should go *bing*.

Unfortunately, buying from a computer dealer doesn't guarantee good support. There are several things you should check out about a dealer before you buy there.

First, visit the store several times, request demonstrations, and ask questions. Are the store personnel knowledgeable about the computers they sell? Are they patient and friendly and unhurried? Do they answer your questions in language you can understand, or do they spout a lot of unintelligible jargon? Unfortunately, even in computer stores salespeople are not always knowledgeable about the computers they sell. After all, anyone who has a good knowledge of computers can make more money doing something else, like consulting. But often a computer science major will work his or her way through school by working part-time in a computer store, either selling or servicing units, and he or she may be an excellent resource. Also, small stores are sometimes operated by the owner, who is available most of the time and who may be very knowledgeable.

Ask the dealer about support. Once you have bought the system, will they promise to answer your questions by phone until you become familiar with it? Do they repair the machines they sell?

Even these precautions don't guarantee safety. Nina Feldman was promised good support by the store she bought her SOL from, but when she called them with problems they put her off and did not return her calls. Later they told her she would have to pay a $100-an-hour consulting fee for their help.

The next thing to do is to visit a users' group for the brand you are considering. Ask the people there what kind of support they receive from their dealers. You'll get an earful. Finding out where to get the best service and support is one of the most valuable benefits of belonging to a users' group. For most things we buy that sometimes require service, we have no way of finding how much support a store provides unless we know someone who has dealt with the store. Usually you discover how good—or bad—a dealer is only after you have made a purchase. But by going to a users'-group meeting *before* you buy, you have the benefit of other people's experience. The store you are considering should be able to tell you about local user groups for the brands they carry.

THE PROS AND CONS OF MAIL-ORDER HOUSES

A Kaypro computer is a Kaypro computer no matter where you buy it, and it will work the same whether you buy it from a mail-order house or a computer dealer. The difference is in service and support. You may save money by buying from a mail-order house, but when you get the computer out of the box and can't figure out how to hook the damn thing up, who will you call? In the long run, it may be worth paying more to a dealer to have free help and advice available when you need it.

But if your finances are tight, a mail-order house may be an alternative you should consider. Many are advertised in computer magazines; you can compare ads for the best prices. Before you buy, make sure there is a service center for the product in your area. Just remember that the reason you are saving so much money is that once you have bought the machine, that mail-order company is not interested in you any longer. Even if you find a local source of service and repair, you will still lack someone you can call and ask, "What do I do now?" You can't expect a local dealer to give you that kind of free help if you didn't buy your system from her.

USED COMPUTERS

Computers have a very low resale value, mainly because technological advances occur so often that last year's hot computer is this year's cold potato, since everyone wants all the latest bells and whistles. But my Osborne 1, first marketed in the early 1980s, runs *WordStar*, *dBase II*, and *SuperCalc*—three major programs for word processing, data-base management, and spreadsheet, respectively; and not one of these programs is going to be outdated anytime soon.

If your funds are limited you might consider a used system. Because of the low resale values you may save hundreds of dollars, even as much as a thousand or more. The Osborne 1 originally sold for $1,795. As I write this, used Osborne 1s go for as little as $400. As an incentive to buy (since used machines are hard to get rid of), the owner will often include all the software she has accumulated—perhaps a couple of thousand dollars' worth.

There's no warranty with a used machine, of course, so be prepared to spend a few dollars fixing something, but even so you might find a very good deal since you will probably get a *lot* of free software with your used machine. However, you should insist that the owner put the machine through its paces for you and demonstrate all the programs, so that you can feel sure there is nothing terribly wrong with it. Look in *Computer Classifieds* (a newsprint magazine) or your local computer paper for ads.

One important caution about buying a used computer: make sure that the model you are considering is still being supported by the manufacturer and software developers. Some models have been phased out, meaning little or no new software will be developed for them, and parts may eventually be hard to find. In general, it's best to buy a used system that is still in production.

Alternatives to Buying— Time Sharing and Leasing

TIME SHARING

Sandy Emerson wanted to use the UNIX operating system, which requires a very large memory (RAM). Since she could not afford to buy a microcomputer that would run UNIX, she bought a terminal and started time sharing on the UNIX system at UC Berkeley.

Terminals cost less than computers and by time sharing on a mainframe you have access to much more computer power than you have on a micro. The tradeoffs are that you may not be able to use the system at the times you want to, and the access charges go on forever, but once you pay for your micro there's no more major cost. You must also live within a local call of a mainframe system that allows time sharing, since long distance phone charges would negate any financial benefit of the time-sharing option. And finally, mainframe software may be harder for a novice to understand and use.

At a photocopy center in Berkeley, an Apple Macintosh can be rented for $8 an hour. The Computer College in Salt Lake City rents computers for $3 to $5 per hour; all the computers are connected to a hard disk with hundreds of programs. Services available (at extra charge) include the printing out of your work. This is an excellent way to become familiar with various brands of micros before you buy. Tutoring is available, and someone is always there to help rental customers with software problems. The Women's Computer Literacy Project in San Francisco also rents computer time at reasonable rates to the graduates of their program. Look for similar resources in your city.

LEASING

Microcomputers can be leased in many cities, but the rates are very high ($200 a month or more) and some companies will not rent to individuals because of the risk of losing the computer. However, leasing is a relatively new development, and both policies and rental rates may change quickly as competition grows. It might be worth $200 to find out if you are going to be compatible with computers—*before* you invest in a system of your own.

EIGHTEEN

Software Primer I: Operating Systems and Programming Languages

A computer without a program is like a body without a brain, or an office without a manager. It has all the potential for doing work but lacks a central authority to tell it what to do.

Software refers to programs in general but is often used interchangeably with *program*. The term *software* makes sense when you know it came into use to distinguish programs from *hardware*—the concrete elements of the computer system. Some programs reside on chips in the computer itself and are called *firmware*, but most of the programs you will be concerned with are recorded on disk or other storage media and must be loaded into the computer before it can be used. A program consists entirely of instructions to the computer that are set in motion by commands from the user.

WHO'S IN CHARGE HERE ANYWAY?

Although software is the central authority from which the computer gets its instructions, there is one higher authority—you. The user rather than the software is the boss; software is the user's administrator. The boss gives orders and provides the proper data; the software then functions as a skilled specialist, carrying out all the details of a particular project. Like any administrator, it also assigns tasks to the workers and sees that

249

they are performed, except in this case the workers are the microprocessor and other components in the computer. *Computers can't do anything that people do not tell them to do.* Software and the microprocessor(s) inside a computer do indeed function like a brain, but a brain without that mysterious power that only living beings have: will.

This fact is important to keep in mind if you feel intimidated by computers. Once you realize that you are the supreme authority, the machines seem less fearsome. It's people we have to worry about, not computers.

Just like people, software specializes, and you must buy programs that are appropriate to the jobs you want to do.

Software can be divided into three general categories: operating systems, programming languages, and applications programs—the programs you use to do your work on the computer.

Operating Systems

As their name implies, operating systems operate the computer. When you turn on the computer it will do a few things automatically. It will accept a message from the keyboard (usually a carriage return or "enter" command) and then activate a disk drive to load a program. The instructions that tell the computer to do these things are the part of the operating system that resides in ROM (read-only memory), and they are said to be "hard-wired" because they are permanently installed. The balance of the operating system is usually loaded from a disk or other storage medium and is the first program you load into the computer every time you use it. Most of the new lap-size computers have the entire operating system in ROM, a great convenience but one that limits you to a single operating system.

Without an operating system, your computer is useless, because this is the software that controls all the mechanical functions such as turning the disk drives on and off, reading from and writing to the disks, and sending data to and from the keyboard, memory, display monitor, printer, and CPU (central processing unit). A few sophisticated programs can be run without the operating system because they address the CPU directly from within the program, but in general, without an operating system, the computer doesn't function. Because it directs all this flow of data, the operating system has been called the "traffic cop" of the computer.

The operating system also does certain housekeeping functions. It allows you to move files from one disk to another or to delete them. It has several other capabilities that you don't need to know about now, but they concern moving data and running the computer, not processing the data itself. Usually the operating system is "transparent" to the user; you aren't even aware of it once you load it into the computer. Your applications software tells the operating system what it wants to do, and the operating system makes the computer do it. The operating system can be thought of as the intermediary between the applications software and the computer. The chain of command goes from you (the boss) to the applications software (the office manager) to the operating system (the gal in the factory with the forklift) to the computer (all the machinery in the assembly line).

The choice of an operating system is an important one because it determines what applications software you will be able to use with your computer. However, the best way to choose an operating system is to select the applications software you want to run first and then buy the operating system that will run it. Any computer you buy has an operating system that comes with it, and since operating systems must be written for the specific microprocessor within your computer, your choice of an operating system also affects your choice of a computer. The selection of either an applications program, an operating system, or a computer automatically reduces your choices for the remaining two elements since all are interdependent. Your choice should begin with the applications software, then the operating system; and finally, the computer, not the other way around, unless a computer has a special feature that is so valuable to you that it overshadows the choice of software.

Increasingly, computer manufacturers are offering the option of adding an additional microprocessor, which allows the use of more than one operating system, and consequently broadens the selection of software you can run on that machine. For example, the Dimension 68000 can run software for five major operating systems. You pay for that flexibility, of course.

Some microprocessors and their operating systems are proprietary, so that software written for them will not run on any other brand of machine. Examples are the Apple, Atari, Commodore, and TRS-80 computers. Other microprocessors and operating systems are found in a number of different computers, and the software for them is transferable, sometimes with some adaptation necessary, among any of these machines. Of these, CP/M and MS-DOS are by far the most popular operating systems. CP/M runs on 8-bit machines, CP/M-86 and MS-DOS on 16-bit. The choice of either of these operating systems assures you a very large selection of software; but on the other hand, Apple, Atari, Commodore, and TRS-80 computers are so popular that a wealth of software has been written for them and you will not be limited if you select any of them. The bottom line still is: select the software you want and then buy a computer that has the operating system that will run it.

Programming Languages

Even if you never intend to do any programming, a little knowledge about how the languages work will help you make better decisions when buying your applications software.

The only language the computer itself understands is machine code—a series of 0s and 1s (known as binary code) arranged in 8- or 16-digit bytes. But machine code is hard to work with because it is tedious and confusing to work for hours with 00100110s and 10010011s and remember what each series means. Computers have no trouble at all remembering such things, but our minds don't work like computers, so a number of languages have been developed that are easier for us to work with and remember. They all involve English words, symbols, and/or mnemonics. Such languages must be translated into machine code before the computer can understand them, and the way languages are translated determines what type of language they are—assembled, compiled, or interpreted. Languages are also classified as "high level" and "low level;" high level if they are written in language and symbols close to those people normally think and write with, and low level if they are close to the representations required by the machine.

Assembly languages are low-level languages consisting of short mnemonic codes, each representing one machine language instruction. An assembler translates the mnemonic codes into machine codes the computer can understand. Each microprocessor (CPU) has its own assembly language, so a program written in assembly language can be used only with the microprocessor for which it is written, which is a disadvantage. However, because assembly programs are tailored to particular microprocessors, programmers can fully utilize any special features of that microprocessor, so that's an advantage. Assembly languages are hard to learn and time-consuming to work with, so they require a high level of expertise (and patience) in programmers and are expensive to produce because they require so much time. Unless the developer can market these programs in high volume, the price to the consumer may be high. Assembly-language programs are also difficult to debug, and the final product is not normally modifiable by the consumer.

But, because assembly-language programs take advantage of each microprocessor's unique capabilities, and because they do not have to be translated from the abstractions of high-level languages like Pascal, they are very fast and efficient. When shopping for applications software, any program that is written in assembly language should receive a big plus. The bigger the program and the more data you have to manipulate with it, the more of an avantage an assembly-language program is likely to be.

Compiled languages are high-level languages that are translated into machine code by a compiler. The version of the program you buy is already compiled—it does not have to be retranslated every time you run the program. Sometimes you can't find an off-the-shelf applications program that will do all the things you want it to do. In that case, you may have to buy the program that comes closest to what you want and modify it. Compiled languages can be modified if (1) the publisher will provide you with the "source code" (a program listing in the original high-level language) and (2) you buy a compiler to retranslate your modified program; but this is not an easy process. Unless you are a programmer, you will probably have to hire a programming consultant to do this for you, which can be expensive.

Although not as fast and efficient as assembly-language programs, compiled-language programs are fast enough for most purposes since they come already translated into machine code, although they may not take full advantage of the special capabilities of your computer's microprocessor.

Interpreted languages translate instructions one line at a time and execute them before going on to the next instruction. So, while assembly-language programs do not need to be assembled every time the program is run, and compiled-language programs do not have to be recompiled, interpreted-language programs have to be retranslated every time they are run, and obviously they must come with an interpreter. Because of this process, interpreted languages are very slow, but a major advantage is that they are easy to modify and to debug (to debug means to find and remove incorrect codes that make a program run incorrectly). If the interpreted language is also an interactive language, it will help you locate program bugs with on-the-screen messages, a great advantage.

As you can see, there is an inverse ratio between (1) the ease of writing and debugging a program and modifying the program once it has been translated, and (2) the speed and efficiency of the program produced.

What you need to remember is that interpreted languages are easy to learn, to debug, and to change, and produce slow programs. Assembled languages are difficult to learn, time-consuming, and hard to debug, but they produce fast, efficient programs. Compiled languages are also hard to debug and to modify, but they are considerably faster than interpreted languages.

For those who intend to learn programming, following are very brief descriptions of the most popular languages. In several cases the name of the language is an acronym of a description of the primary use of the language, and if you learn what the letters stand for you will have no trouble knowing what that particular language does best.

BASIC—Beginner's All-purpose Symbolic Instruction Code. This is the beginner's choice because it's easy to remember, easy to write programs, easy to debug, and easy to change at any stage.

Normally an interpreted language, programs written in BASIC can be speeded up considerably by buying a BASIC compiler. Professional programmers bemoan the popularity of BASIC because good programming technique requires certain conventions of programming structure, and since BASIC generally is an unstructured language, they feel it teaches poor programming habits. However, structured versions of BASIC are available, based on a version of BASIC in development by ANSI (American National Standards Institute). If you want to do serious programming in BASIC, you should buy one of these versions—ask if it is based on the ANSI model. (An official ANSI BASIC may be available by the time you read this.)

But *any* version of BASIC offers an easy and enjoyable entry into the world of programming. Interpreted BASIC is an easy language to learn and use, and programs written in it are easy to debug. That's why BASIC is a popular language with novice programmers, and usually the first programming language a person learns. But interpretted BASIC programs run slowly and are not very efficient compared to assembly-language programs.

COBOL—COmmon Business Oriented Language. This compiled language is the most widely used business-applications language. Experts estimate that 65 percent or more of all data-processing departments' codes are written in COBOL. The fact that COBOL programs read almost like English sentences makes it an easy language to learn and to use, makes it somewhat self-documenting (you don't have to look up obscure command words), and also makes it easy to maintain (correct and update).

For anyone who wants to make a living as a programmer, COBOL is a highly desirable language to learn. Critics say it is too wordy; that wordiness, as we have seen, is also its greatest strength. COBOL will be around a long time because (1) business already has a lot of money invested in COBOL routines and (2) it does very well what it was designed to do.

COBOL was originally designed for mainframes, and micro-computer versions lack some of the features of the original language. Therefore, anyone who intends to buy COBOL for a microcomputer should be careful to check exactly which features are included. As micros become more powerful, however, full-feature COBOL will be available.

FORTRAN—FORmula TRANslator. This was the first widely used compiled language (introduced in the mid-1950s). Its principal use is for scientific and engineering applications. A somewhat antiquated language, it remains popular in spite of outdated features because its structure encourages the development of reusable subroutines (subroutines are blocks of programming code that perform just one function that is part of a larger program) and over the years thousands of scientific, engineering, and mathematical subroutines have been developed for it, and because most of this vast library is available to programmers. These subroutines save a lot of time because you don't have to "reinvent the wheel,"; and FORTRAN will be around a long time because of these resources.

Anyone who wants to program for the scientific and/or engineering segments will find FORTRAN a valuable language to know.

Logo—the children's programming language. Logo has gone through several generations. It was originally developed to teach children math concepts, so simplicity is its keynote, but current versions are also sophisticated enough for artificial intelligence applications. Logo teaches children programming concepts as well as math, and it does so in such an entertaining way that children are barely conscious of their learning processes. Using the "turtle graphics" part of the language, a little triangle or "turtle" draws figures on the screen. Very complex and beautiful designs can be generated quickly with simple commands. To draw the figures, children must use mathematical and geometrical concepts. Logo's turtle graphics has turned out to be an exceptionally powerful educational tool because (1) unlike other programming languages, every command gives immediate results on the screen; (2) it is highly interactive—that is, the child has complete control of the computer; and (3) rather than learning by rote, children learn by thinking. They teach themselves, and they *use* what they learn *while* they are learning it.

Logo is also a powerful general-purpose language. Because of its simplicity it is ideal for novices of any age. If you buy a computer for your children (and I think you should), then certainly you should buy one that runs Logo, and this language should be your first-priority software for your children. Programming in Logo is an activity that the entire family can enjoy together. It's *fun*.

C is a compiled language that is easy to transfer from one computer to another, yet takes full advantage of a particular microprocessor. It has many of the advantages of assembly language but is easier to use. C is very fast and is also a structured language, meaning it is neat—easy to design, read, and debug. Yet, C is also flexible, and it is possible to make errors in programming that may then be hard to find. As you can see, C defies easy categorization by any of the criteria we have used so far. That's why it's so good—it comes close to combining the best of all types.

C is the language in which the operating system UNIX is written (UNIX is a powerful operating system that allows multiple users to access the same computer at the same time). C is probably not for beginners. It is popular with systems programmers and is one of the languages of the future.

APL—A Programming Language. How's that for a straightforward name? Widely used for statistical applications.

LISP—LISt Processing Language. LISP is the most widely used language for artificial intelligence programs. It has the ability to "learn" and to modify itself.

FORTH—really the "fourth" version of a programming language. Forth was designed for engineering, scientific, and mathematical applications, and it allows the programmer to expand the language to include her own commands.

Pascal—a compiled language named after Blaise Pascal, a seventeenth-century French mathematician. Pascal is a *structured* language, meaning that its syntax requires you to write programs in modular form, each module containing a complete procedure in a clear, logical form. Further, these modules can be nested—within any module there can be submodules that are also complete procedures, and these submodules can contain other submodules. However, arrangement is according to a strict hierarchical and logical format. Errors (bugs) in programs are sometimes very hard to find once the program is written; but the strength of structured programming is that it prevents you from making many kinds of errors in the first place. The clear structure also makes it easy to modify and update a Pascal program.

Highly structured languages make it much easier to design, write, and debug very large and complex programs. This is the special attraction of Pascal. It is also a very good language for beginning programmers to learn because it teaches good programming habits that can then be transferred to other languages, even sloppy ol' BASIC.

There are many other programming languages. A detailed discussion of languages and what they can do is beyond the scope of this book, but these few samples will at least make you aware that particular kinds of programming require a language suited to that job.

Most computers are now sold with a language provided, usually a version of BASIC. Once you play around with it, you'll have some notion whether programming appeals to you.

For more information on programming languages and a list of the best books to help you learn, see the *Whole Earth Software Catalog*, edited by Stewart Brand (Doubleday, 1984). (See chapter 19 for a detailed description of this book.)

NINETEEN

Software Primer II: Applications Programs

Applications programs are those programs that do particular kinds of work (or play) for the user. They include games and educational and home-management programs, but for the moment we will consider only those programs that are useful in business.

Applications software falls into two categories. Programs in the general category perform a specific kind of function but can be used for a wide variety of activities. Word processing, accounting systems, spreadsheets, and database managers are common programs of this type. Sometimes a combination of these programs can be bought in one package called an *integrated system*.

A general-purpose word processing program such as *WordStar* can be used to write business letters, a novel, a thesis, technical reports, or anything else that normally is typed. A general-purpose accounting system can be adapted for any kind of business—a dress shop, a gas station, or an optometrist's office.

In the second category are single-purpose programs. A mailing list program is really a database manager that does only one job. Accounting programs are available that are tailored to the particular needs of doctors, lawyers, or real estate brokers.

Each category of applications software has its value. A general-applications program is versatile and adaptable to many different types of businesses, but requires enough knowledge on the part of the user to customize the system to suit specific requirements. A single-purpose or "dedicated" program offers a system designed for a particular type of business or a specific activity and requires much less knowledge on the part of the user, since the program comes already set up (although a certain amount of flexibility may be built in). However, the program is limited in its usefulness. An accounting system designed specifically for a hardware store is of no use to a veterinarian.

Your business needs will define your software needs. To establish a business limited to word processing and accounting service for local attorneys, you would do very well to buy a dedicated package. But to offer word processing to the general public, you will be doing everything from term papers to résumés and will need the most flexible program you can buy—a word processor of the general type.

The distinction between general and specific applications programs is an important one. Salespeople are not always conscious of the importance of the distinction, so keep it in mind when shopping for your software.

Listed below, under the appropriate categories, are the most common types of applications software and what each will do.

General Applications

WORD PROCESSING

I took my first job as a secretary in the early 1950s. If electric typewriters already existed, I didn't know about them, and I know for sure there were no copy machines in the city where I worked. Any documents to be copied had to be photostated at a cost of about two dollars a copy.

I remember a long report I had to type. Nine copies were required. I tried to use nine carbons so I wouldn't have to type the whole thing twice. Have you ever tried to correct a typo on nine carbons? It didn't work, of course, and I did have to type the report a second time—anything beyond four carbons was illegible. I remember that the project took me all day.

Today I could finish the project in less than two hours. With word processing software, no matter how many mistakes I make, no matter how many times I change my mind about the order of sentences or the way I express things, I never retype anything but the words I want to change. The whole document is typed once, and only once—even if I want twenty originals and even if I decide to put the first paragraph last.

On a typewriter, you hit a key that transmits a message, either electrically or mechanically, directly to a mechanism that imprints a character on a piece of paper. What you hit is what you get. Word processing devices insert an intermediate step before anything goes onto paper. What you type goes into a memory, and what is in memory is displayed on a monitor of some kind, so you can see what you typed. But nothing appears on paper until you are satisfied with what you've done. In the memory stage, you can manipulate individual characters, sentences, or whole paragraphs in any way you want. You can correct spelling and grammar, delete words, sentences, or paragraphs, move them around and change their sequence, add new words or new lines, or change the margins and the spacing.

What you put into memory resides *only* in memory until you instruct your computer, with one or two keystrokes, to record the material on disk. You can, if you want, leave the material in memory for further work, and record a revised version over the original on your disk. Or you can save your original version by copying it—again, with just a few keystrokes—to another file, and do a revised version, which you can print out and compare with the first version.

Word processing allows you to write form letters with individual names and personalized messages (a function much abused by the sellers of magazine subscriptions!); print multiple originals; experiment with various formats to see how they look before printing out final copy (how many times have you ended up with just one line that has to go on the last page?); search the entire text for a particular word and replace it; justify right-hand margins; and much more.

Clearly, the beauty of word processing is that once you have typed a document, you need never type the whole thing again, no matter how many changes you make. You need type only what you want to correct or add.

Since I am a writer, I sometimes type several thousand words a day. I am more excited about word processing than any other function of my computer because it eliminates all that boring, repetitive typing to correct errors or to make revisions that once wasted 75 percent of my time—time I resented because it was nothing but drudge work. Now all that remains is the typing I don't mind doing—the creative part—and I am four times more productive. Writers do more retyping and revising than most people, but word processing substantially increases the productivity of *anyone* who spends a significant amount of time typing.

There are a number of programs that augment word processing programs. Such programs will check spelling and grammar, count the number of words in a document, and even check your text for sexist terms. Some programs include a thesaurus and/or a dictionary; others will check your text for the reading level of your vocabulary (useful for people writing for children) or tell you how many times certain words appear.

Probably no type of program is as universally useful as word processing. Whatever business you choose to start with a computer, word processing should be considered an essential program.

SPREADSHEETS

Spreadsheets are to numbers what word processing is to words, and much more.

With a spreadsheet program, data (words and/or numbers) is entered into a grid, or matrix, so that the information appears in columns and rows. Usually, columns are identified by letters and rows by numbers, so that any item of information on the spreadsheet can be identified by coordinates such as A16—column A, row 16—a similar system to the coordinates on a map. The locations are called "cells" and can hold a number of different kinds of information.

Like a word processing program, any number of items can be changed without reworking the entire sheet. With the better programs you can move numbers around, reformat the entire sheet, or experiment with all kinds of plans before deciding on the one for your final copy, or you can print out copies of the same information formatted several different ways, just as you can with words.

But these are just the program's basic functions. You can enter in a certain location a mathematical formula that uses as a factor information that is in another location, and what you see on the screen is not the formula but the result of the computation. If the data in the source location changes, the formula recomputes and displays the new result automatically.

For example: I set up my spreadsheet labeling column A as "Apples," and row 1 as "Quantity on hand," and row 2 as "Retail value of quantity on hand." In location A1 I enter how many apples I have. In location A2, I enter the formula .30*A1, which multiplies the number of apples I have times 30 cents, the price I sell them at. If I enter *10* in location A1, A2 will automatically show "$3.00," the total price of the apples. If I change the number in A1 to *20*, A2 will automatically recompute the total price of the apples and display "$6.00." If I want to enter my cost per apple and have the spreadsheet automatically compute the retail price at a markup of 40 percent, I can enter cost in A1, and the formula .4*A1 in A2 to display the retail price per apple. Then I can do the same thing for column B, "Bananas."

In other locations I can put formulas that show me what I paid for the apples, how many apples I have sold so far, what profit I made on them, the difference between the profit I am making now and the profit I made last year, and just about any other combination of computations imaginable. All of them will be recomputed and displayed anytime a source figure is changed. Even long series of computations are set up only once, and no matter how many times the facts change, only the factors that change need be entered. Yes, you can change the formulas whenever you want, too.

That's a ridiculously simple example. In fact, with a spreadsheet you can do enormously complex calculations. You can compute your income tax so that you can try out several tax strategies, or set up an inventory system that will give you daily tallies and tell you when to reorder. You can also do anything from statistical analysis to calculations for engineers and physicists.

The "what if. . ." function is what spreadsheets are most famous for. Once the spreadsheet is set up for a particular purpose and figures and formulas are entered, one factor at a time can be changed to see what would happen. What if I increase my markup on apples by 1 percent? How much will my profit increase for one month? One year? How will this affect my taxes for the coming year? All these answers are computed automatically within seconds. And I can try as many different percentages as I can think of. To return the spreadsheet to the real record of this year's earnings, I simply reenter my actual markup percentage.

Again, this is an oversimplified example, but you can see the value of this type of program to financial analysts, investors, statisticians, and scientists, as well as to any kind of retail business or service.

One drawback of spreadsheets is that the user has to know how to do what she wants the spreadsheet to do—she has to format the program. Spreadsheet templates (or overlays) that do the formatting for you are now on the market, but then you lose the customizing that is so valuable in the first place. Also, by the time you buy the spreadsheet and then the templates, you have spent quite a bit of money. If you are not already knowledgeable about the processes for which you want to use the spreadsheet—accounting, financial analysis and forecasting, payroll preparation, tax reports, and so on—you might be better off buying a dedicated program for your specific purpose; one in which the format and the calculations are already set up for you.

Offsetting this drawback is the extreme versatility of spreadsheets. Hundreds of uses have been found for them, and more are constantly being developed. When you buy a single-purpose (or dedicated) program, the range of jobs it will do is much narrower than that of a general-purpose spreadsheet, which is an important factor to remember if you are going to use your spreadsheet to perform diverse number-crunching services for clients. The freelance will be better off investing the time to learn to write templates so that the spreadsheet's versatility can be fully exploited.

Spreadsheets are wonderful for people who need sophisticated calculating capability plus a records system that can be perfectly customized to their needs. Examples of this type of program are inventories—which are simple but infinitely variable—to meet the needs of such businesses as auto parts and grocery stores on one end of the scale to research and development facilities requiring complex scientific calculations for unique new products on the other.

Spreadsheets are not difficult to learn to use, but they are time-consuming because they are so powerful and versatile and have many commands and maneuvers to remember. It is wise to buy a popular spreadsheet that has been on the market for some time. Such a program will have support materials available to help you learn to use it. Among the most popular spreadsheet programs are *VisiCalc*, *SuperCalc*, *Lotus 1-2-3*, and *Multiplan*. Many books are available on how to use these programs; in addition, many books feature templates you can enter yourself, although the very best plan is to learn to write your own templates. Seminars are frequently given on these programs. *Multiplan* is a newer spreadsheet on the market, and it has some excellent features, such as the ability to define mathematical functions in English rather than by formulas. For example, *Hours*Payrate* computes the gross wages of an employee (* means *times*). Since it is published by a well-established house, you can expect it to be around awhile and to be well supported with educational materials and templates.

Don't be intimidated by the complexity of spreadsheets. Just because sophisticated functions are available, you don't necessarily have to learn them, and they are invisible until you need them. They don't get in the way of all of the exquisitely simple but powerful jobs you will be able to do within your first hour of experimenting with your spreadsheet.

INFORMATION MANAGERS

A data base is information collected and stored in an orderly manner. An information or database manager allows the user to manipulate that information.

The term *data base* is so general that many people have a hard time understanding precisely what it means; part of the problem is that the term is flexible. Some data bases are like file cabinets where you can store invoices, purchase orders, employee records, and business correspondence. Others are like directories, containing names, addresses, phone numbers, and other useful information on lists of customers, members of organizations, or friends. Some data bases are long lists of things such as parts inventories, record collections, or the names of all the flowers that are native to Georgia. Some data bases are like books that contain a great deal of information on a particular subject such as psychology; others are like encylopedias that have information on almost anything you can think of.

The main thing to remember is that data bases are organized information of one kind or another—it's as simple as that. An information or database *manager* is the program that is used to set up the records and retrieve and manipulate information.

The best database managers allow you to set up your records so that you can retrieve information in any form, with as little or as much of the entire record as you want to include in your report. Reports that would take a person days or weeks to compile working with paper records in file cabinets, a database manager can do in a matter of minutes. For that reason, database managers are among the most useful and popular programs on the market. Names, addresses, and phone numbers can be stored in such a way that they can be sorted, selected, and printed according to zip code, phone number, last name, city, state, street, or even first name or house number. You may select only those records for people whose phone numbers begin with 259-. From a payroll data base you can make a list of all the employees who have not yet taken their vacations this year. Using an inventory data base, you can find out which items in your inventory had fewer than twenty sales this month. From a membership directory you can find all the members of an organization who have not paid their dues this year. This kind of manipulation is possible with any kind of data so long as it is entered according to the rules of the program.

There are three general types of information managers: unstructured (or free-form) indexing systems, file-management systems, and database-management systems (DBMSs).

Unstructured indexing systems are ideal for cataloging information in text form. Suppose you have collected facts about nutrition, and you have used a word processor to write up your information and to store it on a computer disk. You have set up your notes so that they are organized according to nutrients. Under the name of each vitamin and mineral you have written what it does in the body, what the signs of deficiency are, and what its antagonists are. If the nutrient is helpful in treating certain diseases, you have noted that, too. Most important, you have used anecdotal material that can't be expressed any other way than in complete sentences. Over a few years you have collected quite a lot of information, and you now have five disks full of nutrition files.

But there is a problem. It is easy to find the file on vitamin C because that's how your files are organized. But when you want to look up what nutrients are useful in the treatment of arthritis, there is no way to find them except by hunting through each file of text. You also remember that Uncle Henry used some nutrient for his arthritis but you can't remember what it is. Uncle Henry is mentioned in several files since Uncle Henry is always ailing.

Indexing programs allow you to select and enter into each file a set of key words, each key word being a reference to information contained in the file. Then the key words are indexed so that when you want to find out what nutrients help arthritis, you enter "ARTHRITIS" and the index tells you every file in which arthritis is mentioned. Using Boolean (logical) operators, it is possible to search for "ARTHRITIS" *and* "UNCLE HENRY" *or* "VITAMIN C" *or* "CALCIUM" but *not* "RHEUMATOID."

One such indexing program is *SUPERFILE,* published by FYI, Inc. I can take any text file in any form, and by inserting three symbols (*C, *K, and *E) and my choice of key words, I can turn that file into a data base, which I can then index with a few keystrokes. Purchasing this program enabled me to very easily convert years of accumulated notes into data files. It is impossible to calculate how much time I would have spent if I had converted them to the structure required by file managers and data-base-management systems (DBMSs). Some files cannot be converted at all, since the nature of the information requires that it be expressed as thoughts or ideas. For example, I have indexed my journal, which I use as a resource for some of my writing, so that I can find any entry that contains comments on "canyon wrens," the "Moab Rim Trail," "red ants," or "barrel cactus."

Unstructured indexing programs are perfect for anyone who works with ideas rather than with isolated facts. Writers, researchers, psychologists, and anyone who works in the humanities are among those who will find such programs extremely useful. Their single most valuable feature is the ability to quickly convert existing text files into fully indexed data bases.

File managers require that information be entered in a structured manner. The basics of this structure are the same for all data bases; the information is divided into files, records, and fields. Say you are going to use a file manager to record all the names in your address book. The address book itself is equivalent to a file. Each entry in the book (which includes a name, address, and phone number) is a record. Records are divided into fields. A name field may include the full name, or you may have two fields, one for the first name and another for the surname. Another field holds the street address, another the city, and so on. Fields can be set up in a variety of ways, but all require that when the file is first set up each field be assigned a certain length, and once that definition is made, you can't enter anything longer than the defined length. The reason for this limit is that the program requires a precise map of where each item of information resides; to accomplish this, fields must be of uniform length.

This precision allows file managers to do what unstructured indexing programs can't do—manipulate information in a variety of ways. You can print out all the names and phone numbers but omit the address, or you can sort alphabetically or by zip code. File managers are excellent for cataloging, mailing lists, inventory, or any other collection of uniformly structured information. Individual programs vary greatly in how structured they are and in how they set up the relation between records, and it is important to choose a file manager appropriate to the particular job you want it to do. The documentation for each program should describe what functions the program does best.

Database management systems (DBMSs) are classified as hierarchical, networking, or relational, according to the way they structure data relationships, and how the data is structured determines what kinds of jobs each system will do.

The **hierarchical** type is structured like a family tree, and the relationships of the data are just like the relationships on a tree—you can branch out downward but not upward. Hierarchical data bases are hard to change once they are set up, so they lack flexibility. They are suitable for any kind of information that remains relatively stable and that has relationships that fall naturally into a tree-type structure. Botanical and zoological data bases, for example, are well suited for this kind of data base because the classifications are tree-structured: class, order, family, genus, species, and variety. These categories branch in a downward direction only—there may be many varieties of one species, but only one species to a variety.

Network structures are more flexible than hierarchical, since they allow interconnections in more than one direction. However, they are still limited in the number of ways data can be manipulated.

Of the three types of database management systems, relational database managers are by far the most versatile and powerful. A relational data base is one that stores information in such a way that each file can be expressed as a table. Where column A, "Monday," intersects with row 18, "Pizzas Sold," there is a value, "82."

Wherever different files have a certain key field in common (creating a *relation* between the files), the files can be merged into one table, or designated values can be extracted from each file to form a new and different table (and file). These files can be displayed or printed out in many different forms, not just as tables, and information can be extracted to print an invoice, a shipping ticket, or whatever. In the case of your restaurant, the key field "Pizza" from the "Food Sold" file can be used to call up data from another file, "Ingredients," to tell you how much dough was needed to make 82 pizzas.

This relational principle makes possible the kind of system described in chapter 6, where the sale of one item entered in a sales record automatically updates an inventory, monthly sales report, tax records, and any other kind of record you want to incorporate. You can't do that with file managers, and only to a limited degree with hierarchical and network DBMSs.

R:BASE 4000 and *dBaseII* and *III* are examples of relational DBMSs.

dBase II (for 8-bit systems) has been phenomenally popular, largely because it is a programming language as well as a very powerful DBMS. The programming feature makes it almost infinitely adaptable. Other DBMSs can be programmed using whatever standard programming language they were written in—a somewhat tougher task, but customizing DBMSs can be a lucrative specialty.

A file manager has as much power as you need for simple projects like mailing lists or cataloging a record collection or an address book. Relational data base managers are much more expensive but are worth the money if you are going to do extensive record-keeping for your clients. These programs offer great versatility and, as your expertise grows, all the power you need to create large and complex systems. The price you pay for this power is time invested in learning, programming, and maintaining your system—you shouldn't buy more power than you really need.

Unfortunately, information managers are not always clearly identified as to type, and terminology has not yet settled down to a point where everyone uses the same terms to describe the same attributes (these systems are relatively new to microcomputers). In many cases you will have to figure out a program's category by the description of what it does. These distinctions are important, so if you have to, call the program's publisher and ask.

COMMUNICATIONS

If you plan to telecommute to a job, hook up your computer to a network, access data banks and other on-line information services such as The Source or CompuServe, or send text to your friend's computer in Florida, you will need a modem and the software to run it. Communications software controls how information is transmitted and received.

When you buy your communications software, the most important thing to look for is the ability to send and receive both text files and programs. Happily, one of the best programs for doing this is *MODEM7*, a free public-domain program. Any users' group will provide you with a copy. Your computer dealer might provide you with one, also. The documentation that comes with *MODEM7* is awful, but fortunately *MODEM7* has an on-screen help menu that is excellent, and it is such a widely used program that you can always find someone to help you if you get stuck.

GRAPHICS

Graphics programs enable you to produce computer art and design or business graphs and charts. More than any other kind of program, graphics programs must be tailored to specific computers.

Although inexpensive graphics systems are available, high-quality professional graphics capability adds substantially to the cost of your system. You must have a good color monitor and a printer with special capabilities, and both are very expensive. You may need a light pen (for "drawing" directly on the screen) or a graphics pad (you draw on it and the image is displayed on the screen).

Commercial artists can do much of their work on a computer equipped for graphics. The ease of changing a design on the computer almost parallels the ease of revising text with a word processor. I know of one artist who lives on Catalina Island, California, and sells his art and delivers it via modem!

Professional-quality graphics can be a joy as well as a useful tool for anyone who is using the computer primarily for a commercial or fine-arts business, computer-aided design, creating computer games, or generating educational programs.

For the freelance who does reports for business clients, there may be some value in offering business graphics (bar graphs and pie charts) to clients, but there is some question whether you will gain enough income offering this option to pay for the extra hardware and software you will need.

These five categories of general-applications software collectively allow you to do almost any kind of work you can think of with a computer. With any one of them you can start a business. By combining two or more of them you expand your business options as well as provide yourself with the tools to keep your *own* business records.

Single Purpose Programs

Although it's difficult to state with certainty, there are probably thirty thousand software packages on the market, and some experts place the figure much higher than that. The majority of these are single-purpose programs (also known as "dedicated" or "job-specific").

A single-purpose program does only one job. There are too many specific applications even to begin to try to list them all here; a few are described in part 2, "A Multitude of Possibilities." A glance in any software catalog will tell you how many hundreds of options there are. Whether you are a mink breeder wanting to keep track of the genealogies of your minks, or a rock musician who needs to keep track of tour dates, it's a good bet that someone has written a program to meet your needs. (Whether that program will in fact do all you want it to do is another matter.)

Single-purpose programs are excellent for individuals or businesses that need to do a few narrowly defined jobs and do not have the time or inclination to customize a general-purpose program. If a plant nursery can find a commercial program designed for nursery inventories, and that's all they use the computer for, why buy a general program and then have to customize it, especially if they will never need it for anything else? The same reasoning holds for almost any small- to medium-sized business.

For a computer-services business, however, the reasoning goes the other way: you can't afford to buy a dedicated program for every customer. If you confine your services to a special business segment, such as lawyers, then one program might serve them all. But even then, it is hard not to branch occasionally into other areas as opportunities arise. You will need a general-applications program that allows you to adapt it to unlimited variations.

Single-purpose programs do save you from having to learn to use and format complex data bases and spreadsheets. Some are general enough to be used for computer services—for example, mailing-list programs, or accounting programs with some flexibility built in. But a mailing-list program is nothing but a data base designed to do only one job, as is a checkbook balancer or an inventory program. By the time you buy enough single-purpose programs to do all the jobs you want to do for various clients, you will have spent a great deal more money than you would have if you had bought a general-purpose program that you could adapt to do any kind of job you want.

For anyone who is going into business offering any kind of computer service, I recommend buying general-purpose software only, and mastering it. Skills aren't mastered easily, but the ultimate reward—expertise for which you will be very well paid—is worth the investment of time and energy.

Learning to Use Your Software

I have an excellent program for salvaging data from disks that have been damaged, called *Disk Doctor*. The manual that comes with the program is not long, and right up front it says, "Be sure to read this manual carefully before you try to use the program." So I did. I couldn't understand half of it. I got mired in all kinds of overly detailed instructions, so finally I just loaded the program.

Various cues came on the screen. Which drive do I want to put the damaged disk in? Do I want to recover an accidentally erased file, or do I want to salvage what may be left of a file on a damaged disk? Which drive do I want to copy the data to? By choosing my options from an on-screen menu I was able to recover my lost file quickly and easily. I never opened the manual again.

Ideally, the computer novice should be able to learn everything she wants to know about her software and how to use it from the manual that comes with it. You certainly should start there; but, unfortunately, manuals are often very badly written. If that's the case with any of the software you have purchasd, the menu and on-screen "help" options may get you started, as I discovered with *Disk Doctor*.

Procedures for some programs may be too complex and detailed to be handled by menu and help screens, however, and then you are stuck with plowing through the manual or finding help elsewhere. You have several resources.

Because manuals are so bad, many books are published on

how to use specific programs. The more popular a program is, the more books about it are available. I own ten books on *dBase II* because I do consulting on that program, and I know there are others. Most of these books are much better than the manuals and are well worth their price.

Use any of the resources listed in chapter 14 to help you learn to use your software; and, as with hardware, the dealer who sold you the software may be willing to answer questions and help you when you're stuck, although she is under no obligation to give free instruction in the use of a product she has sold to you. (A car salesperson is not obligated to teach you to drive!) Some dealers have responded to the demand for software support by offering classes, and a one-session introductory class is sometimes free. A complete course may be offered for a fee. Such a course might be a good investment.

If you have bought your program from a mail-order house and it is not one of those that offer telephone support, then you still may be able to attend a dealer course if you pay for it.

Recommended Reading

BUYING SOFTWARE

Stewart Brand, *Whole Earth Software Catalog*, Quantum Press/ Doubleday, 1984. A good introductory guide to the most popular programs in all categories, with informal commentary on the strengths and weaknesses of each program. On the most popular programs there are often several opinions. The comments are much like the things your friends would say to you, rather than complete and formal reviews. This is both a strength and a weakness of the book. Sometimes books are recommended to help you learn a particular program. Many important programs are left out; nevertheless, this is a guide and a primer that will help you with your selections. If it's in the *Catalog*, you can be sure it's a decent program.

Philip Frankel and Ann Gras, *The Software Sifter: An Intelligent Shopper's Guide to Software*, Macmillan, 1983. Very detailed lists of features to look for in most types of business programs. Unfortunately, many of the features will be meaningless until you have actually used such programs, but if you use the lists to ask questions of your software dealer, you will learn a great deal about the type of program you are shopping for. This book complements Glossbrenner's nicely, and I recommend that you buy both. It has been my experience that in anything to do with computers, I need to buy two or three books in order to get complete information.

Alfred Glossbrenner, *How to Buy Software: The Master Guide to Picking the Right Program*, St. Martin's Press, 1984. A basic education in what software is and what each type does. This book will answer most of your questions and will remain useful beyond your novice stage. Don't try to read it all at once or your brain will crack at the seams. Use it as a reference book.

Alfred Glossbrenner, *How to Get Free Software*, St. Martin's Press, 1984. The title says it all; incidentally, you will learn a lot about users' groups and networks. Public-domain software is much underrated—we live in a culture that teaches us to value only what we pay for. Don't neglect to look into the world of free software. You'll have a lot of fun, and the programs cost you only a little time.

WORD PROCESSING

Arthur Naiman, *Introduction to WordStar* (updated and revised edition), Sybex, 1983. The best book on *WordStar*, but does not cover the latest revision, *WordStar 3.3*. At the time I write this, Naiman is planning a new edition to include version 3.3, and another separate book for IBM PC users.

Mitchell Waite and Julie Arca, *Word Processing Primer*, BYTE/ McGraw-Hill, 1982. An explanation of word processing for those who are completely unfamiliar with it. Understanding what all the word processing functions are will help you choose a program that has the features you want.

SPREADSHEETS

Douglas Ford Cobb and Gena Berg Cobb, *SuperCalc SuperModels for Business*, Que, 1983. More than twenty "models," i.e., sample spreadsheets, that you can enter yourself. A great way to learn how to set up the spreadsheet to do all kinds of number crunching. Included are models for management of cash, debts, fixed assets, and working capital; financial statements, planning and budgeting, and preparation of quotes. A brief explanation of each model is given, but this is not a primer on using *SuperCalc*. You will need to know the basics of the program before using this book; you can learn those from your *SuperCalc* manual.

Douglas Hergert, *Mastering VisiCalc*, Sybex, 1983. Detailed instruction on how to use *VisiCalc*.

Stanley R. Trost, *Doing Business with SuperCalc*, Sybex, 1983. Complements the Cobbs' book nicely, because it has instructions for setting up spreadsheets, for a different set of business purposes, including real estate, manufacturing, and sales. It also has business-finance, budgeting, and income-tax models.

Stanley R. Trost, *Doing Business with VisiCalc*, Sybex, 1982. Covers the same material as the book above, but for *VisiCalc*. If you look at both these books it will be easy to see the ways in which the two programs differ—and how similar they are.

DATA BASES

Bernard Conrad Cole, *Beyond Word Processing*, McGraw-Hill, 1985. The definitive book on idea-oriented data bases, which Cole calls "knowledge bases." For anyone who needs to organize an index text files or any kind of information that can't be formatted for highly structured data bases, this book is a must. It covers many of the programs that can be used, from unstructured indexing systems to file managers, and tells how to use them. This book will help you select a program that best suits your needs. It even tells you how to use your word processing program to set up a "knowledge base."

C.J. Date, *Database: A Primer*, Addison-Wesley, 1983. The title is a little misleading, since it implies that the book is about data bases in general. In fact, it is a very good explanation of *relational* data bases, and is an excellent book for anyone who is interested in fully understanding the most powerful type of data base available for microcomputers.

Robert A. Byers, *Everyman's Database Primer*, Reston, 1984. For beginning database users, this book focuses on *dBase II*, although there is some information on other types as well. The strength of this particular book is that the author gives examples of *dBase II* models for many different types of applications. Authors of other books on *dBase II* don't seem to know how to do anything but mailing lists. Byers has also written a more advanced book, *dBase II for Every Business*, published by Ashton-Tate. The two books together make a fine course in *dBase II* applications.

TELECOMMUNICATIONS

Alfred Glossbrenner, *The Complete Handbook of Personal Computer Communications: Everything You Need to Know to Go Online with the Word*, St. Martin's Press, 1983. This book is a must for the telecommunicator. It includes information on CBBSs (computer bulletin board systems), on-line information services, communications hardware and software, and almost anything connected with telecommunicating.

There are many other books on particular programs that may be useful to you. It would be impossible to list them all here, even if I chose only the best. I have concentrated on the most popular programs for 8-bit computers. If you buy a 16-bit computer, watch the book-review sections of computing magazines for books on programs of interest to you.

TWENTY

A Strategy for Buying Software

The strategy for buying software is similar to that for buying a computer system, but differs in significant details.

1. Make a shopping list.

In as detailed a manner as possible, and on paper, describe exactly what you want your software to do. This chapter and chapters 18 and 19 will be enough to tell you what types of programs you need; *How to Buy Software*, by Alfred Glossbrenner, and *The Software Sifter*, by Frankel and Gras, are books that will tell you what details you need to make decisions about when choosing between particular programs. (All books mentioned in this chapter are described in detail in chapter 19.)

If you already own a computer, your software choices will be limited to those that are written for your operating system. Therefore, the first thing to consider when researching software is the operating systems on which a particular program will run. If you buy more than one program, you are likely to find that your first choice for word processing runs on a different operating system from your first choice for a database manager. To get around this problem, pick your top *three* choices in each category, each running on a different operating system. This tactic allows you more options when picking a computer as well.

2. Find out what programs meet your requirements.
Now begins some intensive research. Shopping for software is like making love—if you do it in too much of a hurry you're likely to end up dissatisfied.

A users' group is an excellent place to get nitty-gritty information on how well a program works. After all, this is about the only place that does not have a vested interest in selling you a program. You can talk with people who have actually used the program, or better yet, who will allow you to use the program on their machines and instruct you in its use. A person who uses a program in her normal course of business is often more knowledgeable about it than are the people who sell it.

Most computing magazines carry regular reviews of software, supposedly written by knowledgeable people. However, the quality of these reviews varies considerably. You should read at least three reviews of any program you are considering. You can find them in back issues of computer magazines in libraries. If you already own a computer and a modem, you can find magazine software reviews on CompuServe and The Source.

Some magazines are dedicated exclusively to software—here again the quality varies. A magazine review will tell you that a particular program is available, what systems it will run on, and what it does. But do not rely entirely on one review for an evaluation of the quality of a program. Reviews should be only one of several factors in your final decision.

Advertisements for programs in the magazines are curiously lacking in detail and tend to describe programs only in broad terms. But ads do have the publishers' names and addresses, and you can write or call for more detailed information.

The most valuable magazine features on software are the occasional comparative-shopping guides for a particular type of software, comparing various programs feature by feature. These articles will also list the price of each program and what systems it will work with.

Some magazines publish special supplements once a year to reprint and update software reviews that have appeared during the last year. These supplements contain many reviews, but tend to be a potpourri. The most useful are those special issues that contain reviews of all the available software for a particular application, like word processing.

InfoWorld is a magazine that publishes software-review supplements. It appears on newsstands; it is also advertised in the magazines that publish it and may be ordered direct from the magazines. Do *not* trust the reviews that appear in newsstand "buyer's guides" that are not affiliated with computing magazines. These guides never give a program (or a computer) a bad review, which suggests that the reviews may be placed there by the software publishers.

Computer magazines pop up like prairie dogs and disappear just as fast. So many are published that no single general-interest magazine stand can carry more than a few. You may have to visit several sellers to find what you need. If you live in an urban area, find a computer-book store that also carries magazines—that's your best bet.

Computer stores know what software is furnished with the brands of computers they sell, and if they know their business (and sometimes they don't) they will be able to tell you about other programs that will run on their machines. Software stores should be able to give you the most informed advice as well as demonstrations of various software packages.

Software catalogs are published for some of the more popular computers. They can be found in stores that sell that brand of computer and sometimes are advertised in computer magazines and can be ordered by mail. Most tell you very little about a program, but it's a place to start. You can look for the names of programs that do a particular job and then write the manufacturer for more information or search for reviews.

3. Evaluate the most promising programs.
In selecting the package you want to buy, consider the following factors:

A. If you already own a computer, the program must run on your operating system.
B. How completely does the program conform to the list of jobs you want it to do? The shopping checklist at the end of this section is designed to be used in conjunction with your list of requirements and checklists in *How to Buy Software* and/or *The Software Sifter*. My checklist has the

general considerations; the others cover details of particular programs.

C. How long has the software publisher been in business? Is it a successful house that is likely to be in business for a few years to come?

D. How many revisions has the program gone through? It often takes a year or more to discover all the flaws in a program and correct them. When possible, avoid buying a brand-new program or one that has not been updated since it was first published.

E. Examine the documentation (user's manual). If it is not clear, concise, and easy to understand, are there other books on the market to help you learn the program? Many supplementary books on programs are far better than the original documentation.

F. Is the program copy-protected? If it is, you will not be able to make more than one or two copies of it, and you may not be able to use it on a RAM disk or hard disk. Disks do go bad, and one or two backup copies are not enough. Publishers will provide you with a new copy when one is damaged, but replacements can take weeks to arrive. (This is why I personally refuse to buy copy-protected programs.)

4. Use the program before buying it.
A software or computer dealer may have a demonstration copy. Someone in a local users' group may also have the program.

5. Buy more computing power than you need, rather than less, within reason.
As your expertise grows, your uses for the computer will expand. Try to anticipate now what you might need a year from now. It will be cheaper to buy the power you need now than to replace the program later.

6. Select the right source for your software.
A retail store is only one of many options.

I bought my Osborne 1 for several different reasons, but one of them was the fact that *WordStar*, one of the most powerful word processing programs, came with it free, along with *SuperCalc* and MicroSoft BASIC. For $1,800 I got portability without sacrificing any of the standard 8-bit-computer features, and about $1,000 worth of free software. At the time, no other computer manufacturer offered a comparable value; now many of them do. If you can get a major program free by buying a computer you also like, you'll save hundreds of dollars.

Stores that sell only software are now appearing in many cities. The advantage of buying at such a store is that software is their only business and their software customers are important to them. A computer store may sell software as a sideline and a convenience to their customers, and they may not be very knowledgeable about the software they sell or care very much if you have problems. However, stores vary greatly in their attitudes toward customer support. I still buy all I can from a store in Berkeley, even though I have to deal long distance from Utah, because they are so committed to giving their customers good service. I know of other stores that, once they have your money, don't ever want to talk to you again. The best way to find a good dealer is to visit local users groups and ask members about their experiences.

A mail order house may save you a considerable amount of money on a major program such as *dBase II* or *VisiCalc*. Unfortunately, the reason you save so much money is that in most cases you get no after-purchase support. However, some mail-order houses are now offering telephone support. If you choose to buy by mail, be sure to pick a dealer who offers such a service.

One of the best programs I own is *SuperFile*, and I ordered it directly from the publisher (FYI) after reading an ad in a magazine. I felt safe to do that because they offered a thirty-day money-back guarantee (rare). Before I completely understood the program I ran into a problem and got hopelessly stuck with it. I called the publisher and discovered that they employ a person whose sole job is to help users with their problems over the telephone. If you can get such a guarantee (since you must buy the program untested) and a promise of telephone support, there is no reason not to order from a publisher. Be careful, though. Not all publishers are as courteous and helpful as FYI.

Steal it? Software piracy is widely practiced, and ranges from the small-scale trading of software at users' groups to large-scale copying and selling at prices substantially lower than retail.

Software publishers spend a lot of money and time developing good programs, and understandably they want to discourage piracy. They deserve to make a profit on their products. So far, no realistic way has been found to stop pirating. A few companies now code programs so that they can be copied only once (for a backup) and then no more, or they provide you with a backup copy when you buy the program and code both so that they cannot be copied at all. The trouble is that over a period of time a program disk can be expected to crash (computer jargon for "fail") many times. I have had to recopy my main programs as many as six times in the three years I have used my computers. Therefore, I would never buy a program so coded.

I saw one publisher quoted as saying he feels piracy is inevitable, and he simply prices his programs high enough to provide him with a profit even with the losses he suffers from piracy. This is one person's solution, but it is not fair to the scrupulously honest person who wouldn't dream of trading or selling her programs. Must she pay for other people's relaxed ethics?

There are no simple answers for the dilemma. Knowledgeable people have not been able to resolve piracy problems, just as they have not been able to thwart the illegal copying of records and video tapes. To tell people they may not do such copying is unrealistic, but a line has to be drawn somewhere. I don't feel more than the slightest twinge of guilt at having shared or swapped programs with friends. Yet, I'm sure I'd agree with the prosecution of a person who does wholesale copying and selling for profit. I suffer from that universal affliction, the ability to change my ethics to suit the occasion and my personal convenience. Where is the line? Is it okay to share with friends but not to copy for profit? What if the friends stretch to twenty or more members of a users' group?

Fortunately, I don't think the dilemma will exist a few years from now, for two reasons. The cost of developing programs is going to drop dramatically as authoring systems (programs that write programs) make it increasingly easy to do so. Authoring systems will also make it possible for people to develop programs tailored exactly to their own needs without learning to program. Consequently, programs will be so cheap that no one will care if they are copied. Secondly, when separate software marketing becomes less profitable, computer manufacturers will provide a full range of programs with the purchase of their machines. As hardware becomes more and more standardized, competition will focus on the quality and range of the programs provided. The need for software piracy will disappear because everyone will get whatever software they want free with their computer. Also, software will soon be sold in ROM cartridges, which of course can't be copied.

But all these developments are a few years down the road. At the first computer users' group you attend, you will find, unless it is a very exceptional group, that you can get a lot of free software—including some very expensive programs such as *dBase II*—just by copying it. You may even find that everyone takes such things for granted and doesn't think twice about giving away or swapping programs with fellow members. You will just have to apply your personal ethics to the situation, since no one has yet come up with a rule that is acceptable to everyone and, more important, that is enforceable. There is no question that in accepting free copyrighted software from your users' group you will be breaking the law. Whether accepting it is morally wrong is something you have to resolve with your conscience.

Write your own? Programming is fun, and once you have a computer and become reasonably familiar with it, you are bound to be curious about programming.

Almost all schools offer computer science classes, and most of these focus on programming. There are also myriad books on the subject. Programming is something you can teach yourself if you have to, but there is nothing like having an experienced person available to explain things.

However, programming for fun is one thing, programming in earnest is another. Programming is time-consuming and sometimes frustrating. If you have bought a computer to earn money with, your energy is better spent establishing your business. There are programs already available to do almost anything you can think of, and they are probably better than what you can do as a beginner. Why reinvent the wheel? Buy your software, then take a computer programming class at whatever point you become interested in it. By that time you will have discovered how you would like to adapt the programs you already own to your specific needs, and you may be able to modify them.

Thousands of public domain programs are available free through CBBSs, on-line information services such as CompuServe, and users' groups. Many are simple and limited in their capabilities, but others are powerful programs that could compete with major commercial programs. The reason you don't hear about them is, of course, because they are not advertised. One of the best communications programs available is *MODEM7*, a public-domain program.

Once again, our trusty users' group is the first place to inquire, especially if you don't yet own a computer. Many groups maintain an official library of public-domain programs. In addition, individual members are often willing to share programs; you need only provide the disk.

Starting with public-domain software is an excellent plan for a novice—if you have the patience to search for it. For one thing, once you have used a certain type of program, you can make much more knowledgeable choices when you decide to buy a commercial program.

The drawback to public-domain software, however, is that the documentation is often poor or nonexistent. You may need someone to help you learn to use the programs. For an excellent guide to obtaining free software, see *Where to Get Free Software* by Alfred Glossbrenner.

Software Checklist

On the following page is a checklist for use when shopping for software. Photocopy it and take it with you when you shop; it will help you remember what questions to ask. Use a copy for each program you are considering, and you will have an organized comparison of the features of different programs. This checklist is designed to be used in conjunction with your own list of detailed requirements for particular programs, or with the checklists from *How to Buy Software* and/or *The Software Sifter*.

Software Checklist

Name of program _____

Type of program _____

Available from _____

Address _____

Price _____ Phone _____

Program recommended by (reviews, individuals) _____
_____

How long has the program been on the market? _____

How long has the publisher been in business? _____

Is this the latest version, and has it been upgraded from the original? _____

What language is it written in? _____ (give a star to any program written in assembly language)

How much memory (RAM) does it require? _____

What operating system(s) will it run on? _____

Is it copy-protected? _____ (give a star to any program that is *not* copy-protected)

Does it come free with the purchase of any computer? _____

Does the dealer/mail-order house/publisher offer telephone support? _____

Are classes available on its use? _____ Books? _____

Does anyone I know own this program? _____

Is the manual clearly written and easy to understand? _____

Does the program offer on-screen help menus? _____

Is it compatible with other programs? Which ones? _____
_____

Demonstration:

Ask to see a simulation of exactly the kinds of tasks you will be doing with the program. Is the program fast? _____ Is it confusing or complicated? _____

If the person demonstrating the program to you is the person who will be responsible for support, how do you feel about that person? _____

Is she knowledgeable, patient, generous with her time and information? _____

Does she explain things in easy to understand terms? _____

TWENTY ONE

The War Against Technoterror and How It Can Be Won

The Roots of Technoterror

The computer industry has a reputation for being one of the least sexist in the technical fields. Women computer professionals earn 70 to 80 percent of what men earn for the same jobs—an encouraging statistic only because the national average for all occupations is 64 percent. (I feel a trifle schizophrenic to report an essentially depressing statistic as an encouraging one.) Opportunities are so plentiful that whatever barriers do exist against women, though they may be infuriating, can also be circumvented. In no other field of technology can a woman so easily enter the work force at any level for which she can qualify.[1]

Yet government statistics say that only 5 to 8 percent of computer engineers are women (compared to 3 to 5 percent for all industries) and only about 26 percent of computer programmers and systems analysts are women. If the computer industry is so open to women, what accounts for our pitifully low share of the best jobs?

Women aren't going after them, that's what.

Not only are young adult women staying away from computer-science courses in college, but female children and teenagers ignore video-game arcades, summer computer camps, and computer classes at any level—elementary through high school. Women buy only 2 to 4 percent of the personal computers sold. A public-opinion polling-service employee quotes a computer manufacturer explaining why they don't exert any effort to market personal computers to women: "The market is men, so why bother?" Computer manufacturers' ads that present computers being used exclusively by males make this remark a self-fulfilling prophecy. A few computer companies have yielded to pressure from concerned educators and now run ads showing women and girls using computers, but the vast majority of ads are still male-oriented.

It has long been recognized that in general women have an extremely high resistance to math, science, and technology. For a long time there was a myth that women had less innate ability than men for the kinds of thinking necessary in these areas, and women believed it themselves (many still do). But brain researchers looking for right- and left-brain differences between men and women have found that women *surpass* men in the language skills so important to programmers and tech writers, and in linear logic (the logic used in computers). Even keeping in mind that such generalizations are subject to individual exceptions and variations, if innate ability is a determining factor, then women, not men, should predominate in the high technology computer industry jobs! Yet many women continue to believe that even the simplest technology is beyond their ability.

Mary Gaber has her own business, publishing directories and writing programs for *DBase II*, a powerful database manager. Her first experience with computers was with Planned Parenthood, where she worked as a fund-raiser. She told me, "When I became a fund-raiser it took me only one day to realize that the job needed to be computerized. We had an IBM PC, which only one person knew how to use, and she was just learning. She taught me what she knew, but in a few months she left and I was then the computer expert at Planned Parenthood.

"Here is an organization of twenty-five women and no one was relating to the computer at all. They don't understand it. We should have been doing all kinds of jobs with the computer, but no one was listening. There were one or two people who occasionally recognized that a particular task would be easier if they used the computer to do it, and they would ask me to show them how. But their approach was, 'Can you teach the computer to do this single little task?' and they never saw how their whole job would be easier if they learned to use the computer."

Marilyn Frazier of Computer College, who was present, commented, "I think it is 90 percent conditioning. Women are conditioned to think they're incapable."

Mary added, "It's only that feeling that is the obstacle. Once you overcome it, you realize how capable you really are. How many secretaries know how their typewriters work? Most don't even like to change the ribbon, and that's the kind of relationship they've had with machines. The same is true of the vacuum cleaner or the car or anything else. As long as it does the job for them, they don't want to know how it works. But to use a computer, and use it at its capacity, you need to have some interest in how it works—you have to be able to relate to the machine. It's the same kind of thinking you need to do a math problem. It's an objective problem, not a personal one." That's the kind of thinking that most women are not used to doing.

Where resistance is absent, women do very well in technology, as the studies indicate they should. As a matter of fact, women have been on the cutting edge of computer technology from the beginning, and some have been responsible for significant advances. In the mid-1800s Augusta Ada Byron, daughter of the Romantic poet Lord Byron, wrote sophisticated problems for Charles Babbage's Analytical Engine, the world's first mechanical calculator, which made her the world's first programmer.

More recently, Commodore Grace Hopper conceived the first high-level computer language, COBOL, which simplified programming by allowing programmers to write in English rather than in numeric codes. She also wrote the first compiler, which is a program that translates English-language commands into machine language. The amount of time and work the compiler saves for programmers is incalculable. Both developments were major steps forward in programming technique.

Heather Ellin, whose first programming job was in 1958, says, "It was apparent from the start that women were frequently better at programming. There were all sorts of intelligent women in the companies they could train and pay less than the men because so many other fields weren't as open to women as the computer industry."

When women do go into computing, they do well. The trouble is that women at the professional level are still exceptional. If it's not because of lack of ability, and if it's not because of sexism, then what is keeping them away?

In the last few years many thousands of dollars have been spent to find out what you and I could have told them all along if they had asked us: Women are conditioned from birth to be resistant to involvement in mathematics, technology, and science, and they are discouraged from the expression of any innate interests and abilities in those areas. Most of this goes on in the home, and the children carry the attitudes they learn there into the schools, which may or may not try to counteract the initial conditioning. The school itself may have unenlightened teachers or administrators who reinforce the resistance to technology. The sad truth is that it may take a generation or two before the new attitudes brought about by the women's movement are felt in a majority of homes and schools, and the change may never reach some at all.

Clearly, if women are to get their fair share of the jobs in tomorrow's technological society, and advance to whatever level their abilities allow, then something must be done about this massive programmed resistance in women—a resistance that often expresses itself as a terror of anything mechanical.

Fortunately, educators and professional women already established in technological fields—many of whom overcame their own technoterror in order to succeed—are concerned about the future of the next generation of young women and have committed themselves to setting up programs that (1) make girls aware of their options in technology and (2) provide the means to ensure that resistance to technology never develops. Both objectives require reaching girls early in their lives, preferably while they are still in elementary school, since antitechnology conditioning begins even before a child is school age, i.e., the first time brother receives an erector set for Christmas and sister does not.

One such program is EQUALS, dedicated to increasing the participation of female and minority students in mathematics and computer-education courses at all stages of their education, since math, especially, is what is called a "critical filter" for science and technology. That is, people who don't have a good math foundation usually don't end up as engineers, scientists, or technologists.

EQUALS offers workshops for kindergarten to twelfth-grade educators in which teachers are made aware that the avoidance of math has serious implications for women and minority students, resulting in a loss of occupational opportunity and earning potential. EQUALS Director Nancy Kreinberg states that the majority of primary and elementary school teachers have not had preservice or in-service mathematics training and have had to struggle along with their mathematics program as best they can, and that some elementary teachers can't pass a sixth-grade math competency test! (This is a serious indictment of our teacher-training programs.) EQUALS' activities are planned to increase teachers' own math skills as well as to introduce them to activities, tools, and teaching methods that make math more accessible, useful, and fun for students. Finally, women guests working in the fields of science, technology, and skilled trades are brought in to speak and answer questions about opportunities in math- and science-related fields. Teachers learn how they can encourage their female and minority students to consider these options.

Follow-up studies have shown that in the schools participating in the EQUALS program there has been a slow but steady increase of enrollment of young women and minority students in advanced math and computer classes, improved student attitudes toward the study of mathematics, improved skills in problem-solving, enhanced professional growth of teachers, and an increased awareness of nontraditional career options.

EQUALS was originated by Nancy Kreinberg at the Lawrence Hall of Science in Berkeley. The program provides consultation services to schools throughout the country and has helped to establish EQUALS sites in six other states. For those who would like to set up similar programs in their own cities, EQUALS publishes a handbook containing full details of the program, as well as teaching materials. Write:

EQUALS
Lawrence Hall of Science
University of California
Berkeley CA 94720

and ask for the booklet *Use EQUALS to Promote the Participation of Women in Mathematics.* It provides activities and resources for educators, grades kindergarten to twelfth, as well as annotated bibliographies on mathematics and career-education materials.

The Math/Science Network, based at Mills College in Oakland, California, is an association of over twelve hundred educators, scientists, engineers, administrators, and business and community people established to promote the participation of women in mathematics and science and to encourage their entry into nontraditional occupations. Individually and collectively, Network members develop, promote, and conduct innovative math and science programs for women and minorities.

One of the ways in which the Network makes female high-school students aware of nontraditional career options is through their "Expanding Your Horizons in Science and Mathematics" conferences held on campuses throughout the country. Professional women with careers in math, science, and technology volunteer to talk to students about their careers and the opportunities in their fields. Follow-up studies show that these conferences have been successful in shattering negative stereotypes about women in science and technology, and in influencing students to consider nontraditional careers they had not considered before.

The Network also serves as an information clearinghouse and resource for women who are considering career changes and for those who are reentering the job market and need their skills updated in order to get jobs in the fields of math, science, or technology. It is also a support system for any woman who may find herself the only professional woman in a department or company and who feels isolated; the Network is also a conduit through which women can help one another in their careers.

Math/Science Network has a career-education videotape called "Nothing But Options," which profiles five young career women in careers that require a strong math and/or science base: environmental science, computer systems analysis, electrical engineering, computer graphics, and financial investments. The tape rents for $40, deductible from the purchase price of $240 if the tape is purchased within sixty days of rental.

Like EQUALS, the Math/Science Network has encouraged spin-offs all across the country. Check with your local colleges to see if there is a group in your area, or write:

Jan MacDonald
Math/Science Resource Center
Mills College
Oakland CA 94613
(415) 430-2230

Conferences on women and technology are held on college campuses throughout the country, and many degree candidates are writing their theses on women in technology. These students are digging deeply into the problems women face in the techno-logical work market and how to solve them.

These efforts are too new for anyone to know how much good they will do in the long run. Nancy Kreinberg, Director of Math and Science Education for Women at Lawrence Hall of Science, has said, "Progress can be slow in dealing with issues that call traditional attitudes into question. Substantive change takes time, as people must gain confidence that they will be benefited rather than harmed." But so far feedback from students as well as teachers has been enthusiastic and some changes have been seen, so the future looks promising for the girls who are now in school.

But what about those of us whose resistance was set in cement before anyone ever thought of EQUALS or the Math/Science Network—those of us who are sure that if we so much as touch a machine of any sort the great god Thor (that most macho of Scandinavian gods) will fell us with a thunderbolt?

Fortunately, there are some resources for us. Many cities now have computer-literacy seminars designed especially to help women overcome their fears and resistance. It is well estab-lished that women learn to use computers better when taught by other women, and when they are not in a group with men, so these seminars are taught by women and enrollment is limited to women only. The seminars may be given by individuals, through local computer stores, or by the continuing-education programs of colleges. There are also coed seminars—many men have their problems with technology, too—but because so many women have told me how much better they learn when men are not present, I'd suggest you opt for a women-only class if one is available.

The Women's Computer Literacy Project, based in San Francisco, gives introductory computing seminars for women in major cities all across the country. Their primary motivation is unabashedly political. Project director Marcia Freedman is another professional who feels (as I do) that it is essential for women to be involved at all levels of computer applications or they will be "locked out" of the higher levels of the computer field, as they have been in science, medicine, and technology. Freedman believes that "the women's movement's gains can be easily wiped out in this decade if women don't find out about and learn to use advanced technology. For instance, the National Women's Mailing List was established to do for the women's movement what Richard Viguerre did for the antifeminist movement. [Viguerre used computers to compile a mailing list of people who subscribed to conservative magazines and donated money to conservative campaigns, including Right to Life and other movements. He sells this list to conservative causes and Republican party organizations, which have made extremely effective use of it for organizing and fund-raising.] It's the computer that makes mailing lists a viable way of networking. It's fast, cheap, and it's possible to keep and retrieve information in many different ways. There's no way you could have such a mailing list without a computer. You couldn't have it on three-by-five cards. But many women's organizations are not yet prepared to computerize, although attitudes are definitely beginning to change.

"I became involved in founding the Women's Computer Literacy Project because I felt that it was crucial to do something as a feminist activist to bridge the gap between women and computer technology.

"You have to begin with literacy—with how the machine works and what it can do and what it can't do, with learning the terminology so you can read the magazines and the books and the manuals and become familiar with microcomputer applications. Nobody was telling women how very simple it is to use a computer. Most of what you want to do is available in a prepackaged program that you just buy. You don't have to be a programmer. And that, somehow, is a big secret!

"We saw, once we began to check, that educational institutions, manufacturers, and private literacy schools are directing all their outreach to high-level male executives. Women are being hired to do data entry and word processing without understanding that a word processor uses a computer, and that data entry is more than just typing. They don't understand what the machine they're working on does and how it works. 'The office is automating'—what does that mean? Eighty-five percent of all working women are employed as clerical workers; clerical workers handle information, and information handling is what computers do. So, women's jobs are very directly threatened. And the same women are not being offered any training that will enable them to adapt to a new kind of job.

"Beginning about two years ago we began to hear from women's organizations around the country that knew they needed computers but didn't have the vaguest idea of how to begin. When they would walk into computer stores either no one would talk to them or whoever did didn't know enough to tell them what they needed to know. Most computer salespeople don't understand much about them, and if you come in not knowing anything they can't help you very much.

"So these women were at a dead end. There wasn't any kind of community resource for women to learn about computers. We have community resources for many problems, but not that one. There wasn't any literature around that helped much, either, so we came up with our project. We said, 'Okay, this is what we need to do—we need computer literacy for women and we need to empower women to independently develop their computer skills without having to become dependent upon a whole new industry of computer teachers.' And we've done that, very successfully."

WCLP's course was designed by Deborah Brecher, who had been in data processing for seventeen years before joining with Marcia Freedman to found WCLP. Brecher is also a founder of the National Women's Mailing List and the author of *The Women's Computer Literacy Handbook* (New American Library, 1985). Today, Brecher continues to teach the course occasionally, but the staff now includes other teachers.

Brecher believes that women learn differently from men and that they require different things for a productive learning environment. She believes that women are interested in process, while men are more interested in results. So Brecher teaches women how a computer works and that the rules have logic behind them, thus defusing the mystique that makes computers intimidating.

WCLP teachers start each seminar by asking the women why they are taking the class and what they are afraid of. Talking about their fears in a supportive, all-women environment helps to dispel those fears. The women are then introduced to computer concepts and terminology, languages, programming, and the basics of how computers work. The seminar enables women to read any instruction manual, so that they will never need to take another course. All the classes are hands-on, each woman working at her own computer.

Freedman herself is a prime example of what the program can do. She had spent fifteen years in Israel, where she was active with the women's movement and served in the Israeli Knesset (parliament). She returned to the United States to write a book on women and politics. She says, "When I came back to America everything was computers, computers, computers. I had a very strong resistance to them. I am an educated woman, not a particularly frightened woman, and yet as far as this machine was concerned I just said, 'Wow, that's not for me; it's technology and it's responsible for many of the evils in the world and I don't want anything to do with it.' I thought my resistance was ideological, but it was fear more than anything else, and misunderstanding of what the machine is all about. Then I began working with the National Women's Mailing List, and I was very impressed with it, and the computer is what makes it work. I realized that I had to get over my prejudices and fears about this machine and learn to take advantage of it as quickly as possible, because an information revolution is going on and anybody who maintains a prima donna attitude toward computers will be left out of the future."

So Freedman asked Deborah Brecher, who was working on the Mailing List, if she would teach a class if Freedman brought ten or so women together, and Brecher said yes. That was the beginning of the Women's Computer Literacy Project, and Freedman was a graduate of the first class.

Sandy Butler is another WCLP graduate. Sandy is a writer and a counselor who resisted learning about computers for a long time after she recognized their importance. Where her writing was concerned, Sandy says, "I convinced myself that something magical in the creative process would be short-circuited if I made the shift to computers from writing in longhand and on the typewriter. I had all kinds of rationalizations to convince myself I really didn't want to do that."

Sandy was also working as an administrative assistant in an institution. "To those outside the institution I was an administrative assistant, but within the institution I was the 'main girl,' and it fell to me to remember all the things that no one else could possibly remember, and I had developed all kinds of elaborate systems for doing that. But there are only so many tickler files you can do at once, and there are only so many ways to do spreadsheets manually and have them fit in the file drawer for the next month. It became so cumbersome it felt like juggling and I just couldn't keep it all afloat, and my frustration with what I was doing finally exceeded the anxiety that I was not going to be able to master this new body of information about computers."

Sandy heard about the Women's Computer Literacy Project and signed up for a seminar. The story of her experience there is an eloquent argument for seeking out an all-women environment for overcoming the fear of computers:

"Going to a place where I knew in advance there would be only women gave me internal permission to ask more 'stupid' questions than I might have permitted myself in a mixed group. When I got to the class, it was very comforting and reassuring to find women with Ph.D.s who were afraid they would get a shock if they touched the computer. I felt much less stupid immediately.

"The group experience was very important. When I compared my feelings with those of the other women, I could see that one thing that had affected me was a lifetime of the mystification of machinery, and also that the language used to talk about computers is so studiedly arcane that it's like learning a foreign language.

"Deborah made the information available in language that most of us could understand, using the analogy of cookbooks and recipes and ingredients. It wasn't condescending or patronizing, it was just clarifying. She found a way to translate this material so that the language was inclusive instead of exclusive. The point was made that people don't become professionals unless they speak a secret language, and if everybody knows the secret language, then what are the CPAs and the lawyers and the doctors going to do? Professionals have an interest in keeping the language secret."

I told Sandy that when I had studied power and transportation in a California university, I not only had my antitechnology conditioning to contend with, but I had an instructor whose main agenda was to preserve his superiority. To this end he purposefully made his courses as obscure and difficult as he could. It didn't help that the man did not like women, especially in his department. The pyschological obstacle course he erected, compounded by my own inner resistance, made it almost impossible to get through that year. (I did, though.) I commented that I thought mine was a common experience for women who invade male terrain in order to learn technology.

Sandy agreed that such experiences are one reason why an all-women learning environment is so important. "The first thing Deborah did was to deprofessionalize herself. She made herself seem very available, and she made it all seem possible. She said, 'All of us here know a lot about our own specialties, and one of the things I know a lot about is computers and I'm going to teach you what I know.' She spoke in such a way that we felt she would come to *our* seminar to learn what *we* know. She did not separate herself from us in any way that might have been inhibiting.

"She spent the first hour explaining how the computer works. She gave us a sense of the language and what things mean so that it was immediately demystified even if we had not put our hands on the keyboard yet. But after the first hour we did. We didn't touch the machine until we had some intellectual ease with the material.

"So there was almost immediate hands-on experience. When I made my first mistake, all that happened was a little warning beep and no one turned around and pointed scornful fingers at me. Lots of other people were triggering little warning beeps, so mine was perfectly manageable. By the end of the first class I had a reasonable perspective, my anxiety was reduced, and from then on it was just a matter of learning.

"Deborah had designed some entertaining exercises that caught our imagination, so that the exercises did not seem to be about mastery but about play. There is a wonderful element of play in the way she teaches that made the classes lively and compelling for me.

"Unlike the ninety-seven-pound weakling, I was not a whiz after four classes, but I was no longer frightened; I didn't have sophistication and skill with using the computer by any means, but I was able to feel completely comfortable about sitting down at the office with the Hewlett-Packard and the manual and making sense out of it. I would not have done it before. That was the big difference.

"I stayed another seven or eight months at my job after the training. We had a Hewlett-Packard 150, and I mastered as much of that as my boss's anxiety would permit, and there was a great deal more I could have learned had I been permitted to, but certainly I learned enough to manage what I needed to do. It did help me on that job.

"I'm working for myself now, which was another part of the transition I was going through. My specialization is child sexual abuse. I train therapists and do consulting, work with clients, lead groups and seminars, and travel all over the country. I now have a DEC Rainbow and I'm using it for my writing and I keep my records on it. I can gather all the information that I need to do my own work in training and consulting psychotherapists, and I can keep track of all the new monographs that are published, and who's done training for what cities so I can schedule trips—things that I couldn't possibly do manually and still have time to do anything else. I track my status at different points of the year with my work and my finances and my mailings, and it has been an enormous godsend not to have to do all this manually. The computer frees me to do much more

interesting and compelling work. So the computer has taken on
the function of being my 'main girl.' "

WCLP is growing fast; it maintains its own classrooms in San
Francisco and New York and has given seminars in many major
cities across the nation. For information on seminars in your
area, write:

Women's Computer Literacy Project
1195 Valencia St.
San Francisco CA 94110

or call the project at (415) 647–1404 (San Francisco) or
(212) 517-8871 (New York).

Seminars like those given by WCLP can make your introduction to computers a lot easier, but individual women can cure
themselves of technoterror without special help if they want to.
I am one of them. I happened to work out most of my technology resistance on automobiles, but I talked to several women
computer professionals who were at first terrified of computers
but overcame their fears just by getting familiar with them.

When Sandy Emerson first went to work for the Community
Memory Project (CMP) she had never worked on a microcomputer. She says, "When I joined CMP I feared and detested
computers. I had never worked with a microcomputer. While I
did my master's thesis I was feeding cards to a mainframe,
which promptly spat them out again. I thought they were awful
machines and took a lot more time than they needed to. In 1978,
CMP already had microcomputers because the engineer of one
of the first micros [Lee Felsenstein, who designed the SOL and
the Osborne 1] was the engineer for the CMP. So we had some
micros and the programmers and the others on the project
treated them with a mixture of contempt and affection, which
gave me a whole different attitude. It was okay to open them
up. I discovered they weren't engineered very precisely. I was
horrified to find that computers that I had envisioned being
assembled under completely controlled conditions were sloppily
put together. They weren't engineered to be reliable; they were
just engineered to work most of the time, but they were sure to
break.

"More or less by osmosis I lost my fear and started to absorb some knowledge. It was awesome to see someone fix a computer by opening it up and hitting it with a screwdriver—that's called the tap method of computer repair—because the chips in their sockets may be loose, and so you hit the computer and it starts to work again. Seeing that, you can't stay in awe of them."

Marilyn Frazier, co-owner of The Computer College in Salt Lake, says, "I did not end up in this business out of choice. About three years ago my husband had a love affair with computers, and I absolutely detested them. When I say love affair, I really mean it. We would not carry on a conversation that did not relate to computers. I had a small business in my home, typing, and my husband was urging me to get involved, and I did. I learned word processing on my own with documentation that was incredibly bad and incredibly frustrating. I was proceeding by trial and error, reading and not understanding, having fits. But the word processing allowed me to jump from earning five to six dollars an hour to fourteen to fifteen dollars an hour. I'm not going to take any credit, though. My husband forced me into it. I didn't see the light on my own."

Resistance to math, science, and technology is what gets discussed in connection with technoterror, but another, more broad-spectrum element is never talked about: the psychological gestalt of our culture and particularly of the workplace.

Remember how terrified you were the first time you tried to drive a car? Or the first time you appeared on stage to give a speech, act in a play, sing a song, or dance? The root of this kind of fear is the possibility that we might fail: wreck the car, forget our lines, lose our voice, fall down. Only very small children plunge into new experiences without fear. They haven't learned yet that they will be punished for failure by the disapproval of their parents and peers, by hurting themselves, or by finding themselves ridiculed. This punishment for failure is the gestalt I refer to.

The more different a new experience is from our usual routine, the more we fear it. But we did learn to drive the car, give the speech, act in the play, sing the song, and dance the dance.

And every time we did it again our fear lessened. If we did it often enough, our fear disappeared altogether.

The key to the disappearance of fear was that we went ahead and did what we were afraid to do. The payoff was worth the risk. But the risk in getting involved with a computer is far greater than in driving a car for the first time. A car can only mangle and maim us, or perhaps kill us, but a computer can make us look stupid.

How did we become so scared of looking stupid? And how did our reason become so short-circuited that we behave as if not knowing something—not having experience at a certain activity—makes us stupid, when *rationally* we know this is not true?

While we are in school we are not expected to know things or to be experienced. If we are lucky we graduate into jobs as trainees, where we still have license to learn. But our license quickly expires. Competition for jobs and for promotions is based on what we already know, what we can already do, and seldom on our potential. We very quickly learn to cover up when we don't know something or when we lack experience in a certain endeavor. Not to know, to lack experience, is a big black mark. We fear being found out because it means we may lose a chance for promotion, we may lose authority or credibility. We may lose a sale or a contract.

And here they come with a computer, which requires us to make a radical jump, not only in the way we think about getting work done but in the skills we need to do our jobs. We are not prepared: we are not trained, we are ignorant, we have no experience. Our programmed red-alert button goes off: "If you don't already know how, if you can't learn quickly you are going to look stupid and may lose your job."

This response is not rational, of course, but neither is the system. It's what we've been taught to expect. Therefore, the first thing to do is to understand how you came to feel this way, and then consider what the *real* situation is. A primary fact is that everybody else started as ignorant as you are. Look around you at the people you know who have learned to use computers. If *those* boobies learned, surely you can!

The second thing to do is to remember how you have succesfully transcended other fears by forging ahead and doing what you were afraid to do. Unfamiliarity is 90 percent of the threat. The first time you sit down at the computer and find out it doesn't blow up when you press the wrong key, you are on your way.

The third thing to do is to find a safe source of support for yourself. Find a women's computer-literacy group, or a friend, teacher, or computer salesperson with whom you feel comfortable. Don't pick someone who is a showoff or one of those egotists who try to make themselves feel important by making other people look small! There are as many of those in the computer world as there are anywhere else, but you don't have to put up with them.

The fourth and most important thing to do is to slow down and take it easy, give yourself a break. Computers are radically different from what we are used to, so it's reasonable to feel bewildered! Also, computer manuals are notoriously hard to understand because they are poorly written, not because computers are that hard. Methods of teaching have a long way to go, too—many computer-science courses obscure more than they reveal. Not all your difficulties in learning will necessarily be *you*. Computers are not *hard* to learn to use, they are just *different*. Resistance crumbles with demystification, and demystification comes with familiarity. Simply take that first step and give yourself whatever support you need.

What About Our Daughters?

Implicit in the term *basic education* is the idea that it prepares us to go in any direction we want once we are old enough to make choices. We need to be able to read and write and perform elementary math functions no matter what we do with our lives, even if we choose to make marriage and homemaking our career. Typing skills are useful to the scientist as well as to the secretary, and we are somewhat handicapped if we don't know how to drive, even though our career may be horse training.

Computer literacy must be added to that list of essential skills. You are not deciding your daughter's future career for her by insisting that she learn to operate computers now. By the time she gets out of school there will be few business careers that do not require a knowledge of computers, and in science and technological fields these skills will be essential. Even in the arts, computer literacy will give her an advantage over the competition.

The career homemaker/mother will need to understand and use the tools her children take for granted if she is to help them with their studies. She may need to use the computer to earn money or to further her own education. More important, it is no longer feasible for women who want to make home and family their careers to have no job skills. Divorce, a husband's death or disabling accident, and an unreliable economy are always possible, and there are few of us who don't know professional homemakers who have been caught unprepared for such events. Increasingly, one income is not enough to raise a family—an estimated 64 percent of married women work outside the home!

Many women find that life at home is not enough when the children are grown, and they must start from scratch to learn skills so they can find another occupation to make their lives meaningful. Computer literacy will provide the easiest re-entry to the job market at any time of life and should be considered an essential backup skill. "If you know how to type you can always get a job," they told me thirty years ago. It turned out to be true and saved my life several times. Now I tell my daughter, "If you know how to operate a computer you will always get a job," and it's a much better deal than the old typing-pool ghetto.

To give your daughter a fair shot at anything that she might want to do in the future (as well as for her future security), the groundwork must be laid now. Computer literacy is not a frivolous extra and must not be considered an elective, like wood shop. Computer literacy is equal with reading and writing as a vital skill. This situation has come about so fast that schools have been caught with their curricula down. Until schools catch up, parents must take up some of the slack.

From the studies that have been done and the experience of organizations like EQUALS, the Math/Science Network, and the Women's Computer Literacy Project, enough evidence has been compiled to make some general recommendations to parents.

OUR DAUGHTERS NEED AN EARLY START IN
COMPUTER EDUCATION, ON AN EQUAL FOOTING WITH BOYS

In spite of the efforts of programs like EQUALS and the Math/ Science Network and a few enlightened educators, there is a long way to go before girls receive equal encouragement in schools to learn about computers—in spite of the fact that women do the major part of information handling in our society.

Computer manufacturers do as much as can reasonably be expected to get computers into the schools, but they have no control over teachers' and administrators' attitudes toward their use.

Jan MacDonald of the Math/Science Network tells of an incident that spurred her involvement with the issue of equal treatment of boys and girls in the classroom: "I have two children—a son, Angus, who is four years older than my daughter, Suzy. Both my children went to the same school. One afternoon Suzy and I went to her fourth-grade parent-teacher-student conference with the specific purpose of requesting help for Suzy in the classroom science work, since Suzy was having problems with it. Also, she was experiencing the classic syndrome of feeling that she did not measure up to the work that her older sibling—in this case a boy—had done in the same school. When we explained the concern to Mrs. Smith (not her real name), she chuckled warmly and said, 'Oh, Suzy needn't worry about not doing as well in science as her brother. You see, when he grows up, he will have to get a job and support a family. But someone will support Suzy.'

"What Mrs. Smith told Suzy and me was not true. Nine out of ten young women of my daughter's age will work. According to a Bureau of Labor Statistics study, they will spend forty-five percent of their lives in the labor market. So long as they are led to believe that their life's career will be that of housewife and mother, they will be doomed to discover too late that they must enter the work force at a low-level job, with low reward.

"Since that fateful meeting ten years ago, I have learned a great deal about the subject of sex fairness in schools. Much progress has been made, but there are still—unfortunately—unthinking and uninformed teachers and counselors who perpetuate stereotypic beliefs that women don't need to study math, that boys are better than girls at math, and that women couldn't or shouldn't become scientists or technicians."

Until such teachers and counselors are reeducated or retired from the school systems, parents who want their daughters to have equal time and equal opportunity on the schools' computers are going to have to keep a close watch. It is important to check up on how much computer education your daughter is getting, even in the first grade, and to make sure that if computers are taught, your daughter receives equal access.

Teachers resist computers as much as anyone else. One study found that many teachers feel resentful of computers in the classroom; that instead of viewing windfall-grant computers as a blessing, they feel bullied. "They dump this computer in the classroom but they don't tell us what to do with it," said one disgruntled teacher. If that's the case, she has a right to feel resentful. Another teacher asked how she can give any student meaningful experience on a computer when she has only three computers for thirty students.

If your school tends to be reactionary, you and the PTA may have to pressure administrators to provide adequate training for their teachers and see to it that teachers utilize the computers they have.

Computer camps are lots of fun for children and are learning-intensive. A kid who goes to computer camp has an advantage over those who don't. Unfortunately, in many camps girls are in an extreme minority or absent altogether. It would be cruel to pack your daughter off to a computer camp where she may be the only girl, or one of only two or three. But you can persuade parents of your daughter's friends to send their daughters with yours, or organize a girls' camp through your PTA, or persuade the camps themselves to offer and promote a girls-only session.

Implicit in all these suggestions is the idea that you are going to have to get involved with your daughter's education and expend some energy on her behalf. That's what it is going to take. I am convinced that girls and women will not be represented in the computer revolution in significant numbers unless parents take a large part of the responsibility to see that their daughters are adequately prepared.

GIVE YOUR DAUGHTER THE RIGHT PARENTS

I asked the women I interviewed if they had any problems with computer resistance. Many did not, especially those who had entered the computer field in its infancy (the 1950s and 60s). Of course in those days women had even more built-in resistance to defying traditional sex-role boundaries than they do now, which makes it even more puzzling how some escaped the conditioning. I asked these women what they thought accounted for their comfort with technology when so many women have such big problems with it even today.

Almost unanimously, they answered that they were encouraged by their families to feel they could do anything they wanted to do. Some had not even been aware that there were things that, as women, they weren't supposed to be interested in. These women were exceptional in that their parents did not try to mold them into stereotypical female roles.

Computer consultant and writer Miriam Liskin: "I never had the famous female resistance to science and technology because my parents didn't bring me up as a girl doing things that girls are supposed to do. My parents were old-time feminists. I feel it's important for a girl to have a father who supports her as well as a mother who supports her. I learned how to do everything that either of my parents could do, which was not specifically what boys do or what girls do, and by the time I learned about 'proper' gender roles I was already set in my ways.

"The other great help was that my parents brought me up to think I could do anything I wanted, and that I could be right and the rest of the world could be wrong. They believed in me. They were both very intelligent, capable people who had little confidence in themselves. They did everything they could to see that I would have the confidence they lacked."

Law student Kristen Hansen: "I had tremendously supportive parents. My father died when I was ten; he died very quickly, of cancer. My mother feared she might go just as quickly, so she encouraged me to be on my own. I just about supported myself from the time I was ten—put on a neighborhood circus, worked in hamburger joints, mowed the lawn.

"My mother is a diverse and independent person. She is seventy-four years old now, and just left San Francisco on a solo drive back to her home in Mexico. She was a pilot in the early forties, and I am a pilot. My father immigrated from Denmark and went to work as a crane operator; he ended up owning an amusement company—juke boxes and pinball machines. My mother was his partner in the business. When he died, she ran a hamburger drive-in, then a wine shop, and sold real estate.

"I think a wide variety of experiences opens the mind to new possibilities. That's a part of my lack of resistance, too—I've done a lot of different things. The initial attraction was to be a part of the new age. But then you get captivated by, say, the ability to hook up to the Library of Congress and flip through half of their book list, at home, at night. The possibilities for research seem limited only by one's capacity for creative thinking."

Software-store owner and consultant Carol Frazer: "I got a lot of encouragement and support from my family. My father was a self-employed man, a hard-driving man, and my mother was always by his side. He always owned his own business and he very much encouraged me to go out and achieve. My parents must have been free from rigid ideas of masculine and feminine roles, because it was never an issue that came up. My mother was always working with my father in the business or in volunteer work, and it was an environment where sex roles weren't really established."

Freelance programmer and consultant Heather Ellin: "I was raised in a family where I didn't know that women 'don't do those things.' My mother did everything. I think if you raise both boys and girls in an environment where everybody does everything, then they will do this or that because as individuals that's what they like, but not because that's what men do or that's what women do. I didn't find out until women's lib started talking about it that I wasn't supposed to do certain things."

Maxine Wyman: "I have been very fortunate because I've had very strong women in my life as role models. Certainly in the black community women have not had the luxury of staying at home—it's not realistic economically. My mother raised six children and worked as a teacher. Returning to the field of teaching after leaving it to raise six children was very difficult for her. When I consider the difficult problems in my life, I say to myself, 'If my mother can do that, I can do this.'

"I've also been very fortunate to work with some women who

were unique in their fields. In Washington I worked for one of the first women administrative assistants to a U.S. senator—for Frances Henderson, administrative assistant to the late Senator Clifford Case of New Jersey. She ran his office, and she was one of the few women in that position. That's a very strong role model for a young woman in her twenties. Role models are extremely important for young women, so they realize they can do what they want."

Although many of these women agreed that an academic background in math and/or science would be helpful in learning the logical thinking that is necessary for comfort with computers, none of them mentioned such training as being a significant factor in determining their freedom from computer resistance. In every case, the accepting and supportive attitudes of parents, plus an absence of sex-role conditioning, were the key factors.

Obviously, the most important advantage you can give your daughter is the support and encouragement to enable her to pursue her own special interests, even if they are in areas unfamiliar and intimidating to you. Make sure her father or other significant male figure in her life understands the importance of his support and encouragement, as well. Public-relations agency owner Kathryn Hubbell got her first computer because her brother pressured her mother into giving her one!

Avoid reinforcing sex-role stereotyping in the home. Toys and games for boys and girls should be interchangeable until personal inclinations exhibit themselves. A writer whose name I have now forgotten once wrote that the most memorable and important Christmas gift he ever received was a bride doll he asked for at the age of nine. I asked for and received a football for my tenth Christmas. I never played with it. It was a token request, made, I believe, because I wanted to be reassured that I could play football if I wanted to. I feel now that receiving the football was an important symbolic confirmation that I could indeed set foot in the boys' territory if I was audacious enough, and I've been doing it ever since.

Unisex toys won't help much if Dad never does the dishes and Mom won't change a flat. Changing our own well-entrenched sex-role behavior may be the hardest thing we have to do to help our children. Keep in mind that our children learn most of their attitudes from us. We can't expect them to be free of sex-role limitations if we ourselves are not.

ROLE MODELS ARE CRUCIAL

The Math/Science Network and EQUALS have found that role models are of extreme importance to female children; and successful women often cite childhood role models as having been important in their development. The resistance-free women mention that their mothers were active, resourceful, and competent.

Be the best role model you can be. Achieving daughters usually have achieving mothers. That doesn't mean you have to have a career, but in whatever you do, show your daughter how to be a self-reliant, competent person. Expose her to other good role models: participate in programs like the Math/Science Network's "Expanding Your Horizons" workshops when they are available. Buy her books about women who succeed; be sure she sees movies about self-actualized women.

BUY HER A COMPUTER OF HER OWN

A girl's first computer ought to be one that plays games and runs Logo, a computer language designed for children that is extremely easy to use, lots of fun, and teaches mathematical concepts painlessly.

She should not have to compete with her parents or her brothers for computer time. Researchers have found that girls will not compete aggressively enough to win computers away from the boys either in the classroom or in the game arcades, and the same undoubtedly holds true in the home.

Games are a good way to introduce children to computers. The better ones develop hand/eye coordination and sharpen certain kinds of thinking. Unfortunately, it is estimated that 95 percent of games programmers are men, and men usually don't write games girls enjoy. That situation may change by the time you read this book, however. Software developers Elizabeth Scott and Lucy Ewell have developed several games especially for girls that are marketed under the name Rhiannon Software. All are nonviolent adventure games with females as the central characters.

Select educational software that emphasizes problem-solving, rather than the drill type that transfers the very worst of the old rote learning techniques to computers. The best educational software requires complex thinking on the part of the child. It is important to see a demonstration before you buy. The wrong software—too dull or too difficult—can discourage your daughter, and she'll turn off the computer.

When she outgrows her first computer, you can buy her one that runs a simple word processing program and a database management system. When she finds out how much time she saves on her book reports and term papers with word processing, she'll be a committed computer user forever. She can use the database program to catalog almost anything that interests her, and it should soon become an effective learning tool as well as a useful tool for school research and other projects.

Children tend to lose interest in things that no one else participates in. Encourage your daughter's friends to come and play with the computer, and spend some time using it with her yourself.

ENCOURAGE ACTIVITIES THAT
DEVELOP ANALYTICAL THINKING

Most of the computer professionals I interviewed felt that in their own cases a strong background in math or science was not important to their success with computers. What they did see as important is the ability to think logically and analytically. Math and science do provide training in that kind of reasoning, but these women felt logical thinking can be learned in other ways.

Carol Frazer says she was not a strong student in math, but college-level logic courses prepared her for computer procedures. Several professionals commented that women who manage homes and families are expert organizers and that this skill makes them good at programming and systems analysis. I struggled through a year and a half of automotive courses; the most important thing I learned was linear thinking. If you skip steps or work unsystematically when trying to diagnose why a car won't run, you're not likely to find the problem.

Heather Ellin prefers the term *critical thinking* and says it can be learned in traditional women's activities. "You can be teaching your daughter to sew, and you can say, 'See how the fabric pulls? What do you think will happen if we change this dart?' Then you change the dart and see what happens. That's hypothesizing, experimentation, and seeing the result. And that's critical thinking."

There were a few dissenters. Kristen Hansen regrets that she did not have a math background: "I have some facility for computers and I would be so much faster if I had an adequate math background because of the logical relationships, the binary system, and all that. People with a math background immediately see possibilities that take me forever. I don't have all the options; in my mind I don't see the choices, so I can't take advantage of them."

Maxine Wyman has this advice: "If a young woman is focusing on the computer industry and knows where she wants to go, it's important that she have as good a foundation as she can get for herself. If it's not possible to get a four-year degree, then she should take as many classes of a technical nature as she can. For women my age and older, our education was very soft on the math and science. That's something I regret. I had a fear of those fields because I didn't feel I could do well in them. In college I knew I didn't have the background to do well in college-level math and so I skittered around that. Looking back, I wish I had pushed myself farther. I also know, though, that I can learn anything I need to learn."

Kay Gilliland of EQUALS makes a strong argument for making sure your daughters have strong math and science backgrounds, and begin them early: "Math isn't that necessary to doing well in computers, but it becomes a filter that keeps people out. If you don't have the math in high school, then you don't get in the computer-science courses in college. You can find a job programming without the math background, but you won't earn a computer-science degree. Some companies will hire a student just out of high school without even a college course in computer science. But that's going to change—it's getting tougher and tougher, and not everyone is going to find a job that way."

It makes sense to insist that your daughter get some solid math and science courses as well as hands-on computer experience as early as possible. It may well be essential to her success, perhaps even to her survival, in an increasingly technological world and an increasingly competitive job market. Girls who grow up with computers and math will not be intimidated by them, a crucial advantage over those who grow up like so many of us precomputer-era women did—separated from technology and terrified of it.

---

[1] The situation for blue collar workers is dramatically different. Electronics assembly workers are 68 percent female, about one-third of them minority women, who earn very low wages. White males are promoted over women with higher seniority. Attempts to unionize these women have failed (1) because a high percentage of them are illegal aliens who feel that unionizing might result in loss of their jobs, and (2) because they value their freedom to change jobs easily in the volatile electronics job market.

Glossary

Application   The specific use for which a computer or a program is used. "Applications software" is used to differentiate programs that process data from programs that perform computer "housekeeping" or programming functions.

Baud rate   Technically, the number of times per second the electrical state (off/on, high voltage/low voltage) in a communications channel is changed per second, but the term is now commonly used to designate the number of bits per second that can be transmitted by a signal system; for instance, one baud means one bit per second. For microcomputer owners, this term is most often encountered when purchasing modems. The baud rate tells you how fast a modem can transmit data over the telephone line.

Binary code   A coding system using the digits 0 and 1, commonly used to switch circuits on and off in computers. Referred to as "machine language."

Bug   An error in a program that causes it to malfunction.

CBBS   Stands for computer bulletin board system. CBBSs are accessed by telephone, allowing communication between computer users with common interests.

Clock rate   The clock synchronizes the computer's operations, and the higher the frequency of the clock, the faster the machine can process data and instructions. Clock rate is expressed in megahertz (MHz).

Compatibility   The ability of separate units of computer equipment to interact and communicate.

Computer consultant   A person who performs any of a wide range of computer-related services on an independent contractor basis. Some freelance programmers call themselves computer consultants.

Copy protection   Methods used by software publishers to prevent people from making copies of programs to sell or give to their friends. These methods usually consist of imbedding code in the programs that prevents them from working properly once the program has been copied.

Crash   Complete failure of a computer system or software.

CPU   Central processing unit. In microcomputers, the CPU is a microprocessor which executes instructions, controls operations, and performs the built-in functions of the microcomputer.

CRT   Cathode ray tube. Used inaccurately to mean a monitor. See MONITOR.

Cursor   A mark on the display screen that shows you where the next character will be entered. It is usually a small block figure or an arrow, and sometimes blinks on and off so that it is easy to spot.

Data   In computer terminology, data in the strictest sense refers to bits of information processed in binary code; data is also used in its conventional sense as a collective word meaning information.

Data base   Information organized and stored in computerized form.

Database manager   A program for creating and managing data bases.

Data entry   The process of entering information into a computer.

Data processing   Specific procedures—such as sorting, merging, transmitting—performed upon data by computers and associated equipment.

Dedicated   When speaking of computers, dedicated means that the computer is configured to do specialized tasks rather than the wide range of computing operations a nondedicated computer can do. Typesetters and word processors are examples of dedicated computers.

Desktop computer Any computer small enough to fit on a desktop and used principally in a business environment.

Digital An adjective used to describe anything that works by counting numbers. Anything entered into a digital computer is translated into a numerical code (usually binary) before it can be processed.

Disk or Diskette A thin, flat, circular, magnetically charged medium used for recording information with a computer.

Display See MONITOR.

Documentation The written record of technical data pertaining to a piece of equipment or software; also refers to the manuals telling users how to use computer hardware or software.

Download To capture information transmitted to your computer from another computer.

Expandable Describes computers whose work or storage capacities can be increased by adding elements, such as memory chips or disk drives.

File A collection of information saved on disk under a common name, analogous to the traditional paper file folder.

Floppy disk An electromagnetic medium for permanently storing programs and data. Floppy disks come in several sizes and are encased in cartridges or envelopes. The disks themselves resemble small flexible phonograph records.

Hard disk An extremely high-density storage medium for programs and data, with many times the storage capacity of floppy disks. Synonymous with Winchester disk.

Hardware A general term for the mechanical elements in a computer system. To distinguish from "software."

I/O port Input/output port. An interface that can both receive and transmit information. See PORT.

Language See PROGRAMMING LANGUAGE.

Lap computers   A class of computers that are about the size of a notebook and that usually weigh less than ten pounds. They are designed for maximum portability, and can be operated with batteries.

Mainframe   A large, very powerful computer of the class usually found in big businesses or institutions.

Mass storage   Any device used for the permanent storage of programs and data, such as floppy disks, casette tapes, and hard disks.

Microcomputer   A term used to distinguish the small personal (or home) computers from the larger, more powerful mainframe and minicomputers used in big businesses and institutions. These small computers have been made possible by the miniaturization of internal circuitry, and all or most of their control and processing functions are contained on a single chip called a microprocessor. If the computer doesn't have a microprocessor it isn't a microcomputer.

Microprocessor   A single chip that can perform all the control and processing functions of the CPU (central processing unit) of a computer.

Minicomputer   A computer that, in size and power, falls somewhere in the middle between mainframes and microcomputers. Minicomputer is a vague term that is growing even more vague as microcomputers get more powerful.

Modem   A device that translates the digital signals from your computer into pulse signals that can be transmitted over your phone line. A modem connected to a computer at the other end of your telephone connection translates the pulse signals back into digital signals.

Monitor   Anything that allows you to see what you are doing on a computer. Also called a display, video display, display screen, or CRT.

Network   A system of computers hooked up so they can communicate with one another.

On-line   As used in this book, "on-line" pertains to computer services that are accessible by telephone. In more general usage, on-line means under the control of a central computer.

For example, terminals, printers, and modems are on-line when they are connected to a computer.

Operating system   The software interface between your applications programs and the computer. It passes along instructions to the appropriate part of the computer and coordinates processes. In microcomputers, the operating system must usually be loaded into the computer from a disk each time the machine is turned on, and your applications programs will not run until the operating system is loaded.

Peripheral or Peripheral device   Any device that enables your computer to communicate with the outside world, such as the keyboard, display screen, disk drive, modem, and printer.

Port   A built-in interface (plug) that allows you to hook up peripheral devices to your computer. Ports may be input-only, output-only, or input/output. Input/output ports are commonly called I/O ports.

Program   A set of instructions loaded into the computer that cause it to perform a particular set of operations. A program enables the computer to communicate with the user via the screen about the particular task at hand, and the user to communicate with the computer via the keyboard.

Programming language   A set of precise terms used to write programs for computers. All programs must ultimately be broken down into machine language (binary code) that the computer can understand, but machine language is tedious and difficult for the programmer. Programming languages are easier to work with, and can be translated for the computer by programs called assemblers, compilers, and interpreters.

RAM   An acronym for random-access memory. Everything you enter into your microcomputer through the keyboard, input ports, or from disks, whether data or programs, is stored in RAM until you erase it or transfer it to a permanent storage medium. In most microcomputers, everything in RAM is lost when you turn the computer off. Exceptions are the lap computers, which use a memory technology with such low power requirements that contents of memory can be maintained with very tiny batteries; therefore data in memory is saved even when the computer is turned off.

ROM   An acronym for read-only memory. The permanent memory in your computer; the contents are not lost when you turn the computer off. ROM normally contains things that are not usually changed by the computer operator—such as parts of the operating system.

Software   A collective word for computer programs.

Spreadsheet program   A program that allows the entry of mathematical, statistical, and other information in columns and rows, and that can be set up to automatically perform computational functions.

Systems analyst   A person who is an expert at defining information management needs and configuring computer systems to meet those needs. Systems analysts may write special programs to suit their clients' particular purposes, or they may limit themselves to helping clients choose computer systems and commercial software to run them.

Technical writer   A person who writes documentation and/or books and articles on technical subjects. See DOCUMENTATION.

Telecommunications   The transmission of information by any device using electric or electromagnetic signals, such as radio and telephone.

Telecommuting   The substitution of telecommunications for travel to and from a job.

Terminal   The equipment, including a keyboard and monitor, which allows you to operate a computer from a remote location. "Remote" can mean across the room or across the country.

Upload   To send information from your computer to another computer.

VDT   Video display terminal. See MONITOR.

Video display terminal   See MONITOR.

Word processing   The entry of written words into a computer, and the manipulation of them, such as by editing and formatting.

Word processor   A computer configured to do only word processing and related functions; a person who does word processing.

Index

320